Feminist Theory and Pop Culture

Teaching Gender

Scope

Teaching Gender publishes monographs, anthologies and reference books that deal centrally with gender and/or sexuality. The books are intended to be used in undergraduate and graduate classes across the disciplines. The series aims to promote social justice with an emphasis on feminist, multicultural and critical perspectives.

Please consult www.patricialeavy.com for submission requirements (click the book series tab).

VOLUME 13

The titles published in this series are listed at *brill.com/gend*

Feminist Theory and Pop Culture

Second Edition

Edited by

Adrienne Trier-Bieniek

BRILL

SENSE

LEIDEN | BOSTON

All chapters in this book have undergone peer review.

The Library of Congress Cataloging-in-Publication Data is available online at http://catalog.loc.gov

ISSN 2542-9205
ISBN 978-90-04-41423-5 (paperback)
ISBN 978-90-04-41424-2 (hardback)
ISBN 978-90-04-41425-9 (e-book)

This book is printed on acid-free paper and produced in a sustainable manner.

ADVANCE PRAISE FOR
FEMINIST THEORY AND POP CULTURE
(SECOND EDITION)

"This excellent anthology groups feminism as articulated through four waves and features feminists responding to pop culture, while recognizing that popular culture has responded in complicated ways to feminisms. Contributors proffer lucid and engaging critiques of topics ranging from belly dancing to *Fifty Shades of Grey, Scandal, and Orange is the New Black*. This book is a good read as well as an excellent text to enliven and inform in the classroom."
– Jane Caputi, Professor of Women, Gender, and Sexuality Studies and Communication & Multimedia at Florida Atlantic University

"*Feminist Theory and Pop Culture* is destined to be as popular as the culture it critiques! The text plays up the paradoxes of contemporary feminism and requires its readers to ask difficult questions about why the popular brings us pleasure. It is a diverse analysis of women's representations across an impressive swath of popular culture. *Feminist Theory and Pop Culture* is the kind of text that makes me want to redesign my pop culture course."
– Ebony A. Utley, author of *Rap and Religion*

For Dr. Kathleen Underwood,
the woman we should all aspire to be

CONTENTS

CONTENTS

ACKNOWLEDGEMENTS

Thank you to everyone at Brill | Sense, John Bennett and Paul Chambers, and to Patricia Leavy for creating and supporting the *Teaching Gender* series. Thank you, thank you, thank you to Jolanda Karada. Thank you to every contributor for sharing their expertise and talent. It is truly an honor to have you be a part of this work and to have you as a colleague.

I thank my colleagues, mentors, and friends, Chastity Blakenship, Carrie Buist, Michael Gillespie, Jessica Hubbard, Marlene Kowalski-Braun, Random Messesder, Angie Moe, Lee Paulsen, Chanda Postell, Catherine Sheika, Kim Taylor, Judy Whipps, Trisha Whitmire, Jen Wiles, and Bea Yarbrough. I also thank my family, especially my aunt Claudia Sperti, who always has my back. Thank you to all the Trier's, Sperti's, Bieniek's, and Reed's. Thanks to Adelina Sheika for being born to Catherine and Vadzim while I worked on this edition. #futurefeminist

Thank you Tim Bieniek for all the unconditional love. Thanks to my Charlie for laying at my feet while I wrote. And thank you Clara Danvers Trier-Bieniek for needing a home just when we needed you.

Thank you Dr. Kathleen Underwood for your tireless pursuit of equality and your unshakable ability in the face of injustice. Truly, I hope to one day be as incredible as you.

ADRIENNE TRIER-BIENIEK

INTRODUCTION

The problem with gender is that it prescribes how we should be rather than recognizing how we are.

– Chimamanda Ngozi Adichie

Sisters, you are here to learn to serve, to fight, to be fierce, to be fearless.

– Aneka, to the Dora Milaje initiates in
Black Panther: World of Wakanda

Recently, several moments in media have indicated that feminism is alive and well in popular culture. Thanks to streaming services coupled with network television, shows such as *Shrill, Orange is the New Black, Parks and Recreation, Scandal, One Day at a Time, 30 Rock, The Mindy Project, Unbreakable Kimmy Schmidt,* and *Superstore* have given viewers exposure to smart, funny and diverse women and men. In music, one doesn't have to look any further than Beyoncé standing in front of a massive sign reading "Feminist" while performing at the 2014 MTV Video Music Awards. A statement that, as Amanda Morcotte from Slate notes, in an image-driven culture where the five second sound bite rules and meme's are more popular than books, the image of Beyoncé declaring her feminism to the world just felt amazing.

What may have had the largest feminist impact on popular culture in recent memory comes from a duo of super hero films, 2017's *Wonder Woman* and 2019's *Captain Marvel. Wonder Woman*, directed by Patti Jenkins and staring Gal Gadot, was an unrivaled success when it hit theaters. As Angela Jade Bastien describes the character,

> Wonder Woman has always been at her best when her stories lean into the feminist ethos at her core. When artists treat her compassion as the key to understanding her – rather than her brutality in battle – audiences are privy to a superhero who offers what no other can: a power fantasy that privileges the interiority and desires of women. (2017, para. 1)

In the book *The Secret History of Wonder Woman*, Jill Lepore chronicles the history of the character and the man who created her. She writes,

> Wonder Woman isn't only an Amazonian princess with badass boots. She's the missing link in a chain of events that begins with the woman suffrage campaigns of the 1910s and ends with the troubled place of feminism fully a century later. Feminism made Wonder Woman. (2015, p. xiii)

For generations, Wonder Woman had been linked with feminist messages whether it was through the comic strip, or through the countless number of Wonder Woman merchandise available. And yet, when it came to film renditions of Justice League characters, Batman and Superman received much more attention. When Gadot's Wonder Woman makes her appearance in the 2016 film *Batman vs. Superman*, many people sat up in their seats at the introduction of a new warrior princess. (Even if she was only "new" to this series of films.) In 2017, upon the release of her own film, the audience was treated to more images of women warriors on screen than most people have seen in their lifetime. As the images of Amazonian women practicing their battle skills, juxtaposed with women in positions of political authority, and women leading the island of Themyscira, it became clear to the viewer that Wonder Women's story stands on the shoulders of many iterations of femininity. Add to this the diversity present in the casting of the Amazon women, including Gadot, an Israeli actress, and audiences were treated to the power of intersectional images present on a screen. Further, the character of Wonder Woman was portrayed as compassionate, curious, intellectual (she speaks dozens of languages) as well as strong, and relentless.

These characteristics are also present in 2019's *Captain Marvel*, part of the Marvel Universe series based on the comic characters. Captain Marvel, aka Carol Danvers, has become known throughout the Marvel Universe as the most powerful Avenger. During the film follows her origin story the viewer learns that Marvel's powers have been suppressed by her male mentor, Yon Rogg. A realization that leads to a quite satisfactory fight scene in which Yon Rogg tells Captain Marvel that she has learned all of her skills from him, taking credit and challenging her to fight without her powers. Captain Marvel sends him flying into a mountain.

Naturally, as one of two super hero movies which feature women as leads, comparisons have been made between Wonder Woman and Captain Marvel. In his review of Captain Marvel, Peter Travers writes,

A Riot Grrrl power pulses through every frame, not to mention humor, heart and the thrill that comes from watching a genuine game-changer. *Wonder Woman*, the 2017 epic from DC Comics, may have thrown the first punch for comic-book-movie equality among the sexes. But *Captain Marvel* should have its detractors on the ropes. (2019, para. 2)

Yet, the largest similarity that both movies share is the gender-based treatment they have received online. When *Wonder Woman* premiered in 2017 David Edelstein, reviewer for the website Vulture, was widely criticized for his write-up of the film. Edelstein's remarks focused widely on Gadot's looks, describing her as a former model, with a "superbabe-in-the-woods innocence and mouthiness." What seemingly upset readers the most was the comment,

She looks fabulous in her suffragette outfit with little specs, but it's not until she strips down to her superheroine bodice and shorts, pulls out her sword, and leaps into the fray, that she comes into her own. (para. 5)

Edelstein's use of gendered language presented an image of a woman removing her clothes in a suggestive manner. (Which the character does not do.) Additionally, the critique placed emphasis on the character's body and looks, two things which are overwhelmingly dominant in discussions of female characters. Backlash on Edelstein was swift, he printed an explanation defending his review a few days later. But, this dynamic is emblematic of a larger issue for gender and film. Does the sex, gender, race, age, sexual orientation, etc. of the reviewer affect the way they see a film? With *Captain Marvel*, we got the answer. Of course it does.

Prior to its release in March of 2019, *Captain Marvel's* Rotten Tomatoes page began to see a downward spiral of reviews. At one point, the film was rated as "29% fresh." Considering the film had yet to be released, many were curious about the source of these reviews. All signs pointed to trolls attempting to tank the film's box office numbers. Seemingly, their motivation was to spite Brie Larson, the star of the film, who had spoken out against the dominant narrative of white, male, filmmakers, reviewers, and storytellers.

Captain Marvel found itself in the crosshairs with some largely in response to Larson's advocacy for diversity in film and in those who write about it. A USC Annenberg Inclusion Initiative study last year found that, for the 100 top grossing films in 2017, 77.8 percent of the critics counted on Rotten Tomatoes were male and 86 percent were white. (Coyle, 2019, para. 13)

These examples of *Wonder Woman* and *Captain Marvel* are easily connectable to the roots of feminist theory. Essentially, feminist theory is associated with women's inequality and subordination. However, as you will see in these pages and in the history of feminism, as culture has developed and changed so has feminist theory. It is not surprising to see feminist theory linked with concepts like queer theory (aimed at gender identity in heteronormative societies) or theories related to women of color which are often based in how race and ethnicity shape experiences. Additionally, theories of masculinity, such as C.J. Pascoe's 2007 book *Dude You're a Fag: Masculinity and Sexuality in High Schools*, posit that there are many different approaches to masculinity and that men simultaneously benefit and suffer from patriarchal culture. (Thus the troll reaction to *Captain Marvel*.) Regardless, each incarnation has roots in similar parts of history. As bell hooks writes "Before women's studies classes, before feminist literature, individual women learned about feminism in groups. The women in the groups were the first to begin to create feminist theory which included both an analysis of sexism, strategies for challenging patriarchy, and new models of social interaction" (2000, p. 19). Congregating in groups to talk about feminist theory was also how activism and consciousness raising became synonymous with feminism. Consciousness raising, or raising awareness of a topic/idea/revolution in order to get a better understanding is often the link between theory and activism. This is why feminist theory and feminist activism often work in tandem.

What is more, defining feminism has become especially difficult in contemporary society as many women now arrive at adulthood having gone their entire lives benefiting from feminist movements and scholarship. When asked "Who is a feminist?", responses will probably vary depending on how one conceptualizes the term. However, most people will say that there are characteristics of feminists, founded in personal politics or the need to dismantle patriarchal structures, which are indicators of feminist identity.

Additionally, the juxtaposition of feminist theory and popular culture has an inevitable impact on the consumption of culture mainly because popular culture has the power to put up a mirror to our lives and show connections between media, socialization and identity. Pop culture is generally the images, narratives and ideas that circulate widely in contemporary culture. What makes something "popular" is its general availability to the masses and, from a social science point of view, it is usually something that we can consume (Trier-Bieniek, 2019). Additionally, the impact of pop culture is often subject to debate in academic communities. While some feel that the masses get a say in production of culture and the direction of media, like Theodor Adorno and Max Horkheimer find that pop culture works to support the interests of those in power (Milestone & Meyer, 2011). This text is largely situated in the latter, particularly when we consider the definition of feminism as a movement focused on the political and economic equality of the sexes. Pop culture's tendency to simultaneously celebrate and neglect this concept is one of the reasons why it is so ripe for exploration. To that end, a grasp of feminism becomes necessary in order to see how inequality and gender are linked in culture. Understanding how feminism came to be is key, especially so that we can deconstruct the ways feminism has been received by diverse groups of women.

THE WAVES OF FEMINISM AS A HISTORY OF FEMINIST THEORY

Feminism is defined as happening in "waves." Just like a literal wave, as one wave moves out another moves forward, retaining much of the structure of the original wave. As such, feminist movements are characterized as first, second and third waves respectively, with recent discussions happening regarding what makes a fourth wave. Perhaps the intention behind the wave analogy was a demonstration that women have not yet received equal rights and the women's movement is an ongoing process. If this was the case, the analogy for the waves of feminism can also act as a perfect illustration for the generations of women who make it up.

Historically, the work of Mary Wollstonecraft is often cited as the beginning of the first wave of feminism as it is one of the first writings which discuss women's liberation. In her 1792 essay, *A Vindication of the Rights of Women*, she writes "I may be accused of arrogance; still I must declare what I firmly believe, that all the writers who have written on the subject of female education and manners from Rousseau to Dr. Gregory, have contrived to render women more artificial, weak characters, then they would otherwise have been; and, consequently, more useless members of society" (1986, p. 7). Wollstonecraft began a discussion of women's place in society, a conversation which evolved into the Seneca Falls Convention of 1848.

The Seneca Falls Convention produced the *Declaration of Sentiments*. Based on the *Declaration of Independence*, the *Declaration of Sentiments* was primarily authored by Elizabeth Cady Stanton. In part it reads "The history of mankind is a history of repeated injuries and usurpations on the part of man toward woman, having in direct object the establishment of an absolute tyranny over her" (2000, p. 64). The purpose of this declaration was to establish a list of ways women have been deprived of rights and ends with resolutions, mainly contending that women must receive the right to vote. It was with this declaration that the first plans were made for suffrage and the convention lead to the work of suffragette women like Susan B. Anthony, Elizabeth Cady Stanton and eventually Alice Paul and Lucy Burns and ending with the 19th amendment.

While for most this period of feminist history is marked with women fighting for the right to vote, simultaneously there were rumblings of freedom for the enslaved. Perhaps the most noted women who had a hand in both movements was the African-American abolitionist Sorjourner Truth, a former slave and the first women of color to successfully sue a white slave-owner to reclaim the child he owned.

Truth's famous speech "Ain't I a Woman?" an extemporaneous speech given to the Women's Convention in Akron, Ohio in 1951, was a response to men in the audience discussing how women are delicate and should be treated as such. In part, Truth stated "That man over there says that women need to be helped into carriage, and lifted over ditches and to have the best place everywhere. Nobody ever helps me into carriages or over mud-puddles, or gives me any best place! And ain't I a woman?" (2000, p. 66) She goes on to respond to a man who asserted that women cannot have the same rights as men because Jesus Christ was a man. Truth states, "Where did your Christ come from? From God and a woman! Man had nothing to do with Him" (2000, p. 66). Truth's legacy is indefinitely linked with the foundation of feminist theory. It connects the activism of women of color to the role they often played by being on society's margins, something that became a focus of later waves of feminism. Many years later, Kerry Washington, an American actress, would perform this speech as part of Voices of People's History of the United States gathering.

Some notable works and events to emerge from the first wave:

- The book *Women in the Nineteenth Century* by Margaret Fuller in 1845.
- *Married Women's Property Act*-first passed in New York 1839, extending rights of property and to earn a salary.
- Oberlin College, the first American co-educational college/university, was founded in 1833.
- First birth control clinic was founded in Brooklyn, New York in 1916 and Planned Parenthood was incarnated as the American Birth Control League in 1938. (It would become Planned Parenthood in 1942.)

Some notable works and events in first wave pop culture:

- Mary Shelly publishes the novel *Frankenstein* in 1818, first anonymously and then under Shelly's name in 1823. Shelly, is also the daughter of Mary Wollstonecraft and Frankenstein contains many references to her mother's writing and ideas.
- Jane Austin publishes multiple stories centered on female characters and their resistance to depend on men.
- Charlotte Perkins Gilman publishes *The Yellow Wallpaper* in 1892, address the lack of attention paid to women's physical and mental well-being.
- Hattie McDaniel becomes the first African-American to win an Academy Award for her portrayal of Mammy in *Gone with the Wind* in 1939.
- The 2004 film *Iron Jawed Angels* depicts suffragette Alice Paul's crusade in the ten years before women were awarded the right to vote. Alice Paul is played by Academy Award winner Hilary Swank.
- In 2015 Meryl Streep and Carry Mulligan starred in the film *Suffragette*.

Feminism's second wave is characterized by the women's rights movements of the 1960s and 1970s with the mantra "The Personal is Political." This wave became focused on women pursuing careers, reproductive rights, addressing violence against women and pay equality (to name a few) as well as a focus on laws like the Equal Rights Amendment. Spurred by Betty Friedan's 1963 book, *The Feminine Mystique*, many women of this time read about and related to the "problem which has no name." A graduate of Smith College, with a degree in psychology, Friedan was dismissed from her journalism job in 1952 because she was pregnant with her second child. While she was a stay-at-home mom Friedan began to question why women were shelving their education in order to raise families. In 1957 she surveyed women at her college reunion, asking about their education and satisfaction with life. What she found was that, while women were more likely than their mothers to attend college, they were also shelving their careers to stay at home and, as a result, felt under stimulated, constantly asking the question "Is this all?" Seemingly these women had everything, but found themselves intellectually unfilled, wanting careers and feeling guilty for not being thankful for their lives.

One of the main theoretical frameworks which characterized the second wave of feminism is Simone de Beauvoir's book *The Second Sex* in which de Beauvoir declares that women are categorized as the Other. She writes, "The category of the Other is as primordial as consciousness itself. In the most primitive societies, in the most ancient mythologies, one finds the expression of a duality-that is of the Self and Other" (1948, p. xxii). Simone de Beauvoir writes of women's position in society as secondary, almost as an afterthought and, as a result, women involuntarily participate in oppressive social norms. She writes, "Why is it that women do not dispute male sovereignty? No subject will readily volunteer to become the object, the inessential..." (1948, p. xxiv). What makes this work central to the second wave of feminism is Simone de Beauvoir's contention that women stay in a subordinate position because they have been made to feel complacent. The work of women like Friedan and de Beauvoir, combined with the changing political climate of the 1960s, created a sense of urgency for feminists to develop a second generation of women who were willing to carry on, and expand upon the work of previous generations of women. Commonly referred to as "women's lib," the second wave took on many areas of women's rights, particularly violence against women, prostitution and pornography, birth control and access to contraception and the growing need for more women in the work force and in political office.

However, criticism of the second wave has focused on its contradictions, particularly relating to race, sexuality, and social class. Women of color have reported feeling like they were placed on the margins of the waves of feminism in general and the second wave of feminism in particular. Kinser writes, "Second-wave feminism may have been better at making decisions about what was in the purview of feminism, but it may have silenced voices that should have been part of the feminist dialogue" (2004, p. 145).

Perhaps it is best to start with bell hooks's critique of Betty Friedan, particularly her essay's on feminist theory in *Feminist Theory: From Margin to Center* which discusses the marginalized experiences women of color have with feminism. hooks writes, "Betty Friedan's *The Feminine Mystique* is still heralded as having paved the way for contemporary feminist movement-it was written as if these women did not exist... (It) actually referred to the plight of a select group of college-educated, middle and upper class, married white women-housewives bored with leisure, with the home, with children..." (1984, p. 1). hooks, and many women of color theorists, found much fault with the work of Friedan whose pool of interviews, friends and neighbor's she knew, were (for the most part) white, middle class women living in affluent neighborhoods. The assertion that these women wanted to step away from their homes and work was almost offensive to hooks because, as she contended, women of color have always worked. "She did not discuss who would be called in to take care of the children and maintain the home if more women like herself were freed from their house labor..." (1984, p. 1). Whether it be in the fields, or as a caregiver to white women's children (see Ehrenreich & Hoschild, 2003), or on the front lines of equality battles women of color were present in the work world, mainly because the choice to stay at home and raise children was something that, hooks argues, was left to white, upper class women.

Patricia Hill Collins 1990 book, *Black Feminist Thought*, while not specifically situated in the second wave but certainly influenced by it, addressed the need to place the voices and experiences of women of color at the forefront of feminist theory. *Black Feminist Thought* became situated in critical social theory as it was born out of a critique of oppression and aimed to find ways to survive in economic injustice. Hill Collins argues that, particularly for African-American women, critical social theory is about bodies of knowledge and industrial practices that struggle with questions facing Black women. *Black Feminist Thought* catapulted questions of contradictions between dominant ideologies and their devalued status. Topics like the merit of "good" mothering being based on stay-at-home motherhood, a standard rooted in race and class, became part of discussions of feminism. Hill Collins connected these scenarios to being "the outsider looking in," defining Black Feminist Thought as a metaphorical margin, a place where Black women could see the world they are supposed to exist in but could not quite participate. The experiences of women of color produce their own category of knowledge which can be used to advance understanding of what it is like to be a marginalized group within an already marginalized group.

Gloria Anzaldua's contribution to feminist theory, and the second wave, rested in the U.S. borderlands as physical and metaphorical boundaries faced by women of color. She uses the examples of human trafficking to illustrate Mexican women being used as monetary gain. "The Mexican women is especially at risk. Often the coyote doesn't feed her for days or let her go to the bathroom. Often he rapes her or sells her into prostitution" (1987, p. 34). Additionally, Audre Lorde's 1984 book *Sister Outsider: Essays and Speeches* chronicled her journey to discover her sexuality through the lens of identifying as a Black feminist poet. Lorde contends that the feminist movement, which had largely been comprised of white women, ignored the aspects of race and class present in the struggle for women's rights. She also contends that Black and Third World people, people who are the working poor and who are elderly took on the role of the "dehumanized inferior." She questioned why it must be that members of oppressed groups should be the ones reaching out to educate White America.

Essentially, writing like Lorde, Hill Collins, hooks and Anzaldua laid the groundwork for an intersectional approach to future discussions in feminist theory. Intersectionality, as it is commonly called, can be traced to the work of Kimberle Crenshaw but may have deeper roots in a statement by the Combahee River Collective (CRC) who wrote *A Black Feminist Statement* in 1977. Crenshaw's contention is that forms of oppression are connected, as the CRC said, they are interlocking. Thus, it becomes difficult to address oppression simply based on one category of oppression (i.e. race, gender, social class, sexuality etc.) This theory argues that examining the oppression of women cannot happen in a vacuum, rather we must be examining the whole of women's experiences using their standpoint.

Some notable works and events to emerge from the second wave:

- Mass production of oral contraceptives.
- Equal Pay Act of 1963, Civil Rights Act of 1964, Title IX is passed in 1972 and Roe vs. Wade is passed in 1973. Additionally, Laws passed against marital rape, limiting access to contraception and repealing "help wanted" ads which were arranged by sex.
- Creation of the National Organization of Women (Originally headed by Betty Friedan) in 1966.
- The Redstockings Group, who will later publish the radical feminist work, *The Redstockings Manifesto* is formed in 1969.
- *Sexual Politics* by Kate Millett is published in 1970, critiquing sexual theory posited by researchers such as Sigmond Freud and John Stuart Mill.
- *Against Our Will: Men, Women and Rape* is published in 1975 by Susan Brownmiller. The book is one of the first to address rape myths in contemporary society.
- Laura Mulvey publishes *Visual Pleasure and Narrative Cinema* in 1972, addressing the male gaze and its prevalence in film.

Some notable works and events in second wave pop culture:

- Gloria Steinem and Letty Cottin Pogrebin founded *Ms. Magazine* in 1972.
- Tennis player Billie Jean King defeats Bobby Riggs in the televised "Battle of the Sexes" in 1973.
- *The Mary Tyler Moore* show premieres in 1970, depicting the single woman as independent, career driven and politically aware.
- The television show *Maude* becomes one of the first to address abortion as a story line.
- In 2016 the film *Hidden Figures* would chronicle the women of color mathematicians who worked at NASA during the Space Race of the 1950s and 1960s.

Many feminist writers relate the beginning of the third wave of feminism to 1991 and the work of Naomi Wolf who, in *The Beauty Myth,* stated that feminism needed a rekindling. Others point to a statement made by Rebecca Walker in *Ms. Magazine* in 1992. Walker, infuriated by the Clarence Thomas hearings and the implications they had for minority women, declared that "I am not a post-feminism feminist, I am the Third Wave" (Walker, 1992, p. 41).

Amy Richards and Jennifer Baumgardner, via their 2000 book *Manifesta: Young Women, Feminism and the Future* are also credited with bringing the third wave of feminism into the forefront. In *Manifesta* they argue that feminist and political theory has as much a place in third wave feminism as the impact of pop culture. Third wave's use of activism via pop culture was particularly evident in much of the music in the early to mid 1990s, especially with the Riot Grrrl movement. The Riot Grrrl music scene was a grouping of bands which started in the Washington D.C. area in the early 1990s as a way for young women to participate in the male-dominated punk rock scene. (Trier-Bieniek, 2013) The "Riot Grrrl" title was conceptualized as a way to "[r]eclaim the validity and power of youth with an added growl to replace the perceived passitivity of 'girl'" (Rosenberg & Garofalo, 2001, p. 810). Essentially, the combination of pop culture and feminism signified the third wave because it allowed new generations of feminist women to be who they want to be, but with a political consciousness.

The third wave of feminism has had a broad focus as it is the first generation of feminists to grow up in the cyber age and because there has been much focus on eliminating notions of post-feminism and contentions that feminism is for white women. Because current generations of women have grown up with feminism perhaps it is for this reason that the emergence of the third wave of feminism is often confused with the "post feminist" era. "For these women, and for anyone born after the early 1960's, the presence of feminism in our lives is taken for granted. For our generation, feminism is like fluoride. We scarcely notice that we have it – it's simply in the water" (Richards & Baumgardner, 2000, p. 17). Because young women growing up around this time were benefiting from the second wave's work by having the ability to play sports, get birth control etc. there was a concern that the rights they had were being taken for granted. In fact, Richards and Baumgardner write in their dedication to *Manifesta* "To feminists everywhere-including those of our generation who say, 'I'm not a feminist, but...' (2000, p. vii). A result of this contention is the third wave's focus on allowing feminists to define the term for themselves.

At the forefront for the third wave has been the inclusion of non-Western women in discussions of women's rights. Particularly through the work of Chandra Talpade Mohanty whose 1986 essay *Under Western Eyes: Feminist Scholarship and Colonial Discourses* took a postcolonialist view of Western feminism and critiqued the view of "Third World woman" as hegemonic. Mohanty states that Western feminisms have tended to gloss over the differences between women of the global South, ignoring the diverse experiences of oppression, particularly how they are contingent on geography, history, and culture. Vandana Shiva's work is another example of the impact of non-Western women in feminism. Shiva's collection of research and theoretical positions was the basis of her 2008 work *Soil Not Oil*, which addresses the growing environmental problems in India and uses an ecofeminist approach to the environment. Ecofeminim contends that when women-focused systems are used to solve community problems there are higher rates of success.

Some notable events and works to emerge from the third wave:

- Family Medical Leave Act becomes law in 1992.
- Violence Against Women act becomes law in 1995.
- The Fourth World Conference on Women was held in China in 1995. Here Hillary Clinton gave a speech contenting that "Women's rights are human rights and human rights are women's rights."
- In 2004 the March for Women's Lives was held on the Washington D.C. National Mall in support of reproductive health.
- Judith Butler publishes her seminal work on gender, *Gender Trouble*, in 1999.

Some notable works and events in third wave pop culture:

- Eve Ensler, writer of *The Vagina Monologues*, founds V-Day, an international effort to end violence against women. V-Day, to date, has raised over 100 million dollars for local, national and international women's groups via performance of *The Vagina Monologues*.
- BUST magazine enters into publication with a focus on feminism and pop culture in 1993.
- *Buffy the Vampire Slayer* (TV show) premiers in 1997 giving audiences a feminist, female character on a major television show.
- *30 Rock* premiers in 2006 with the character of Liz Lemon (Tina Fey) declaring her third wave feminism in the pilot episode. Leslie Knope (Amy Poehler) would soon follow in *Parks and Recreation*.

- The combination of Tori Amos, Ani DiFranco, Liz Phlair and Sarah MacLachlan mark a changing tide in music during the early 1990s.
- Queen Latifah selects of number of historical Black women's images in her 1992 video for *Ladies First*.
- Madonna cultivates discussions of sex, "artistic integrity" and feminism with her albums and concerts.

While there are few major declarations supporting the idea, there is a push for a fourth wave of feminism, including a chapter in this text. Currently, two major schools of thought have been proposed to define this wave. One, as discussed by Wyre (2009) contends that

> The Fourth Wave of feminism brings us into the 21st century as women who focus our attention on a question that earlier waves may have addressed but not to the extent now required: the limits of materialism; the need to turn from concerns about 'me' to concern for the planet and all its beings; and the sense that, for us in the Fourth Wave, what is most important is to put ourselves in the service of the world. (p. 187)

Indeed, understanding not only how inequality affects us locally but world-wide as well has been examined in the third wave but does merit more study by new generations of scholars. However, perhaps the most agreed upon aspect of the fourth wave of feminism is the use of technology and digital culture.

Twitter, Facebook, YouTube, blogs are just a few of the ways contemporary feminism has taken to the internet. Activism and feminist theory present themselves in the form of websites like *Feminist Frequency* which is dedicated to addressing gender's representation in media. Run by Anita Sarkeesian, *Feminist Frequency* presents videos breaking down troupes such as the presentation of women in video games or the use of violence against women as a backdrop in gaming communities. In a 2014 interview with *Rolling Stone* Sarkeesian relays that *Feminist Frequency* was founded as a way to move feminist theory out of academia and into the public sphere. Feminist theory is also present in the use of meme's with websites such as *Beyoncé Voters* which takes quotes from Beyoncé songs and repurposes them with images of powerful political women. Blogs such as Girl W/Pen and the Gender & Society Blog work to connect feminist theory and research with contemporary culture. Facebook pages like *Pop Culture Feminism* present scholarly ideas about feminism with current pop culture icons. Yet, one could hardly argue that this is exhaustive. There needs to be much more exploration of what this new generation of feminists is and what they can be. While some may contend that this can happen under the heading of the third wave, others declare that a fourth wave is here (i.e. Baumgarnder, 2011).

A few examples of works and events constructing the fourth wave are:

- Jessica Valenti creates the feminist blog Feministing.
- Malala Yousafzai's image and message of education for girls world-wide goes viral after a 2012 assassination attempt. In 2014 she become the youngest recipient of the Nobel Peace Prize.
- Patrick Stewart (of *Star Trek: The Next Generation*) declares his feminism and support for lgbt rights while also speaking out against violence against women.
- Beyoncé stands in front of a glowing "Feminist" sign at the 2014 MTV Video Music Awards.
- The film *Frozen* becomes the number one animated film of all time.
- Lena Dunham creates, stars in and directs the HBO series *Girls* in 2012 and releases a book of essays on feminism and young women in 2014.
- The 2017 (and subsequent) women's march on Washington in protest of the Trump Presidency.
- The rise of blog writers and activists like Luvvie Ajayi, and Glennon Doyle.
- The use of social media by celebrities to circulate intersectional feminist ideas. (For a few examples, see the accounts of Aidy Bryant, Busy Phillips, Aisling Bea, Alison Desir, Amy Poehler's Smart Girls, America Ferrera, Dax Shepard, Kristin Bell, Jameela Jamil, Ronan Farrow, and John Legend.
- More women in comedy are featured on streaming platforms. (For a few examples, see *Nanette* by Hannah Gadsby and *Baby Cobra* by Ali Wong.)

FEMINIST APPROACHES TO RESEARCH

When discussing feminist theory it becomes necessary to mention how theory connects to research. Feminist methodology was constructed as a response to sexism in research, particularly the ways women were treated while being studied. A main argument is that those who participate in social research should be viewed not as "subjects" but as key components to understanding social phenomena. By considering the people we study from a feminist point of view, we place the stories and positions of these people at the forefront of our research. These positions are particularly important when researching popular culture. As Leavy writes, "By investigating culture in general, and popular culture more specifically, dominant narratives, images, ideas and stereotyped representations can be exposed and challenged" (2007, p. 224).

One of the theoretical approaches feminist researchers take as a tool to combat patriarchal foundations and critiques of feminist methods is to argue for a feminist standpoint, a theory used to state the importance of all women's voices being brought to the forefront. One purpose of a feminist standpoint is to create a situated knowledge. Starting from the position of women's lives who are different than our own allows us to understand a great deal about the impact of dominant groups. When feminist analysis is done from the perspective of a marginalized woman, or her standpoint, the research becomes enhanced and strengthened by her point of view.

Situated knowledge leads to Harding's concept of strong objectivity. Essentially, when considering research from a feminist standpoint, strong objectivity "Requires that the subject of knowledge be placed in the same critical causal plane as the objects of knowledge" (2004, p. 36). In order for a researcher to truly begin to understand a phenomena, she must start from the position of people (in this case, women) who have traditionally been left out of research. Strong objectivity happens when there is an increased motivation for the researcher to become knowledgeable of power structures within their methodologies and research. Additionally, understanding how our positions affect our research is key because researcher position leads to the introspective element found in feminist analysis. Identity cannot be ignored in feminist research because part of conducting feminist research is understanding where and how the standpoint of women has been neglected.

CONSTRUCTION OF FEMINIST THEORY AND POP CULTURE

Feminist Theory and Pop Culture is composed of a combination of chapters addressing many of the theories and topics covered in this introduction. The book begins with "Unveiling the Gaze: Belly Dance as a Site of Refuge, Re-Envisioning and Resistance" by Angela M. Moe. In this chapter Moe deconstructs the male gaze through an extremely in-depth research on the history, use and contemporary popularity of belly dance, particularly in Western communities. The chapter utilizes the theoretical components of Laura Mulvey's concept of the gaze and addresses how belly dance fits with the "to be looked at ness" described in Mulvey's seminal work.

In Chapter 2, "Lena Dunham, *GIRLS,* and the Contradictions of Fourth-Wave Feminism" April Kalogeropoulos Householder addresses the changing tides of feminism, a point in history when the lyrics of pop songs are as connected to feminist theory as the writing of historical feminist theorists. Using the HBO series *Girls*, Householder contends that new generations of women are finding their feminism in pop culture and that the future of feminist theory might be reflected in celebrity.

Chapter 3, "Olivia Pope as Problematic and Paradoxical: A Black Feminist Critique of *Scandal's* 'Mammification'" relates the theoretical approach of Black feminist thought with the wildly popular television show *Scandal*. In this chapter, Rachel Alicia Griffin explores both sides of the Mammy image presented by the show's main character, Olivia Pope. Connecting Black feminist thought with images in pop culture is also present in Chapter 4, "The Un-Quiet Queen: An Analysis of Rapper Nicki Minaj in the *Fame* Comic Book." Here Melvin Williams and Tia Tyree utilize the images of Nicki Minaj in the *Fame* comic book series as examples of both Black feminist theory and the sexual scripts present for women of color. Williams and Tyree contend that these sexual scripts are present through a lens which receives popular culture as a source of power heavily based in preconceived racial and gender roles.

Addressing theories of power and the position of power in popular culture is central to Chapter 5, "Queerness (Un)Shackled: Theorizing *Orange is the New Black*." Using queer theory present in the work of Judith Butler and Adrienne Rich, Lauren J. DeCarvalho and Nicole B. Cox consider how the Netflix series *Orange is the New Black* utilizes both gender performance and compulsory heterosexuality. They contend that the queer-based storylines and narratives of the show often act as morality tales combining queer theory with contemporary characters.

Examining gender roles in television shows is also a focus of Chapter 6, "Warning! Social Construction Zone!: Exploring Masculinities, Femininities and Gender Roles in Cop Shows." Here Carrie Buist and Jean-Anne Sutherland deconstruct the television shows *Chicago P.D.*, *The Shield* and *Rookies* in order to expose the many layers of hegemonic masculinity on television. Buist and Sutherland argue that masculinity and femininity on these shows are mutually exclusive and that the performance of manhood found in police-themed shows is also linked to how masculinity will be interpreted by viewers.

Chapter 7, "*Girl Rising* and the Problematic 'Other': Celebritizing Third-World Girlhoods" by Emily Bent analyzes the popular documentary *Girl Rising*. Through the use of feminist standpoint theory, Bent contends that the use of celebrity in telling the story of third world girls' experiences shapes humanitarian aid efforts for girls' education. This juxtaposition problematizes the ways in which experience, identity, and voice can result in 'celebritized' knowledge about third world girls, rather than their stories being told in their own voices.

With Chapter 8, Patricia Boyd utilizes postfeminist theory to address contemporary views of sex. "Paradoxes of Postfeminism: Coercion and Consent in *Fifty Shades of Grey*" uses the conflicting feelings found in the popular novel *Fifty Shades of Grey* to illustrate complicated choices present when navigating a feminist identity. She contends that, in part because feminism has had its conflicts, that this tension is reflected in the book and in the reception of the book. These themes, which are a growing part of defining the fourth wave, are also present in Chapter 9, "From Street to Tweet: Popular Culture and Feminist Activism." In this chapter Jenn Brandt and Sam Kizer explore the future of feminism in the face of its current challenges and potential identity crisis. Brandt and Kizer address cyberfeminism as a potential marker of the fourth wave of feminism and assert that digital culture is the future of feminist activism.

While *Feminist Theory and Pop Culture* consists of many diverse essays, it is not meant to be an exhaustive anthology. Rather, this text should serve as introductory discussions of feminism reflected in popular culture. Much is still to be learned about the impact of pop culture on feminism and, because culture is ever-evolving, so will theories of feminism. If a fourth wave is upon us, perhaps this text can be a jumping off point into the next ocean of knowledge relating feminism, gender and pop culture.

DISCUSSION QUESTIONS

1. What examples of feminism in pop culture can you think of?
2. What social media pages, blogs, or websites do you follow that relate to feminism and pop culture?
3. How can feminist theory be used to explore contemporary gender roles?
4. Discuss song lyrics which you relate to gender and/or feminism. Are there musicians who are challenging patriarchal standards through their music?

REFERENCES

Bastien, A. J. (2017). *Review: Wonder Woman*. Retrieved on March 15, 2019, from https://www.rogerebert.com/reviews/wonder-woman-2017

Baumgardner, J. (2011). *F'em!: Goo goo, gaga and some thoughts on balls*. New York, NY: Seal Press.

Baumgardner, J., & Richards, A. (2000). *Manifesta: Young women, feminism and the future.* New York, NY: Farrar, Straus and Giroux.

de Beauvoir, S. (1948). *The second sex.* New York, NY: Knopf.

Coyle, J. (2019). *In success for Captain Marvel, a defeat for trolls.* Retrieved March 15, 2019, from https://www.apnews.com/b5212d2607574b7796f7fcdb74c7ec29

Edelstein, D. (2016). *Wonder Woman is a star turn for Gal Gadot, but the rest is pretty clunky.* Retrieved March 15, 2019, from https://www.vulture.com/2017/06/movie-review-wonder-woman-is-a-star-turn-for-gal-gadot.html

Ehrenreich, B., & Hoshschild, A. R. (2002). *Global woman.* New York, NY: Metropolitan Books.

Friedan, B. (1963). *The feminine mystique.* New York, NY: W.W. Norton.

Harding, S. (2004). Rethinking standpoint epistemology: What is 'strong objectivity'? In S. Harding (Ed.), *The feminist standpoint theory reader* (pp. 127–140). New York, NY: Routledge.

Hill Collins, P. (1990). *Black feminist thought: Knowledge, consciousness, and the politics of empowerment.* New York, NY: Routledge.

hooks, b. (1984). *Feminist theory from margin to center.* Cambridge, MA: SouthEnd Press.

hooks, b. (2000). *Feminism is for everybody.* Cambridge, MA: SouthEnd Press.

Lapore, J. (2015). *The secret history of Wonder Woman.* New York, NY: Vintage Books.

Leavy, P. L. (2007). The feminist practice of content analysis. In S. Hesse-Biber & P. L. Leavy (Eds.), *Feminist research methods* (pp. 223–249). New York, NY: Oxford University Press.

Kinser, A. (2004). Negotiating space for/through third-wave feminism. *NWSA Journal, 16*(1), 124–153.

Milestone, K., & Meyer, A. (2011). *Gender and popular culture.* Boston, MA: Polity.

Pascoe, C. J. (2007). *Dude, you're a fag: Masculinity and sexuality in high school.* Berkley, CA: University of California Press.

Rosenberg, J., & Garofalo, G. (2001). Riot Grrrl: Revolutions from within. *Signs, 23*(3), 809–841.

Travers, P. (2019). *Captain Marvel review: Brie Larson takes on cosmic villians, sexist trolls, and wins.* Retrieved March 15, 2019, from https://www.rollingstone.com/movies/movie-reviews/captain-marvel-movie-review-brie-larson-802831/

Trier-Bieniek, A. (2013). *Sing us a song, piano woman: Female fans and the music of Tori Amos.* Lanham, MD: Scarecrow Press.

Trier-Bieniek, A. (2019). *Gender & pop culture: A text-reader* (2nd ed.) Dordrecht, The Netherlands: Brill Publishers.

Walker, R. (1992, January–February). Becoming the third wave. *Ms. Magazine*, 39–41.

Wollstonecraft, M. (1986). *A vindication of the rights of woman.* London, England: Everyman's Library.

Wyre, H. K. (2009). The fourth wave of feminism: Psychoanalytic perspectives introductory remarks. *Studies in Gender and Sexuality, 10*(4), 185–189.

ANGELA M. MOE

1. UNVEILING THE GAZE

Belly Dance as a Site of Refuge, Re-Envisioning and Resistance

A central concept within feminist theory and pop culture is "the gaze" – the realization of being seen and interpreted by others, and adjusting one's conduct accordingly. Stated differently, the gaze represents the notion that something happens inside of us (within our cognitive and psychological processes) when we become conscious of others' observations of us, and that we often alter our physical presentation, language, demeanor and behavior in response to such changes. Analyses of the gaze have occurred through various cultural contexts over the last several decades, including media (e.g., television, advertising), fine art (e.g., paintings, sculpture) and graphic literature (e.g., comics). When applied to settings where women feel observed, assessed and judged primarily on their physical appearance by others, predominantly heterosexual men (or the presumed lens through which a heterosexual man would look at a woman), the analyses becomes one of "the male gaze."

This chapter applies the theory of the male gaze to performance art, particularly belly dance (aka, oriental or Middle Eastern dance), which is laden with stereotypes relating to eroticism and sexuality. I argue that such stereotypes are direct products of the male gaze, as manifested through an interconnected stream of political, economic and cultural factors related to gender, women's role, and the Middle and Near East. I then go on to illustrate how American belly dancers today recognize and negotiate the male gaze.

EVOLUTION OF GAZE THEORY

The foundation for the concept of the gaze arose primarily from two distinct mid-20th century French intellectuals, Jean-Paul Sartre and Jacques Lacan. Sartre (1958/2003) discussed the notion of subjectivity, or the condition of being a subject of another's consciousness or awareness. He illustrates the point by describing the scenario where one comes across a life-like mannequin and, for a brief moment, believes that it is another person. Sartre

© KONINKLIJKE BRILL NV, LEIDEN, 2019 | DOI:10.1163/9789004414259_001

was specifically interested in the change in consciousness a person has in such a moment, when becoming aware that she/he is not alone and may be observed by others. Likewise, the controversial French psychiatrist, Jacques Lacan (2006), spent decades of his life lecturing on various incarnations of Freudian-based psychology. Among some of his more noteworthy commentary was his belief about the effects of being observed. He noted that the realization that others may gaze upon us often facilitates greater self-conscious and that this may be both unsettling and anxiety producing.

To illustrate, think about how you act when you are alone versus amongst others. Many people will freely admit that they act differently when all alone, perhaps in the comfort and privacy of their own home. Being alone in a private setting, we might not worry so much about how we look or behave. We assume nobody else is watching, and thus we feel freer do what we want to do and to keep our attention focused inward rather than on outward appearances. However, when outside of our homes in public settings, or just around others, we may act and present ourselves differently based on where we are, who we are with, and how we believe we are supposed to behave (or at least we have become aware, through socialization, of such expectations). These private-to-public modifications may be conceptualized as products of the gaze. Gaze theory encompasses efforts to understand and apply the notion of the gaze in various settings. It provides a framework for analyzing how people learn about, create and maintain power differences within a culture based on visual cues.

Becoming aware of the gaze is not necessarily a bad thing. It does, after all, help us to understand how to function most successfully in the world. However, it is possible that the gaze becomes harmful and oppressive. Such has been the perspective of theorists who have advanced gaze theory. Michel Foucault (1975), another contemporary French social theorist, discussed the gaze in relation to penology (the study of punishment and use of prisons). By studying the structure of early penitentiaries, he found that inmates within the panopticon design, where a guard station sits in the center of several outward expanding cellblocks (imagine the hub and spokes of an old wagon wheel), were especially conscious of the gaze. In Foucault's use of the concept, the gaze represents the effect of constant observation by others and the subsequent lack of privacy. In such prison structures, he theorized, inmates were apt to begin self-regulating since they assumed their behavior was always being monitored, even if it wasn't (i.e., the prison guard was turned away from the cellblock), so as to avoid reprimand for inappropriate conduct. He argued that such practices affected a person not just physically, but also emotionally, mentally and spiritually.

While Foucault's work occurred predominantly within the guise of penal practice, the implications of it spanned much further. Many believe he was not talking so much about prisons and correctional strategy as much as observing changes in the modern world. Think about how much less privacy we have today, compared to the past, with the various technological advances that allow us to stay connected with (plugged into) the outside-public world 24/7. Indeed, the self-regulatory effects of the gaze have had widespread influence on the development of contemporary feminist theory (see Bordo, 1989). Laura Mulvey was among the first and most influential of feminists to extend the concept of the gaze to the oppressive effects of society and socialization on women.

Writing during the time of the second wave women's movement, Mulvey's (1975) objective in the essay "Visual Pleasure and Narrative Cinema" was to recognize and question gender asymmetry (power differences) within the visual arts and entertainment industries. Like Foucault, her focus on one element of society was meant to suggest something about general social conditions – in this case, gendered power differences between men and women. Mulvey argued that the portrayal of women in various forms of film were primarily aesthetic in purpose. They are presented in ways that appeal to others, notably heterosexual men. (Note that most of the arts and entertainment industries were, and remain, controlled by heterosexual, as well as white, men.) From their perspective, sexualizing women (portraying them as objects of heterosexual male desire) was assumed to be most aesthetically pleasing (and by extension, more profitable).

To illustrate her points, Mulvey (1975, 2009) discussed camera angles within cinematography, highlighting the common technique of pausing or focusing the lens on certain parts of women's bodies, namely those associated with sexual appeal (e.g., breasts, buttocks, legs). Those watching the film must accept this portrayal, regardless of who they are or to whom they are sexually attracted. In this way, the heterosexual male perspective arises as the predominant, if not only, one. Alternative perspectives are secondary or irrelevant. Consequently, women's perspectives and worth, both in the entertainment industry and larger society, also appear secondary or irrelevant. The consequences are both interactional and relational. Women become accustomed to hegemonic views of their physicality. They learn that talent, skill, knowledge, ability and experience are secondary to physical appearance (Lorber & Moore, 2007). As adaptation they may look at themselves through the eyes of (heterosexual) men. The gaze is internalized. Those whomever best embodies normative definitions of beauty (thin yet curvaceous, slender/

3

toned, white and youthful) are most likely to be hired, and highlighted, in entertainment productions, and elsewhere. All others are left chasing the aesthetic ideal or settling with less desirable options. As American feminist philosopher, Judith Butler (1999) has attested, this process is about enacting, or performing, one's gender according to social expectations. In time, it becomes seemingly natural and routine – the status quo. What early feminist sociologists termed "doing gender" (West & Zimmerman, 1987).

As with all discussions of power differences, gender cannot be divorced from race, ethnicity, age, size, and so on. Thus the women who most readily found secure and lucrative roles, in cinema and elsewhere, fit ideal notions of beauty and sexual allure. Just as Foucault (1975) suggested of inmates within the panopticon, one of the effects of this situation were that women more readily regulated themselves, striving at sometimes unhealthy and unsafe levels to fit the narrow hegemonic vision of aesthetic beauty. As a result, women expect to be viewed, judged and visually consumed as objects. It is not a far leap from here to see how women might be inclined to play a role in their own exploitation. The male gaze inundates us, especially today. It is an expected, and too often unquestioned, aspect of our culture. Women's worth becomes quite literally tied to their physical attractiveness. Beauty, as defined by Western, heterosexual, white male standards, is a commodity – something that they may leverage for opportunities and benefits (Lorber & Moore, 2007).

SOCIAL CONTEXT OF BELLY DANCE

Belly dance (known by various other names, including oriental dance, Middle Eastern dance, and Arab dance) is a recreational activity that has generated considerable interest by women (and those who would like to gaze upon women) for millennia. It generally represents an amalgamation of dance styles originating in and around the Middle East (northern Africa, southeastern Mediterranean, Arab peninsula, and southeastern Asia), that are used in community celebrations, religious ceremonies, and various other aspects of daily life (Shay & Sellers-Young, 2005). Given such a vast region of origination, belly dance is by necessity an eclectic form of movement that has remained largely uncodified – meaning there are few set movements, with standardized names and agreed upon lineage. It is largely seen as expressive, easily personalized, and adaptable. It is also considered to be a derivative of the oldest documented dances within civilization, with archeological evidence in Egypt and the eastern Mediterranean region dating to 3400 BCE. While its historical uses are subject to much debate, it has been suggested that belly dance played a role in rituals and celebrations related to god/goddess worship, harvest celebrations, holidays, courtship, sex education, marriage ceremonies, pregnancy and birthing preparations, and funeral rites (Dox, 2005; Mourat, 2000).

However, this is not what a lot of people think of as belly dance today. Rather than an indigenous form of celebration or ritual, belly dance is more often associated with obscene eroticism and impropriety. (Picture the long-haired, ample breasted and barely clothed woman who shamelessly undulates and shimmies for tips or a hookup at the local Middle Eastern restaurant.) Such connotations have evolved over time, as a product of various gendered social, economic and political forces related to tourism, Orientalism, and European colonialism. Space does not permit a full historical review, but suffice it to say that women have often served as the conduit of cross-cultural trade and tourism, as well as colonialist expansion and exploitation. The greater Middle Eastern region has suffered its share of this, and so too has belly dance. The last several hundred years are especially telling.

Take, for example, the myriad writings and paintings to emerge during Orientalism (1700s–1800s) where women were often depicted as well-endowed, partially nude performers within harem or outdoor slave markets. Such images portrayed women as wanton objects of male desire – explicitly present for the titillating gaze of (heterosexual) men (Alloula, 1986). Never mind the fact that women were imported from various colonized outposts and sold largely as domestic servants or sex slaves, or that Ottoman harems were highly secretive and completely private, the goings on in which are largely speculative. Those who were dancers by trade were (and still are) heavily scrutinized and often ostracized legally and socially (Dougherty, 2005; Karayanni, 2004; MacMaster & Lewis, 1998).

The United States has had a direct hand in shaping contemporary perceptions of belly dance. "Dancing girls" from the Middle and Near East were brought to Chicago in 1893 for the World Columbian Exposition (World's Fair). Their disreputable gyrations, though performed under layers of modest clothing, became known as the "hootchy kootchy" dance and helped bolster ticket sales by conservative Victorian fair-goers (AlZayer, 2010; Carlton 1994). Moreover, Oscar Wilde's play, Salome, in 1894, along with Richard Strauss' 1905 operatic adaptation, contributed further to the stigma associated with belly dance. Both depicted the infamous "dance of the seven veils," an alleged striptease/seduction of King Herod by his step-daughter (Carlton, 1994; Deagon, 2005). Regardless of its historical inaccuracy, the dance was popular within concert and vaudeville stages throughout the early 1900s (Deagon, 2005). Equally popular were negative portrayals of belly dancers (as seductresses, home-wreckers, tricksters, villains, prostitutes, and harem slaves) within the several hundred films shot on location in North Africa throughout the first half of the 20th century (Dougherty, 2005; MacMaster & Lewis, 1998). Colonial-orientalist spins on the portrayal of female dancers easily became a characteristic of the productions, as Egyptian cinema (known best for such films), in particular, became increasingly popular in the mid-1900s and was heavily influenced by Western financing (Dougherty, 2005).

Through such destructive influences, belly dance has become a largely stigmatized genre of creative movement. Curiously, however, it has also become increasingly popular among women in various parts of the world in recent decades. Countries such as the United States, Australia, Japan, Germany, France, England, Canada and Brazil all have flourishing belly dance communities involving both professionals (those who perform or teach for payment) and amateurs (those who practice it as a hobby or recreation). I have been examining this phenomenon through various means for the past ten years, finding that indeed most women use belly dance for leisure, exercise, recreation (Moe, 2012). The genre seems correlated with greater confidence, body acceptance, and self-esteem (Paul, 2006); is associated with reducing stress as well as encouraging physical fitness, personal growth, and spirituality (Bock & Borland, 2011; Kraus, 2010; Moe, 2011); and provides an important outlet for social support (Moe, 2012, 2014).

The above referenced research has focused explicitly on standpoint (Harding, 1987), honoring what women have to say about their perceptions and experiences with belly dancing, as opposed to other non-involved individuals and entities. Thus, a distinct and alternative portrayal of belly dance has emerged, predicated on embodied experience as opposed to the external gaze. Nonetheless, belly dancers understand and frequently encounter the gaze. The second half of this chapter focuses on their recognition and negotiation of the male gaze via belly dance, as well as their resistance to it.

APPLYING GAZE THEORY

My analysis of belly dance arose from personal experience. I have been belly dancing semi-professionally for over ten years as a soloist, troupe member and instructor. Such activities have allowed me to travel regionally, nationally and internationally in pursuit of my craft. Like many others, I came to belly dance as an adult without previous dance training, out of both curiosity and a search for an alternative form of recreation. Many women have a difficult time benefitting and enjoying formal dance classes without prior training (which often would have occurring during their childhood). Belly dance seemed different. It was malleable and easily conformed to various body types and skill sets. There was little expectation of conformity, standardization of movements, or body type.

It did not take long for my observations to turn into a research project. I began formal field research by documenting my observations of others, accumulating over 1000 hours between 2003 and 2010. Additional data were collected in 2006 and 2007 through the collection of journals narratives I asked women to write regarding the meaning of belly dance in their lives. For this endeavor, about 500 people were reached via recruitment, 150 expressed interest in participating, and 20 completed journals (these involved over 50 entries). Initial findings provided the foundation for the content analysis of 160 online statements from women on two popular US-based discussion boards during the same years (2006–2007). These efforts culminated in a series of 67 qualitative, semi-structured interviews with American belly dancers throughout 2009 and 2010. I have recently begun lecturing to the American belly dance community on these findings and have found acceptance and agreement with my findings, which I believe is a testament to the credibility and validity of this cumulative work. While full methodological details may be found in my previous publications (see Moe, 2011, 2012, 2014), suffice it to say here that the women represented in this analysis are diverse and appear generally representative of the American population of belly dancers. They are mostly white and not necessarily associated via ancestral lineage to the Middle East. They are generally middle to upper-middle class (belly dancing is an expensive endeavor) and highly educated (college and graduate degrees are commonplace). Various religious and spiritual identifications are represented, as well as sexual orientation/identities and partner/marriage statuses. Age ranges are also quite broad.

PERCEPTIONS OF THE GAZE

To say that American belly dancers are conscious of the male gaze is an understatement. They (we) are well aware of the negative perceptions the general public has of the genre, as well as the women who practice it. As Elzbieta noted, "There's the old fashioned view that belly dancing women are just hartlets and that you shouldn't be doing that sort of thing." Indeed, many of us have had experiences similar to Genevieve, who commented within the context of directing a belly dance troupe: "People make comments about the morality of it, like I was promoting something that was immoral or exploiting the women. I was concerned that people would think I was like a stripper or something. All those crazy ideas they get tossed around." In such insinuations, belly dance is portrayed, as has been the case throughout history, as a form of sex work akin to prostitution or striptease – certainly not an acceptable activity for reputable women.

While belly dancers take issue with such insinuations (as well as the larger socio-political context of sex work which often condemns women's roles while condoning men's), they are not surprised by them. As Jherico explains "Our culture is so much more free than many in the world, but still our world is dominated by males… You can't blame people for having that misconception because that's what the media would have you think everything in life is about. Why else would people undulate and move their torsos in dance?" It is understood that "in America, belly dance is sexualized and that the youthfulness and the sexuality of belly dance is what our culture is used to responding to" (Jeela). As such, belly dancers' reactions to the gaze fall into three generalized categories: (1) belly dancing as a refuge from the gaze; (2) belly dancing as a means of re-envisioning the gaze; and (3) belly dancing as active resistance to the gaze.

Refuge

Indeed, a primary motivation for belling dancing is the fact that instructional classes, as well as many of the earlier and informal performance opportunities, are geared specifically toward women. Such contexts are seen as having a protective factor, shielding women from the harsh judgment associated with the male gaze. As Angela described:

> I never really thought there would be a type of dance that I would feel comfortable with, but when I came in and started doing this there was no comment about my weight. I'm a bigger girl and I just thought that no one would want to see that, that's not something that's really readily acceptable. But after just a little while dancing with these girls and everything, it's kind of helped me accept my body and the way that I look. It gives me the confidence that made me feel that all body types can be beautiful. That's why I call it liberating and freeing.

Likewise, Jordana, who described herself as "heavy" indicated:

Society tells you what beautiful is and what attractive is and what sensual or sexual is and they bombard you every day with all this information. Especially growing up, I mean as a teenager and whatnot, you see it so much, you hear it so much. It's just so engrained in the back of your psyche. The community of belly dance says "It's okay! Everyone's different and it's okay. We can all belly dance from whatever level. We're all doing this together and we're all doing it to have a good time. It doesn't matter how big or how small you are.

Such sentiments were echoed by many others. When practiced amongst other belly dancers, this is largely interpreted as a safe and supportive space where women are free to examine, perhaps confront, and accept their bodies. Thus, comments such as Audrey's are common:

I know so many women out there who hate themselves, they hate their body, hate the way they look. Anytime you put that women in a position where you can get her to start loving herself and loving her body and loving what she's doing then she will heal.

In other words, belly dance "becomes a refuge from so many aspects of life for a female" (Jherico). Zaheen, who has been belly dancing for nine years and is mentored by a well-known veteran of the genre, provided greater backdrop to such commentary:

This dance was created by women for women. It was a way for us to express our love and our enjoyment for each other. It had nothing to do with men. Of course one guy sees it and says "I wanna see" and it's open to all of them. But this was not for them. I really do believe that makes a difference because we can express ourselves towards each other and not have to worry about what the guy is thinking or what he wants out of this.

Another aspect of the gaze is important to note here. While much of what is assumed about belly dance arises within the context of a patriarchal male gaze, within the space of a belly dance class or practice, women have the opportunity to gaze upon themselves on their own terms, with greater reflection and social support. Caroline's description was illustrative: "I can stand in front of a dance mirror and watch myself and notice that I'm beautiful. That is an incredibly empowering moment. I was transfixed from the first lesson and I hear that again and again." Gazing at one's own body (whether with supportive others or alone) was a practice that many women described as a direct product of belly dance. Bella, for instance, recounted the following scenario about gazing upon her postpartum body ten years prior:

> I remember this like it was yesterday. I went down to my studio by myself, turned the music on and stood there and looked at my body. I thought, "I still look pregnant." I started doing figure-8s. I watched the movement roll across the belly. It was one of the most beautiful things I have ever seen in my life. I was thirty-five pounds heavier and I looked at myself and said "Look at my body. This is so beautiful! This is what God has created. This is what we should praising!"

Bella describes an experience of letting go, both emotionally and physically, of the self-judgment spurred as a consequence of the gaze. The result is a sense of liberation. Indeed, recognizing what fellow dancer and author Wendy Buonaventura (1998) notes as the "West's perception of the body as something inferior which needs to be played down, even apologized for" (p. 201), I noted the following (under the pseudonym "Zamani") early in my field research:

> Another aspect of belly dancing that immediately struck me was the way we were moving our bodies. American women, moving in ways that seemed strangely erotic and emphasizing the areas of our bodies that we had been socialized to cover up, be afraid of and ashamed of – our hips, butt and belly.

> I couldn't get over that. We're taught from such an early age to suck them up, trim them down, keep things tight. Here we were jiggling them, and bouncing them around and on top of that, wearing hip scarves to emphasize our hips and butts!

While refuge from the male gaze is prominent within belly dance classes and the like, the situation changes a great deal as women advance into semi-professional or professional roles, which involve contractual obligations and exchange of payment for teaching and performance. Under these pretenses, handling the male gaze becomes a constant struggle, which is concerning for dancers. As Samantha noted:

> I am fuzzy about whether I want to perform or not. Going to class is so satisfying, fun and rewarding. I love moving my body and I love looking in the mirror at myself during class. There are certain presentations or ways you have to be to make yourself presentable for your audience. I'm not sure I want to struggle with that.

Re-Envisioning.

Many women spoke of encountering the male gaze within professional and semi-professional contexts, predominantly those involving public performances such as Middle Eastern restaurants, wedding receptions and other paid "gigs." Some spoke of such encounters with resignation, accepting that with more public exposure came a loss of control over the context of their dancing. While there are many components to making "yourself presentable," as Samantha noted, the one that has been recognize most frequently is age, followed closely by size. Race, ethnicity and ethnic heritage (whether Middle Eastern or not) also bear mentioning, though age and size seem most salient to the gaze. Gail described:

> I'm older, six feet tall and really light (skin toned), and I demand what should be the market rate for my performances. I live in [a large urban area] and there are huge amounts of dancers here including "desperate darlings" who have taken six weeks of lessons and have bought a costume. They're willing to dance for free. I know they're not as good as me but if a restaurant owner can get two people who are dancing for free who are short and cute, and for me they'll have to pay more, financially they're just going to go with the freebees. So I don't even bother.

Related to size, many women belly dance during and soon after pregnancy (including myself). This has also been a source of ambivalence regarding the male gaze, as pregnancy and early motherhood seem at odds with the erotic nature associated with belly dance (see Moe, 2011). Elissa described her experience of negotiating the male gaze during pregnancy:

> With my final pregnancy I was dancing in more of a hip hookah [Middle Eastern water pipe] lounge setting and I knew for sure they would not want to see my pregnancy there. I performed there like three to four months into the pregnancy. It was smoky... and I knew they were looking for more just like hot, sexy women. In fact there was a woman that I was performing with at the time who went a little too long into her pregnancy and they were kind of like, "What's up with the pregnant belly dancer? That's not what we ordered."

Those who are members of professional belly dance troupes are also subject to the standards set via the male gaze. African American and larger set, Mariska discussed her suspicions about not advancing into a professional troupe at the dance school she attended, despite having danced consistently for many years and illustrating requisite skills. Again, while Mariska was the only woman of color in the troupe (she was eventually asked to join it), she did not recognize this as a factor in her prior exclusion. For her, it came down to size:

> I have to admit that at one point I believed that I was being skipped over in being considered a member of the troupe. Granted all those who moved up were talented, however various members in the different levels of dance expressed to me that I should have already advanced. I felt as though I deserved a shot. I attributed my not being moved up to my weight and the fact that I would limit the troupe in costuming.

As the above quotes illustrate, there was a sort of acceptance of the gaze (as inevitable) within these contexts. Beyond such resignation, however, some have attempted to re-envision, or alter, public perceptions of the dance by approaching their performances differently than stereotype would dictate, yet in ways they hope are still attractive and entertaining (so as to not completely unsettle the audience's gaze). For Vicki, age was a driving force in her change of performance venue. She accepted this and moved on to other venues that were more open to what she had to offer:

> I was with an Egyptian restaurant until 2006 and I retired because of my age. Not that I can't dance. I just wasn't cute anymore. You don't get invited to dance, even though I kept my weight down, if you look like you're over 50. I'll be 58 in June and actually I'm probably a better dancer now than I ever was. It's just that time runs out for you as far as being hired, so I'm not performing the way that I did. I will do benefits, haflas [informal Arabic dance parties], and things like that, educational things. Showing how beautiful the dance is and that it is every woman's dance. You don't have to be, you know, 21 with a knock-out figure.

As Vicki also indicates, it is common for seasoned belly dancers to hold out for the possibility that their talent and skill will overcome narrow expectations and negative perceptions. On this point, Casmir maintains:

> It really doesn't matter what your body shape is or your skin type or anything. Once you start dancing, people forget all that. They see the beauty and the grace and the passion come through and all of the sudden there's a beautiful person dancing on that stage. It's a complete transformation. It comes out and everybody can see how beautiful you are.

As such, the objective for women who attempt to re-envision the gaze is to help spectators see more of what the dancers want them to see, to work with them in altering the gaze. Often this comes down to the emotion and feeling expressed through the dance, which women like Casmir believe is possible. Sometimes they come to this conclusion by watching others whom they believe successfully did it. For example, Joanna described the awe and appreciation she gained from watching her teacher perform:

> I developed, through belly dancing, a great appreciation of the female form and all its shapes and sizes. My teacher was a large, fleshy curvaceous woman and I just loved to watch her dance. She was so incredible, so I had seen firsthand these beautiful large bodies. Maybe that helped me feel better about my own body. Just a sense of wonder at the way our bodies work and they change. Maybe I wouldn't have felt the same way if I hadn't been exposed to these big beautiful bodies of the belly dancing women around me.

As Casmir hinted, focusing less on outward appearances and expectations, and more on internal experiences and joy, is a means through the gaze may be re-envisioned. Rika, for instance, described "get[ting] to the point where I just don't care what they're thinking" and to assist in this, Gale admitted that she "dances without glasses so I tend not to notice looks…" Focusing internally can also allow women to reach what is described as a "high" or "flow" while dancing. Alexandria described this phenomenon:

> I enter a state of forgetfulness and intensification… getting to a point where you're not thinking about what you're doing but you're still very much experiencing what you're doing. When things start coming out right, the audience and the dancer enter this kind of state of exchange and everyone is drawn into this shared emotional state. I think a lot of dancers now aim at that.

While the women who attempt this may or may not successfully change the perspectives of others, they are hopeful that they are and otherwise prefer to focus on their own internalized adjustment to the gaze's omnipresence. Such is not always the case though.

Resistance

Many belly dancers have found that despite efforts to negotiate the male gaze, it is more often the case that the public applies its rigid and objectifying criteria on them and the entire genre. For such women, whose dedication to performing is strong, the best means of combatting the gaze is to actively challenge it. Their goal is to push the public to see the dance, and its practitioners, in ways with which they are not comfortable. This often assumes a rather confrontational tone. For example, Zaheen recalled an exchange common to many a belly dancer: "Some of my friends who've seen me dance are like 'Wow, I would have never have seen you as a belly dancer.' I'm like 'What's a belly dancer supposed to look like?!?'"

In her quick come back, Zaheen essentially dares others to expose, explain and defend their stereotypes. The same is true with debates around terminology. Many are aware of how the name "belly dance" may contribute to longstanding misconceptions about the genre. However, rather than deny what is likely the most recognized and widely used name for this dance (see the endnote in Moe, 2012 for a discussion on names and labels), many consciously reclaim it. Caroline's provides a justification for doing so:

> I know that it's a bit of a political hot potato about what to call it and there's a school of thought that says that "belly dance" is denigrating and helps keep it pigeon-holed as something low on the totem pole, just one step up from stripping. I tend to be more of the "grab it by the throat and push it in their face" school. So I call it "belly dance" and I say "What's wrong with that, 'cause that's what we do?" It is a dance of the torso. That is its distinctive characteristic.

Perhaps because of the heightened awareness belly dance brings to the gaze, and the obvious contradiction between it and women's actual experiences, some feel there is little choice than to be confrontational. Again, size and age are prominent factors in determining which women feel especially judged. Underscoring the continued salience of size, Sarah discussed her response to both viewers' and troupe leaders' comments about her postpartum appearance:

> I can't count the times that people have made comments about my stretch marks, especially photographers, and it's just been obnoxious. However that's when I expanded my business and formed a performance troupe of my own. I responded to an email about auditions for a troupe and had met this instructor a few times. I got an email back and she says, "Well I know who you are and my specifications are…" She gave me height, a weight, a cup size and said "I'll tell you, you're nowhere near meeting those, so don't even bother showing up." And after that I decided that

I'd form my own troupe and I did and all of my women were mothers and they all had stretch marks! I wanted to make a statement. I will definitely challenge the status quo when it comes to the perception of what a beautiful female should act like and look like.

In similar fashion, Jeela made sure to celebrate the beauty of size within her classes: My big girls were right up in front of the class. They were not hiding out in the back all self-conscious of their bigness. It was just "Look at MY shimmies." You had to stop to watch because when you get a big girl shimmying, it is so fantastic to watch. It is so exciting. The whole quivering and control, and the smile on her face. It is so beautiful to see.

She went on to discuss what she sees as the larger socio-political backdrop to honoring what women bring to belly dance and why she cares little for what others think of it:

I think we've got something here that's pretty right on. If you're gonna overlay religious or political prejudices on top of it, that's your thing. There's a lot of religious people in our culture and in our country and they come with all sorts of agendas. My thing is, I am rooting myself back to something that women have done for hundreds of years. Something that has felt wonderful to their bodies, looks wonderful, shares the joy with their friends and their family and their husbands and lovers. It's your problem if you're uncomfortable... I think it's great when women are just like "Yeah, I'm gonna do what is natural. I'm not going to listen to guys. I'm gonna dance..."

Likewise, Lois described her thoughts on audience expectations about age, especially those involving men:

A lot of the men look at it as a sexual thing. They want this little smooth-skinned cutie up there in a bare costume. They don't want to see a 74 year old dancer. "Why should I look at that old lady?" But I don't dance for them and I laugh at them when they pay for tickets. I say, "You're the one paying money to watch a 74 year old dancer!"

Highlighting the narrowness with which the gaze allows the viewing of women's "aged" bodies, Jherico, 68 at the time of her interview, recalled her early motivation for belly dancing:

I had a big fight with my boyfriend at the time. He made some crack about me being forty and it really upset me. I signed up for the beginning and intermediate class and submerged myself in it. Belly dancing seemed like something I could do to authenticate the fact that I was still alive, young, and had something going for myself. I just felt like being a maverick. Women in our culture generally become more invisible with the passage of time. It just feels great to put on a sparkly outfit, get up there and dance, and get paid for it and applauded. It's very nourishing to my spirit.

Resisting the male gaze through belly dancing helped many women honor not only their individual spirit, but the historical and cultural spirit on which the dance is premised. In this regard, belly dance is seen as much less about distinct technique and outward skill, and more about emotive quality and embodied experience. It is generally believed, based on understandings of the dance in the Middle East (minus current Western pop-cultural infiltration), that a dancer becomes better with age, life experience, and a bit of girth:

> To an American audience it might be fun and gratifying to watch a twenty year old body. In the Middle Eastern idea, that's nothing. It's the soul. It's the emotion. The concept of making art of who you are and that it's available to anyone. You don't have to be twenty years old and thin and gorgeous. (Caroline)

Obviously this is at odds with perceptions of the dance vis-à-vis the Western male gaze. It is also likely part of the historical, political and cultural disconnect discussed earlier regarding the roots of this dance and its contemporary reputation. For the most part, the women in my research understood this cultural heritage and found validation in its implications for resisting the gaze.

CONCLUSION

This chapter held several objectives, the first of which was to describe the evolution of the male gaze as a theoretical concept within feminism. I discussed the primary mid-twentieth century thinkers who developed the construct through various disciplines. Regarding the feminist take on gaze theory, I relied most heavily on Laura Mulvey's (1975, 2009) early work which analyzed the sexist and objectifying nature of cinematography within the film industry. My second objective was to start a conversation on how the gaze may aid understandings of the interconnected socio-historical-political factors undergirding contemporary belly dance. This process is a difficult one to tease out in a couple of paragraphs, but my hope is that some increased awareness about the complexity of the genre was gained through it. Indeed, what we often think of and see as belly dance today, especially in the United States and other Western nations, is but a sliver of what the genre comprises.

My third objective was to apply these discussions to the words and experiences of contemporary women who belly dance and routinely encounter the gaze. I organized this discussion around three themes, distinguishable based on their various means of adaptation: refuge, re-envisioning and resistance. I premised the discussion of these themes by recognizing that belly dancers do indeed understand something about the gaze and what it means to their craft. Some consequently choose to use the more private or informal spaces of belly dance, such as instructional classes, as a way of finding refuge from the gaze that is present in other aspects of their lives, and which they would expect to encounter if they belly danced publicly. In such a setting, they are freer to experience and express the dance on their own terms, exploring their physicality and creativity in a safe and self-defined space without the presumed constraints of public viewing. As such they are able to dodge some of the gendered expectations Butler (1999) argues are so inhibitive to contemporary social scripts. This is not to suggest that a belly dance class is some sort of feminist utopia (though some of us try to make it so), it is simply to highlight the ways in which some contemporary Western women seek refuge from societal constraints regarding use of the body and performativity.

The second theme, re-envisioning, represents attempts at accepting the gaze to some degree, and working within its parameters to subtly change perceptions of the dance. There are many women out there who love belly dance and enjoy showing their interpretations of it to others. They may use small events and classes as a refuge, of course, but they also do not shy away from performance. It is more that they hope to adjust the perceptions of those who gaze upon them in subtle and unthreatening ways. Consequently, some will select certain performance venues over others (an educational based event versus restaurant gig) so as to have better odds of a mutually enjoyable and entertaining experience. It is also common here to focus less on what audience members may be doing and more on what the individual, as the performer-dancer is doing. The focus inward allows women to tune some portions of the gaze out and to possibly transcend them with the beauty and skill they hope to embody.

The third theme concerned more overt and active resistance. Women who challenge the gaze take conscious and intentional steps toward threatening contemporary expectations of "doing gender" (West & Zimmerman, 1987). Their goal is to subvert public stereotypes about the dance and the women who perform it. This often entails embracing the misconceptions surrounding the genre and figuratively turning them on their heads (e.g., forming troupes of women with stretch marks, wearing revealing costumes over the age of 60). They rely on the negative byproducts of the gaze as motivation for pushing the boundaries of social scripts. In other words, their experiences serve as reminders of the juxtaposition between gendered socialization and belly dance, wherein "body parts that are ordered by cultural norms to remain subdued and covered suddenly acquire a voice and a privilege as they carry the beat and 'speak'" (Stavrou, 1999, p. 14).

Taken together, these adaptations to the male gaze suggest a nuanced characteristic of contemporary Western belly dancing that has not previously been examined. While I would argue that these findings are valid based on my ongoing and multi-effort research in the area, much more could be done to examine this issue. The content matter seems ripe for further investigation, either within the context of belly dance, or other seemingly erotic performance outlets. Burlesque, for example, is experiencing a recent surge of interest, as is studio-taught pole dancing. Indeed, much remains to be learned regarding why and how women negotiate the gaze when opting to learn or perform presumably sexually laden movement genres.

DISCUSSION QUESTIONS

1. While this chapter applies gaze theory to belly dance, what other similar types of endeavors could be analyzed through gaze theory? Are there other forms of creative movement or recreation that seem relevant to this type of critique?

2. Do you engage in any activities that would be relevant to an analysis of the gaze? If so, what are they and what would this analysis look like? If not, can you think of a relevant activity?

3. As the author suggests, the gaze is so entrenched in our culture that it is almost invisible. Thus, we may not even think twice about camera angles and such that are objectifying to women. Do you think this discussion will change the way you view movies and the like? How so?

4. Given how entrenched the gaze is in our culture, it could be difficult to convince someone not in this class (or who has otherwise not read this book) of its merit. Imagine you are speaking to a good friend. How would you explain the gaze in your own words?

5. Imagine that the male gaze worked in reverse – that it was more of a female gaze. How would camera angles in movies change? What do you think the cultural response would be?

REFERENCES

Alloula, M. (1986). *The colonial harem*. Minneapolis, MN: University of Minnesota Press.

AlZayer, P. (2010). *World of dance: Middle Eastern dance* (2nd ed.). New York, NY: InfoBase.

Bock, S., & Borland, K. (2011). Exotic identities: Dance, difference and self-fashioning. *Journal of Folklore Research, 48*(1), 1–36.

Bordo, S. R. (1989). The body and the reproduction of femininity: A feminist appropriation of Foucault. In S. Border & A. Jagger (Eds.), *Gender/body/knowledge: Feminist reconstructions of being and knowing* (pp. 13 34). New Brunswick, NJ: Rutgers.

Butler, J. (1999). *Gender trouble: Feminism & the subversion of identity*. London: Routledge.

Carlton, D. (1994). *Looking for little Egypt*. Bloomington, IN: IDD Books.

Deagon, A. (2005). Dance of the seven veils: The revision and revelation in the oriental dance community. In A. Shay & B. Sellers-Young (Eds.), *Belly dance: Orientalism, transnationalism and harem fantasy* (pp. 244–275). Costa Mesa, CA: Mazda.

Dougherty, R. L. (2005). Dance and the dancer in Egyptian film. In A. Shay & B. Sellers-Young (Eds.), *Belly dance: Orientalism, transnationalism and harem fantasy* (pp. 145–171). Costa Mesa, CA: Mazda.

Dox, D. (2005). Spirit from the body: Belly dance as a spiritual practice. In A. Shay & B. Sellers-Young (Eds.), *Belly dance: Orientalism, transnationalism and harem fantasy* (pp. 303–340). Costa Mesa, CA. Mazda.

Foucault, M. (1975). *Discipline and punish: The birth of the prison*. New York, NY: Vintage.

Harding, S. (1987). *Feminism and methodology: Social science issues* (pp. 1–14). Bloomington, IN: Indiana University.

Karayanni, S. S. (2004). *Dancing fear and desire: Race, sexuality, and imperial politics in Middle Eastern dance*. Waterloo, ON: Wilfrid Laurier University Press.

Kraus, R. (2010). "We are not strippers": How belly dancers manage a (soft) stigmatized serious leisure activity. *Symbolic Interaction, 33*(1), 435–455.

Lacan, J. (2006). *Écrits: The first complete edition in English* (B. Fink, Trans.). New York, NY: W.W. Norton.

Lorber, J., & Moore, L. J. (2007). *Gendered bodies: Feminist perspectives*. Los Angeles, CA: Roxbury.

MacMaster, N., & Lewis, T. (1998). Orientalism: From unveiling to hyperveiling. *Journal of European Studies, 28*(1), 121–136.

Moe, A. M. (2011). Belly dancing mommas: Challenging cultural discourses of maternity. In C. Bobel & S. Kwan (Eds.), *Embodied resistance: Challenging the norms, breaking the rules* (pp. 88–98). Nashville, TN: Vanderbilt University Press.

Moe, A. M. (2012). Beyond the belly: An appraisal of Middle Eastern dance (aka belly dance) as leisure. *Journal of Leisure Research, 44*(2), 201–233.

Moe, A. M. (2014). Sequins, sass and sisterhood: An exploration of older women's belly dancing. *Journal of Women & Aging, 26*(1), 39–65.

Mourat, E. A. (2000). Dances of ancient Egypt. In T. Richards (Ed.), *The bellydance book: Rediscovering the oldest dance* (pp. 42–51). Concord, CA: Backbeat Press.

Mulvey, L. (1975). Visual pleasure and narrative cinema. *Screen, 16*(3), 6–18.

Mulvey, L. (2009). *Visual and other pleasures* (2nd ed.). New York, NY: Palgrave Macmillan.

Paul, B. (2006). *Physical and psychological effects of belly dancing: A multiple case study* (Unpublished doctoral dissertation). Saybrook Graduate School and Research Center, San Francisco, CA.

Sartre, J.-P. (2003). *Being and nothingness* (H. E. Barnes, Trans.). London: Routledge. (Original work published in 1958)

Shay, A., & Sellers-Young, B. (Eds.). (2005). *Belly dance: Orientalism, transnationalism and harem fantasy*. Costa Mesa, CA: Mazda.

West, C., & Zimmerman, D. (1987). Doing gender. *Gender, 1*, 125–151.

APRIL KALOGEROPOULOS HOUSEHOLDER

2. LENA DUNHAM, *GIRLS*, AND THE CONTRADICTIONS OF FOURTH WAVE FEMINISM

One of the foundational theories of feminism argues that imagery in media and popular culture often degrades and objectifies women, creating unrealistic social expectations which can hurt relationships between men and women, limit women's relationships with one another, and even distort women's relationships to their own bodies. Magazine advertisements feature young, skinny, white models who uphold unattainable standards of beauty; music videos show sexy, nearly-naked backup dancers whose sole purpose is to prop up male performers; reality television pits women against each other as they fight for the attention of male suitors; pornography dehumanizes women by fragmenting their bodies into fetishized parts, rather than depicting them as whole beings. But contemporary feminist movements such as #MeToo, #TimesUp, and the Women's March, approach media as a site for critique, as well as a powerful tool for organization and activism. For young feminists who have grown up with feminism "in the water" (Baumgardner & Richards, 2000) and with media at their fingertips, definitions of women's "empowerment" and "autonomy" may be radically different from those of previous generations. As feminism has filtered into mainstream consciousness, Millennials have come of age in a time when feminist theories have been absorbed by pop culture in a way that makes Beyoncé's lyrics almost indistinguishable from the writings of Simone de Beauvoir.

As Ariel Levy (2005) observes, "Many of the conflicts between the women's liberation movement and the sexual revolution and within the women's movement itself were left unresolved thirty years ago. What we are seeing today is the residue of that confusion" (p. 74). Eighteen year-old college Freshman "Belle Knox," a Women's Studies major at Duke University and self-made "porn star," made headlines in 2014 when it was revealed that she paid for her first year of college by making internet porn in her dorm room. In an interview with xojane.com (2014), she framed her choices within a feminist discourse about women's sexual autonomy and self-expression:

© KONINKLIJKE BRILL NV, LEIDEN, 2019 | DOI:10.1163/9789004414259_002

"We play around with roles and identities while we are working out issues that are long buried in our subconscious. I'm an ambitious young woman. I'm a student at Duke. I'm a slut who needs to be punished. Feminism means I can take ownership of what I enjoy sexually *and* that sexuality does not have to determine anything else about me. Because feminism is *not* a one size fits all movement." For young women, the contradictions of feminism in the twenty-first century are confusing, to say the least. As Levy asks, why is this the new feminism, and not what it looks like: the old objectification (p. 81)? Why does contemporary feminism appear so conflicted on the question of how to represent women, and how is this reflected in our media and popular culture?

This essay investigates how the contradictions of the feminist movement are honestly explored in the HBO series *GIRLS* (2012–2017), and offers a perspective on the current state of feminism in relation to representations of gender in the contemporary media landscape. Specifically, it explores how *GIRLS* embodies a feminism in which issues of body image, sex, and women's solidarity remain unresolved, signaling the need for continued and nuanced theories on the themes explored in the show. In the pilot episode of *GIRLS*, while trying to convince her parents not to cut her off financially while she struggles to find a job as a writer, Lena Dunham's protagonist, Hannah, tells her parents that she thinks she may be the voice of her generation. Or at least *a* voice. Of *a* generation. What does this generation's feminism look like? What compromises is the show willing to make in order to raise this question? And, how does the show embody the unresolved conflicts of the feminist movement?

THE WAVES OF FEMINISM

The "waves" model has been used as a shorthand structuring device to organize feminist history and to track the "progress" of feminist interventions into social, political, and economic change for women. Typically, the first wave is conceived of as addressing nineteenth and twentieth century social and political inequalities for women in North America and the U.K., starting with the struggle for women's full citizenship and the right to vote.

The second wave is the era of "women's liberation" (1960s–1980s), and sought social transformation through a critique of patriarchy and the ethos of "the personal is the political." During this time, Betty Friedan founded the National Organization for Women and published *The Feminine Mystique,* exposing the limits of suburban motherhood and the domestic slavery of women who gave up their own ambitions and educations in order to fulfill the social role of becoming housewives and mothers. *Ms.* founder Gloria Steinem became the face of the movement when she went undercover at Hugh Heffner's Playboy Club and wrote about the exploitation she experienced in her exposé, "A Bunny's Tale" (1963). In 1968, feminists protested the Miss America Pageant, where activists burned feminine products like mops, false eyelashes, and *Playboy* magazines, and the myth of the burning bra was born. A critical eye was given to the study of popular culture when Laura Mulvey's essay "Visual Pleasure and Narrative Cinema" (1975) established the theory of the "male gaze" and called for the destruction of visual pleasure found in dominant media as a radical weapon against the objectifying ways of seeing women in visual culture. In continuity with the civil rights and counter-culture movements, the second wave featured a reclaiming of lost "herstories," the formation of consciousness-raising groups, and the concept of solidarity ("sisterhood") as a preface to activism: "Women would tap into their voices when they once again formed strong relationships with other women – our most powerful weapon against sexism" (Gilligan, 1982, p. 175). At the same time, this period was marked by contention over the exclusion of lesbians ("the lavender menace," in Friedan's words), and women of color from the movement.

While continuing to fight against structural inequalities, third wave feminism (1990 2010) challenged what it deemed as the second wave's "essentialist" definitions of gender, which often assumed a universal female identity and over-emphasized the experiences of upper-middle class white women. Rebecca Walker urged young women to become involved in politics by organizing voter registration campaigns to counter youth apathy and, with Amy Richards, co-founded the Third Wave Foundation. Richards' and Jennifer Baumgardner's book *Manifesta: Young Women, Feminism, and the Future* (2000), revisited the goals of feminism at a generational crossroads in the 1990s and detailed the political objectives that still needed to be achieved. The third wave redefined the infantilized and apolitical term "girl," and turned feminism into a movement about riotous "grrrls," reclaiming once pejorative terms like "cunt," "bitch," and "slut." It gave rise to judgment-free pleasure and sex, initiated a discussion of masculinity, and worked to transform men. The third wave tackled issues including voter registration, women in music and other creative arts, reproductive rights, LGBT rights and the politicizing of "queerness," globalization, date rape organizing, sexual harassment, and DIY culture. The biggest contribution of the third wave critique has been to point out the marginalization of women of color and lesbians, and examine feminism as a white, middle class, heterosexual women's movement. Judith Butler's work on performativity and gendered bodies helped redefine gender terms and categories, and ushered in an emphasis on queer theory, transgender politics, and a rejection of the gender binary, unlinking sex, gender, and the heterosexual matrix (Butler, 1990, 1993). This wave sees race, gender, class, and sexuality as interlocking identities, and asserts that oppression is experienced along these "intersectional" axes of power (Crenshaw, 1991).

Tech-savvy and gender-literate young feminists like Lena Dunham constitute a budding fourth wave. "In place of zines and songs, young feminists created blogs, Twitter campaigns, and online media with names like Racialicious and Feministing, or wrote for Jezebel and Salon's Broadsheet... Transgenderism, male feminists, sex work, and complex relationships within the media characterized their feminism" (Baumgardner, 2011, p. 251). They embody the residue of the unfinished tensions between the second and third waves. They are acutely aware of their inner feminist conflicts, but unresolved about things like whether shaving their legs is a personal choice, or constitutes being brainwashed by the patriarchy, or whether admitting their desire to be married and raise children over "leaning in" (Sandberg, 2013) to a high-powered career makes them un-feminist. If older feminists accused third wavers of being superficial in their relationship to pop culture, ungrateful of the gains fought for by their foremothers, apathetic to politics and organizing, overly empowered and spoiled, the millennial "selfie" generation is defined by an even more pronounced individualist approach to feminism. Dunham's characters express many of these fourth wave anxieties over how to be "good" feminists in *GIRLS*; that is, over aligning themselves with their mothers' generation of feminist values which reject sexist ideas about women and their roles, or with a contemporary feminism that embraces pop culture and personal choice. During a drug-induced moment of honesty in the episode, "Bad Friend" (S2: 03), Hannah shamefully exclaims that she wants to get married wearing a veil, and taste, like, *fifteen* cakes before she does it. And she knows that she said that she was against the marriage industrial complex, but that's what she really wants. She is, in Roxane Gay's words, a "bad feminist" – "I am human. I am messy. I am not trying to be an example... a woman who loves pink and likes to get freaky and sometimes dances her ass off to music she knows is terrible for women and who sometimes plays dumb with repairmen. I am a bad feminist. I regularly fuck it up" (p. xi).

To complicate things, the mainstream media's backlash against feminism popularized the term "post-feminism" and constructs the movement as an obsolete undertaking of a past generation, or as an unnecessary and "finished" project (after all, we have Hillary and Oprah, clearly women have arrived!) and emphasizes the theoretical tensions between the waves. It paints older feminists as ugly, old-fashioned, man-hating, anti-sex lesbians, or, in an updated version of the stereotype, as young, sex-crazed, birth control-pill-popping "sluts," who emasculate men and are responsible for the "crisis in masculinity" that makes men unable to relate to women or know their true roles. In its most divisive form, the public image of feminism is constructed as an elitist movement for and about white women, and uses race as a divider to repress alliances between women of different races and classes. Young women, wanting to identify with the movement but not seeing themselves reflected in the image of the race-blind, bra-burning generation of their mothers, have rebelled against their feminist predecessors and distanced themselves from the "F" word. As B. Ruby Rich (2003) explains, "Feminism has become a mother figure, and what we are seeing is a daughter's revolt" (p. 209).

Nowhere was this sentiment more apparent than in the 2016 presidential election of Donald Trump over Hilary Clinton, who, despite being the most qualified candidate to ever run, and with a history of championing women's rights, was seen by many millennial feminist voters as an "establishment" candidate. "These young women weren't going to rush to order a plastic "woman card" for a candidate that had been portrayed… as a hack of the establishment. They didn't believe in sisterhood– a relic of a time when, as they had been told (often in women's studies courses) privileged, white feminists clasped hands in imagined gender solidarity, ignoring racial injustice and the problems of the working class. They didn't want to be dealt any cards at a bridge game organised by Gloria Steinem or Madeleine Albright – or Hillary Clinton" (Bordo, 2018). In Bordo's analysis, millennial feminists' support of Bernie Sanders and refusal to vote for Clinton in the general election helped Trump, a self-proclaimed "pussy grabber," who also referred to Dunham as a "B-list actor with no mojo," win the 2016 presidency. According to Bordo, the "Bernie or bust" sentiment among young women voters, who disavowed voting at all if it meant supporting a candidate associated with second wave feminism, helped elect one of the most misogynistic presidents in American history.

LENA DUNHAM AND CONTEMPORARY FEMINISM

When Lena Dunham accepted the 2013 Golden Globe award for her series *GIRLS*, for many, it was their first introduction to the show's twenty-five year old writer, producer, director, and star. Dunham was young, curvy, short-haired, tattooed, and wore little make up—miles away from the glamorous awards-show look of the other female celebrities in the room. More compelling than her unconventional-for-television appearance was what she said when she gave her acceptance speech, honoring the legacy of the other women nominees, and foregrounding her identity as an unapologetic, self-proclaimed feminist: "This award is for every woman who has ever felt like there wasn't a space for her. This show has made a space for me… making this show and the response to it has been the most validating thing that I have ever felt. It's made me feel so much less alone in this world." The speech catapulted Dunham and the show to become feminist icons of the millennial generation.

As the title indicates, *GIRLS* foregrounds the experiences of four young women living in New York City immediately after college, as they negotiate life, work, sex, and relationships. Hannah Horvath, a privileged, intelligent, yet self-doubting writer, played by Dunham, is the main character in *GIRLS*. She lives in the hipster neighborhood of Greenpoint, Brooklyn, with Marnie, her uptight roommate and best friend from Oberlin College (where Dunham herself went to college as a creative writing major and made short films). The other girls of the cast include Jessa, a free-spirited British transplant, recently returning to New York City where she moves in with her cousin Shoshanna. Shoshanna is a rambling, naive New York University student, whose "biggest baggage" is that she is a virgin. The "boys" of *GIRLS* include Adam, Hannah's detached, sexually sadistic boyfriend; Charlie, Marnie's over-sensitive boyfriend whom she outgrows then regrets losing; and Ray, Charlie's coffee-shop manager friend. The characters are inspired by of some of Dunham's real-life experiences and writings.

The title itself signifies a new feminist horizon. In the 1990s, "girl power" defined feminism's third wave, from The Spice Girls to the underground feminist punk rock movement known as Riot Grrrl. In using *GIRLS* as her title, Dunham continues the feminist project of reclaiming language: "Calling an adult woman a 'girl' was once insulting, like calling an adult black man 'boy.' But now that we can choose and use the word ourselves, and not have it forced on us, 'girl' is increasingly rehabilitated as a term of relaxed familiarity, comfy confidence, the female analogue to 'guy' – and not a way of belittling adult women" (Baumgardner & Richards, 2000, p. 52). Dunham's twist is to capitalize and pluralize the term, announcing a resolute version of feminism that is not fixed, but fluid and diverse, but also ripe with contradiction. But it has also been widely noted that the girls in *GIRLS* refers only to privileged, white women. Like other shows set in New York

City (*Friends, Seinfeld, Sex in the City, How I Met Your Mother*), the all-white cast is unrepresentative of the show's ethnically diverse setting. While intersectionality is the calling card of fourth wave feminism, the invisibility of women of color, lesbians, and trans women on *GIRLS* highlights ongoing feminist debates about identity politics and inclusion.

But in its construction and content, the show represents a radical break from dominant tele-visual representations of women's lives. *GIRLS* has been critically praised for exploring themes relevant to feminism in a way that is novel to the small screen, and radically different from other all-girl shows set in New York City, like its HBO predecessor, *Sex and the City*. As the showrunner, Dunham uses her creative control to give a uniquely feminist voice to the show. Her feminist values extend beyond the storylines, and into the show's production. Dunham hires first-time actresses and creates complex characters for them to play. In a culture obsessed with youth, she writes roles for older women and gives them a sexuality. She gives exposure to female musicians whom she features on the soundtrack. She hires independent female filmmakers like Claudia Weill and Jamie Babbit to direct episodes. Co-producer Judd Apatow has stated that he was drawn to Dunham's writing because it "would provide men with a unique window into the psyche of women" (Goldberg, 2012). The simple sets, thrift store costumes, gritty stock, and subdued color palate are deliberate choices that reflect the DIY riot grrrl aesthetic of the show.

The stories, taken from Dunham's life as a twenty-something college graduate with a women's studies education, have allowed her to explore feminist issues ranging from navigating sexual relationships; friendships between women (including their mothers); friendships between women and men; body image and self-esteem; sexual harassment and equality in the workplace; women's reproductive health; race and class dynamics; masculinity, rape, and pornography. In her writing, Dunham breaks down stereotypes, like when Hannah dates a complex African American character named "Sandy," who also happens to be an Ayn Rand-toting Republican (she dumps him when she realizes that she "can't be with someone who is not an ally to gays and women") (S2:02). Dunham has also actively engaged in feminist discussions on social media, campaigned for Hillary Clinton's 2016 presidential election, and been an outspoken supporter of feminist issues: "There was a sense that I and many women I knew had been led astray by Hollywood and television depictions of sexuality. I want people ultimately, even if they're disturbed by certain moments, to feel bolstered and normalized by the sex that's on the show" (Heller, 2014). By foregrounding issues that are relevant to young women, the show navigates the uneasy, sometimes contradictory terrain of contemporary feminism, highlighting the tensions between second and third wave feminist themes. For young, college-educated women of the fourth wave who have been raised by second and third wave values, there is a theoretical understanding of feminism that is grounded in the idea of the struggle for justice and equality – that the personal is the political, and that feminism emerges from everyday life. What isn't always clear is the map for navigating those everyday interactions in the "real" world. When the final season of *GIRLS* aired in January of 2017, Dunham noted the impasse between the politics of representation on her show, and the political realities of women in the Trump era: "It's going to be interesting promoting this show right after Trump is inaugurated. Hopefully it'll bring up important conversations. The confluence, for me, of the show ending and this new era beginning, in which I know that we as public women are going to have to fight harder than we ever have before, is a really interesting, complicated moment" (Wappler).

BODY IMAGE

Speaking at the Democratic National Convention in 2016, Dunham used her feminist brand of comedy to introduce herself: "Hi, I'm Lena Dunham and according to Donald Trump, my body is probably, like, a '2'." Much controversy has been generated by *GIRLS*' treatment of body image, because of its female-centered perspective on sex and nudity, and its irreverent focus on imperfect bodies. Howard Stern called Dunham "a little fat chick" on his radio show, and men's magazines have described her body as "funny," contending that it is her body that provides the comedy of the show (Schrodt, 2014). *GIRLS* confronts this type of sexism in the media by foregrounding Dunham's own naked body to explore a fat-positive body image. Dunham's body is photographed in realistic situations and in unflattering angles. She often spills over the edge of the frame, and things are constantly overflowing from her body – the icing from a half-eaten cupcake on her lips; her body stuffed into an outfit that looks like it was made for someone else's much thinner frame; her words, that seem to come out before her thoughts have been fully formed. Dunham shows her off thick thighs and round belly, rather than using lighting and makeup to mask the "imperfections." Her breasts are not perfectly augmented; they are small, and have even been described as "misshapen" (Mead, 2010), but they are exposed in scenes where the story calls for it, which is in almost every episode. When Adam sees her naked body and asks about her tattoos, Hannah explains that they are her way of using a riot grrrl idea to take control of her own shape. Feminist discourse is prevalent in both the dialog and visual representations of abject bodies on the show. With Dunham behind the script and the camera, bodies are rendered from a distinctly female gaze, providing alternative ways for spectators of the show to see and take pleasure in women's bodies.

Dunham combats a media culture that continually promotes the message that women's bodies aren't good enough, and where makeover shows, dieting, cosmetic surgery, the beauty industry, and the male-dominated media have defined standards of beauty for women. Hannah wears thrift store clothes and baggy, full-cut underwear, which, as she explains, are mostly stained with blood because she never knows when to expect her period. This is not the lace-bra-and-thong type of nudity usually found on late night cable television. John Berger (1972) makes a distinction between depictions of nudity and nakedness in visual culture: "the nude is always conventionalized – and the authority for its conventions derives from a certain tradition of art. To be naked is to be oneself. A naked body has to been seen as an object in order to become nude" (pp. 53–54). The pornographic imagination that stylizes nudity as a fantasy which is constructed as passive, posed, and presented on display as a subject of male idealization and desire is subverted by Hannah's non-conforming body and its treatment as a naked fact. Hannah is shown bathing with her female friends, but it is not sexualized. As in real life, the sex on *GIRLS* is awkward, and not always orgasmically fulfilling. And sex has consequences, unlike the way that it is presented in most media, including pornography. Dunham balances some of the most graphic sex on the show with scenes of Hannah in a gynecology clinic, getting tested for HPV (she's positive), while her friends gather to accompany Jessa to her abortion. By showcasing these de-romanticized versions of sexuality, the show features characters and creators who understand and challenge dominant body images.

However, one of the feminist contradictions of the show is that part of its popularity comes from its exploitation of the cable television format that allows for explicit sexual imagery and the incorporation of other, more conventionally attractive bodies, like those of actors Allison Williams (the all-American beauty, Marnie), Jemima Kirke (whose character Jessa has been described as having "the face of Brigitte Bardot and the ass of Rhianna") (S1:04), Christopher Abbott (Charlie), Andrew Rannells (Elijah), and model/actor Adam Driver (Adam). Adam often walks around his apartment shirtless with his jeans unbuttoned, looking like he just stepped out of an Abercrombie & Fitch advertisement. Jessa, Marnie, and Shoshanna are all involved in made-for-the-male-gaze sex scenes, including a girl-on-girl kiss between Marnie and Jessa, used to tease a man in an almost-threesome, Shoshanna's quest to lose her virginity, and a Jessa's Lolita-like seduction of a married man for whom she babysits. Elijah, a gay man, is heterosexualized in a scene when has sex with Marnie, a straight woman, in what Dunham has described as "one of the most traditionally sexy sex scenes we've seen...in the show" (Dunham, 2013). Season three opens with another pseudo-queer sex scene: Jessa performing oral sex on a black lesbian she meets in rehab (played by actress Danielle Brooks, who plays Taystee on *Orange is the New Black*). The explicit sex contributes to high ratings, which results in more subscriptions for HBO. The show appeals to straight and queer audiences alike, combining HBO's commercial interests with some of the more subversive aspects of sex and sexuality featured in the show. According to Jennifer Baumgardner (2011), these contradictions are a defining aspect of late-wave feminism: "Transparency about whether a feminist had worked out her body image issues, felt upset by an abortion, or believed that any hair could be unwanted, replaced strong, black-and-white statements. Activists spoke from personal places, not to overshare, but to tell the truth about their lives and what had happened to them" (p. 249). But by including so many conventional depictions of bodies, the show also appeals to mainstream audiences, making a commercial compromise to the sex-driven cable market, despite the centering of Dunham's atypical body.

SEX

One of the main schisms between second and third wave feminism happened around divergent ideas regarding sex – how to have it, with whom to have it, and how to represent it. Known as the "sex wars," "two distinct and passionately oppositional factions developed. On the one hand there were the anti-porn feminists, and on the other, there were the women who felt that if feminism was about freedom for women, then women should be free to look at or appear in pornography" (Levy, 2005, pp. 62–63). Whereas for radical feminists like Robin Morgan (1977) "pornography is the theory, and rape is the practice" (p. 169), "pro-sex" feminists celebrate sex as a positive, not repressive aspect of the lives of women, with broader definitions of what sex, oppression, and empowerment can mean. For example, many third and fourth wave feminists have reconsidered oppositions to pornography and prostitution, and challenge existing beliefs that participants in pornography and sex work cannot be empowered. As a free speech issue, they ask, who gets to decide was is "good" or acceptable porn, and what is not? In the context of sexual liberation, they see pornography as contributing to diverse expressions of sexuality and pleasure, including sadomasochism, butch/femme role play, and representing lesbian and gay sexuality, which has been systematically erased from visual culture. On the other side of the debate, some feminists maintain that the media, including the multi-billion dollar porn industry, sexualizes violence against women and normalizes it, contributing to a rape culture in which women and girls are treated as sex objects both on screen and in real life. They argue that under the guise of "liberation," today's neoliberal feminism garbles the vocabularies of sexual revolution and feminist radicalism, parading regressive throwback postures as innovatory and avant-garde (Siegel, 2007, p. 157). The feminist movement remains deeply polarized over the issue of sex.

GIRLS embodies the contradictions of the sex wars is in the sexual relationships on the show. They tell us a lot about how young women both reject and buy into their objectification, but also about men's roles in those experiences. Contemporary feminist critiques of masculinity see gender as an oppressive ideological structure that also harms men. Jessica Valenti (2007) explains: "Men are affected by sexism too, but it's not often talked about – especially among men themselves. That's where feminism should step in. Men aren't born to rape and commit violence. Men aren't 'tougher' emotionally. These gendered expectations hurt men like they hurt us" (p. 183). For a show about girls, Dunham spends a lot of time working out gender issues by creating complex depictions of men and holding them up for critique. One place where this is evident is in Dunham's juxtaposition of Adam and Charlie's versions of masculinity.

There couldn't be a more challenging relationship for a feminist than Hannah's relationship with Adam Sackler (an anagram for "slacker"). By most accounts, he is any self-respecting woman's worst nightmare. When Hannah runs into one of Adam's ex-girlfriends in a coffee shop she describes him as an off-the-wagon Neanderthal sex addict sociopath who's gonna fuck her like he's never met her and like he's never loved his own mother (S3: 01). Unlike Charlie, Marnie's attentive, sensitive "new man" boyfriend, in whom she loses interest because she is "sick of eating him out... because he has a vagina," Adam is closer to the classical version of a Man's Man, which Dunham draws attention to as equally flawed and regressive.

Charlie is often pictured in the women's spaces of the show, hanging around the bathroom, or sitting in the kitchen while he explains that he shaved his head to show support for a coworker who has cancer. Adam, however, vacillates between being gruffly charming and totally repulsive. He physically towers over Hannah and refers to her in a paternalistic way, calling her "doll" and "kid." Adam's relationship to food and exercise is the exact opposite of Hannah's. His chiseled body is the result of a maniacal obsession with physical perfection. He borders on being emotionally abusive, and stalks Hannah after she breaks up with him. He is silent and unemotional, grunting impulsively to express his feelings. He sends Hannah a "dick pic" in a text message that was intended for another woman, and doesn't apologize for it. He urinates on her leg in the shower and laughs about it. Adam's hobby is woodworking, and his dimly lit apartment is filled with menacing tools, broken pieces of wood and metal, and sloppy second-hand furniture. In the pilot episode, it's difficult to tell if he is a serial killer planning an attack, or a pensive, hipster artist building something beautiful.

It's clear that Adam's sexual vocabulary comes directly from the world of pornography. Adam seems consumed by his own sexual fantasies and unconcerned about his partners' sexual pleasure. In the pilot episode, he tells Hannah to lie on her stomach and grab her legs, so he can have sex with her from behind, like a bound animal. When she asks him to wear a condom, he arrogantly replies, "I'll consider it." His confusing attitudes towards women are revealed when he tells Hannah, in an attempt to be supportive about a work decision, that she should never be anyone's slave. Except his. "Vagina Panic" (S1: 02) opens with Adam and Hannah having sex, Adam on top, Hannah lying motionlessly on her back. Without her consent, Adam launches into a pedophilic version of role playing, telling her that he found her in the street, walking alone, and that she "wanted it." Confused, Hannah reminds him that they actually met at a party. Adam ignores her and continues with the fantasy of her as an eleven-year old junkie with a Cabbage Patch lunchbox. Perplexed but feeling like she should play into his fantasy, Hannah reluctantly joins in by telling him that she was "really scared." Before he ejaculates on her arm, he calls her a "dirty little whore" and tells her that he's going to send her home to her parents covered in come. The confused expression on Hannah's face leaves viewers wondering whether what they've just witnessed is intended to be arousing, or if it constitutes sexual assault.

In this scene, Adam's schoolgirl fantasy is taken directly from one of the tropes of pornographic imagery, the sexualization of young girls. No matter how many slut walks Hannah may have participated in as a college student, her feminist ideals seem to be at odds with her life experiences, in which it's not always easy to apply and reclaim the label of "slut," when she is actually being treated like one without her consent. As the title comes up, Dunham, who also directs the episode, cuts to Charlie and Marnie "making love" – a scene softly lit with candles, quiet music playing, and Charlie politely whispering to Marnie that they should look each other in the face when they climax. Disgusted by Charlie's ultra-sensitive lovemaking, Marnie turns around, so she doesn't have to look at him. Aroused by the "doggie style" positioning, Charlie quickly ejaculates, and the scene ends with Marnie shaking her head in frustration. By juxtaposing the two sex scenes and showing them from Hannah's and Marnie's perspectives, Dunham reveals how both women struggle to understand various versions of masculinity in a post-feminist world, and how women's sexual pleasure is still secondary to men's.

Toxic masculinity is explored on the show as a topic that is intrinsically linked to feminist values. Exposing Adam's sexual dark side is Dunham's way of showing how his sexual relationships with women have been influenced by porn and rape culture, and how extreme, sadistic images which may have once been considered degrading to women are now something that women are expected to buy into if they are to be considered desirable or "hot." Not to excuse Adam's behaviors, but to humanize him by exploring how the confines of gender also limit men, the show slowly reveals clues about the potential sources of Adam's misogyny – his relationship with his mentally ill sister, his sobriety, his lonely adolescence. Hannah endures Adam's chauvinistic attitudes about sex, but she also refuses to be victimized by him. She challenges him. She communicates with him. And they grow as a couple.

WOMEN'S SOLIDARITY

If Hannah is confused by the objectification she experiences in her personal relationships, she is equally puzzled by how she should react, as a woman working with other women, to sexual harassment in the workplace. In season two, Hannah finally lands a job as a freelance writer for a fictional blog site, jazzhate.com, which parodies the online women's magazine, xojane.com. While they are discussing ideas for what Hannah should write about, her female boss suggests that she should have a threesome with some people she meets on Craigslist, or "do a whole bunch of coke, and just write about it!" The female boss is no less sexually exploitive than the men she has encountered in the workplace, including a male boss whom she threatens with an "Erin Brockovich-style" class action law suit after he gropes her breasts, and a gay male boss who refers to her work as the writing of a "pudgy-faced girl slicked with semen and sadness." Women exploiting other women's sexuality in the name of feminism is a recent feminist phenomenon, which favors individualism over solidarity with other women. In her study of female media producers like HBO's Sheila Nivens and *Playboy* CEO Christie Heffner, Levy (2005) observes, "Women who have wanted to be perceived as powerful have long found it more efficient to identify with men than to try and elevate the entire female sex to their level" (p. 95). Hannah doesn't take the advice of her female boss and have a threesome, but she does snort a lot of cocaine, and the episode ends with her making out with Laird, an ex-junkie who lives in her building, "for the story." Showing no signs of inter-generational solidarity, Hannah's experiences are exploited by older women in positions of power formerly held by men.

Dunham provides viewers with an uncomfortable portrait of a young woman exploiting her own sexuality in order to have something "sexy" and "edgy" to write about for the media, even when that media is controlled by other women, including herself. By the third season, Hannah goes to work at a mainstream men's magazine (*GQ*), which further challenges her integrity as a writer and a feminist. The show presents a meta-narrative about representations of women in the media and women's compliance with their own oppression by showing Hannah exploiting herself as a character *within* the show, as well as Dunham's role in exploiting herself as an actor *on* the show. It's a show struggling to represent women against television's sexist stereotypes, about a woman struggling to write her own life with authenticity, within the sexist world of the publishing industry.

Intersectionality is a hallmark of contemporary feminist theory, but in *GIRLS*, Dunham shows us that the gulf between feminist theory and practice isn't always easy to navigate. Hannah learns that you can't expect all women to have the same reactions to feminist issues like sexual harassment, especially among women of different classes and races. When discussing the "dick pic" that Adam sent to Hannah, the Latina women with whom she works support her in solidarity, telling her that the picture is disgusting and that she should get a little self-respect and leave him (S1:04). But, in the same episode, when Hannah's boss touches her breasts while giving her a "massage," the same female co-workers walk by and look the other way. When she enquires about his groping to the Latina office women (whose Spanglish accents also signify their working-class identities), they tell her that it's gross, but she'll get used to it, and that the health insurance benefits outweigh the abuse. Hannah's private school women's studies education has not prepared her for the real-world challenges of navigating race and class as a lived experience. This scene helps her learn that not everyone understands or has the privilege to participate in feminism in the same way, because feminist values evolve from specific historical, cultural, and material conditions. The office women can't resist their boss' sexual harassment and organize with other women because they need their jobs to survive, and because they benefit from the abuse. Hannah's ignorance about race relations is supposed to be a joke, and she makes her whiteness visible to audiences for critique, disdain, discourse. Hannah's universalist feminism collides with the class-specific perspectives of her co-workers, leaving her perplexed, but opening up a space for audiences to critique her privileged assumptions about what feminism means in the real world.

CONCLUSION

Looking at HBO's most popular shows such as *The Sopranos, Six Feet Under, Entourage, Game of Thrones,* and *Sex and the City,* it becomes clear that the network isn't necessarily in the business of promoting radical representations of gender. HBO's depictions parallel other media images of powerful women that are almost always inscribed with a complementary message of sexual objectification. When *GIRLS* first aired, Miley Cyrus was twerking her way to fame and fortune by using a racist, sexist MTV performance to catapult her to success in the music industry. She was at once celebrated and shamed for using her naked body to sell her music – proving that being a woman who takes off her clothes and subjugates other women (particularly women of color) is still the fastest way to the top. The fourth wave is the inconsistent portrayal of submissive female sexuality in the best-selling novel, *Fifty Shades of Grey.* And, even though there are more women participating in political leadership than ever before, after almost one hundred years, the Equal Rights Amendment to the U.S. Constitution still hasn't been passed into law by Congress. During this wave, our desire to celebrate women's involvement in politics had to grapple with the contradictions of vice presidential candidate Sarah Palin urging women to "rise up" like "mama grizzlies" and push aside liberal feminists, to launch a "new, conservative feminist movement" that supports only political candidates who oppose abortion and reinforce traditional marriage and the family. In 2012, Oprah Winfrey – a black woman – was one of the wealthiest women in the world, but women still made seventy-seven cents to the dollar compared to men (and women of color made only seventy cents). Beyoncé appeared on the cover of *Time* magazine as one of its "most influential people," but did so in her bra and underwear. Danica Patrick drove race cars in the Indy 500, while in the middle east, 32-year-old engineer Manal al-Sharif broke Saudi Arabia's unwritten law banning women from driving a car in an act of defiance against a culture which prohibits women from being mobile and autonomous. Teenager Belle Knox articulated her embracing of pornography as a feminist "choice," and used it as a way to overcome the high costs of a college education in the absence of viable options for employment that pay a fair and equal wage to women.

But we also saw Senator Wendy Davis stand in her running shoes for eleven hours to filibuster a bill that would limit female reproductive rights in Texas. Jennifer Siebel Newsom's 2011 documentary *Miss Representation*, exposed how mainstream media contributes to the under-representation of women in positions of power and influence in America. Georgetown law student Sandra Fluke demanded that medical insurance should have a contraception mandate. Feminists created blogs and websites like feministing.com, the Crunk Feminist Collective, The Feminist Wire, Women and Hollywood, the Hollaback movement to end street harassment, Ryan Gosling Feminist tumblr, and "Binders Full of Women" tumblr. Jezebel.com posted un-retouched images of Lena Dunham's spread for *Vogue* magazine to expose the paradox of Dunham's self-image and the one the media constructed without her consent. Feminist occupiers took to Wall Street and participated in the in the Arab Spring. The U.S. Women's Soccer team, Amy Poehler, Tina Fey, Mindy Kaling, Rachel Maddow, Shonda Rhimes, *Orange is the New Black* and Laverne Cox rose to prominence. Eighty-three-year-old lesbian widow Edie Windsor, brought her case all the way to the Supreme Court and struck down the Defense of Marriage Act. Sixteen-year-old Pakistani activist and Nobel Peace Prize laureate Malala Yousafzai challenged the Taliban and published a best-selling autobiography about the right to education for women. And Lena Dunham unapologetically called herself a feminist and consistently asked us to grapple with what that means on her show, *GIRLS*. In her willingness to use her own body as a battleground in the politics of representation, her raw portrayals of sexuality from a young woman's perspective, and her messy but honest stories about female friendships, Dunham created a space for some of the most important conversations of fourth wave feminism to emerge.

DISCUSSION QUESTIONS

1. Do you think the "waves" model of feminist history is a good one? Where is it helpful and what does it fail to take into account? What are the overlaps between second and third wave feminism that should be foregrounded in the fourth wave? What is unique about the fourth wave?

2. Use the Bechdel test to determine if *GIRLS* is a feminist text. What is the significance of the female relationships on the show? What other contemporary television shows would you describe as "feminist"? What criteria should be used to determine this?

3. The essay argues that intersectionality is a hallmark of fourth wave feminism. How are race and class depicted on the show? Does *GIRLS* treat these issues in a feminist way?

4. Who is the intended audience for *GIRLS* and does the sex on the show pander to certain audiences (men, women, queer viewers)? What commercial pressures does the show succumb to, in order to make its feminist themes palatable to popular audiences?

5. In one episode of *GIRLS*, Hannah expresses her anxiety over her desire to get married and have a big wedding, despite her feminist values which oppose the marriage industrial complex. What does a feminist heterosexual relationship look like? Is Hannah successful at achieving this kind of relationship on the show?

6. Watch the public dialog between bell hooks and Laverne Cox hosted by the New School (2014): https://www.youtube.com/watch?v=9oMmZIJijgY. What are the contradictions that emerge between second and fourth wave feminists? How do each define themselves, as women, as feminists? Are there ways to reconcile these differences?

7. Watch the "Boys" episode of *GIRLS* (S:2 06). How do Dunham's male characters (Adam, Ray, Booth Jonathan) embody anxieties over their masculinity? How is the discourse on masculinity part of the feminist perspective of the show?

REFERENCES

Baumgardner, J. (2011). *F'em! Goo goo, Gaga, and some thoughts on balls*. New York, NY: Seal Press.

Baumgardner, J., & Richards, A. (2000). *Manifesta: Young women, feminism, and the future*. New York, NY: Farrar, Straus and Giroux.

Berger, J (1972). *Ways of seeing*. New York, NY: Penguin.

Bordo, S. (2018). *The destruction of Hillary Clinton: Untangling the political forces, media culture, and assault on fact that decided the 2016 election*. Brooklyn, NY: Melville House.

Butler, J. (1990). *Gender Trouble: Feminism and the Subversion of Identity*. New York, NY: Routledge.

Butler, J. (1993). *Bodies that matter: On the discursive limits of sex*. New York, NY: Routledge.

Crenshaw, K. (1991). Mapping the margins: Intersectionality, identity politics, and violence against women of color. *Stanford Law Review, 43*(6), 1241–1299.

Duggan, L., & Hunter, N. D. (1995). *Sex wars: Sexual dissent and political culture*. New York, NY: Routledge.

Dunham, L. (2013). *GIRLS: Inside the episode*. HBO. Season 2, episode 1.

Findlen, B. (2001). *Listen up: Voices from the next feminist generation*. New York, NY: Seal Press.

Freedman, E. B. (2007). *The essential feminist reader*. New York, NY: Modern Library Classics.

Gay, R. (2014). *Bad feminist: Essays*. New York, NY: Harper Collins.

Gilligan, C. (1982). *In a different voice: Psychological theory and women's development*. Cambridge, MA: Harvard University Press.

Goldberg, L. (2012, January 13). TCA: Lena Dunham says HBO's 'girls' isn't 'sex and the city'. *The Hollywood Reporter*. Retrieved from http://www.hollywoodreporter.com/live feed/tca-hbo-girls-lena-dunham-judd-apatow-281483

Heller, N. (2014, February). Interview with Lena Dunham. *Vogue*, 196–200.

Henry, A. (2004). *Not my mother's sister: Generational conflict and third wave feminism*. Bloomington, IN: Indiana University Press.

Heywood, L., & Drake, J. (Eds.). (1997). *Third wave agenda: Being feminist, doing feminism*. Minneapolis, MI: University of Minnesota Press.

Knox, B. (2014, March 18). In defense of kink: My first role as the duke porn star was on a rough sex website, and no, that doesn't make me a bad feminist. *xojane.com*. Retrieved from http://www.xojane.com/sex/belle-knox-duke-porn-star-rough-sex-feminism-kink

Levy, A. (2005). *Female chauvinist pigs: Women and the rise of raunch culture*. New York, NY: Free Press.

Mead, R. (2010, November 15). Downtown's daughter: Lena Dunham cheerfully exposes her privileged life. *New Yorker*. Retrieved from http://www.newyorker.com/reporting/2010/11/15/101115fa_fact_mead?currentPage=all

Morgan, R. (1977). *Theory and practice: Pornography and rape. Going too far: The personal chronicle of a feminist*. New York, NY: Random House.

Reger, J. (Ed.). (2005). *Different wavelengths: Studies of the contemporary women's movement*. New York, NY: Routledge.

Rich, B. R. (2003). Feminism and sexuality in the 1980s. In R. Dicker & A. Piepmeier (Eds.), *Catching a wave: Reclaiming feminism for the 21st century*. Boston, MA: Northeastern University Press.

Sandberg, S. (2013). *Lean in: Women, work, and the will to lead*. New York, NY: Knopf.

Schrodt, P. (2014, January 15). Lena Dunham's body is funny. *Esquire*. Retrieved from http://www.esquire.com/blogs/culture/lena-dunham-body-funny

Siegel, D. (2007). *Sisterhood, interrupted: From radical women to grrrls gone wild*. New York, NY: Palgrave.

Valenti, J. (2007). *Full frontal feminism: A young woman's guide to why feminism matters*. New York, NY: Seal Press.

Walker, R. (1995). *To be real: Telling the truth and changing the face of feminism*. New York, NY: Anchor.

Wappler, M. (2017, January 11). Dunham talks the end of 'Girls,' our new president, and being a workaholic. *Nylon*. Retrieved from https://nylon.com/articles/lena-dunham-nylon-february-cover

RACHEL ALICIA GRIFFIN

3. OLIVIA POPE AS PROBLEMATIC AND PARADOXICAL

A Black Feminist Critique of Scandal's "Mammification"

For seven seasons, ABC's *Scandal* (Rhimes, 2012–2018) flourished as a primetime Washington D.C./Beltway thriller that millions watched weekly. Of great significance amid *Scandal's* success is that Olivia Pope, played by Kerry Washington, was the first Black female lead character in a network drama since Teresa Graves in *Get Christie Love!* in 1974 (Powell, 2013). Articulating the Shondaland show's significance, Obell (2018) says, "there have been more black women leads on network TV... since *Scandal's* debut than ever in history, suggesting that increasing blackness on television may be OPA's [Olivia Pope & Associates] greatest "fix" of all." Exemplary of this shift in television are the enduring lead and supporting roles of Viola Davis and Aja Naomi King on *How to Get Away with Murder* (2014–), Tracee Ellis Ross and Yara Shahidi on ABC's *black-ish* (2014–), Taraji P. Henson on *Empire* (2015–), and Angela Bassett on Fox's *9-1-1* (2018–). As such, *Scandal* can be understood as a phenomenal turning point of cultural progress with regard to Black female representation. Alongside *Scandal's* trailblazing industry influence, it has also been critiqued as highly problematic insofar as its advocacy for colorblind and post-racial ideology (Chaney & Robertson, 2016; Washington & Harris, 2018). Equally troubling are the pronounced traces of "controlling images" (Collins, 2009, p. 76), such as the mammy and jezebel, which toil to confine Olivia to historically situated and oppressive caricatures of Black femininity.

To situate *Scandal* as emblematic of paradoxical popular culture (i.e., a television show that is both progressive and problematic), I begin with an overview of the presence and absence of Black women in U.S. American television followed by a description of the show focused primarily on Olivia Pope. Second, I situate Black feminist thought (Collins, 2009, 2016) as theory and Black feminist spectatorship (hooks, 1992) as method to foster a critical interpretation of Olivia at the intersections of race, gender, and class. Next,

© KONINKLIJKE BRILL NV, LEIDEN, 2019 | DOI:10.1163/9789004414259_003

I theorize how *Scandal's* storylines, Olivia's character, and the series' finale evoke and undermine the mammy archetype. Embracing the paradox, I first interrogate the "mammification" (Omolade, 1994, p. 54) of Olivia's career as a political fixer, and then highlight how the personal and professional intricacies of her life incite "de-mammification" (Omolade, 1994, p. 37). Finally, I reflect on *Scandal* as a show that, albeit paradoxically troubling, importantly challenges essentialist portrayals of Black womanhood.

BLACK WOMEN, MEDIATED REPRESENTATION, AND OUR PRESENT ABSENCE

Critical scholars concerned with representations of marginalized identity groups, such as Black women, insist upon the critique of media as a powerful social institution (Allison, 2016; Goldman, Ford, Harris, & Howard, 2014; hooks, 1992; Smith-Shomade, 2002; Squires, 2009). Underscoring media as a means to ideologically denigrate Black femininity, scholars have long challenged negative representations of Black women and girls (Bennett & Griffin, 2016; Coleman, 2000; Griffin, 2012, 2013, 2014, 2015; Smith-Shomade, 2002). Despite such efforts, controlling imagery remains customary and profitable. Drawing upon Mullings (1997), Collins (2009) defines controlling images as stereotypical scripts that "not only subjugate U.S. Black women but are key in maintaining intersecting oppressions" (p. 77).

Foundationally established via slavery and continually reproduced and repurposed ever since, controlling images function to justify (at minimum) racist and sexist oppression (Collins, 2009). For Black women, such imagery includes the: mammy, jezebel, sapphire, amazon, matriarch, welfare queen, gold digger, Black bitch, superwoman, freak, hoe, and hoodrat (Collins, 2005, 2009; Jordan-Zachery, 2009). While each controlling image is contextually unique, they are also interrelated and can overlap (Collins, 2009). Of importance to underscore is that they all necessitate culturally deficient representations of Black femininity in that each is characterized by at least one trait that naturalizes Black female inferiority, deviance, and/ or contemptibility. Therefore, when depicted in alignment with controlling imagery, Black women are never fully within reach of dignity, integrity, intelligence, respect, admiration, or compassion.

While Black female characters may not be fully confined to any one controlling image, it is vital to expose how controlling images problematically linger in contemporary media, particularly in depictions of powerful, awe-inspiring cisgender Black women like Olivia Pope. Pronounced traces of the mammy and jezebel are present within *Scandal's* storylines and Pope's characteristics, interactions, and relationships (Washington & Harris, 2018; Wright, 2014). Relevant to this chapter is how Pope's character both evokes and undermines the mammy caricature. According to Anderson (1997), "The icon of the mammy is probably the most recognizable and longest perpetuated image of African American women in American society, and it has been reproduced again and again on stage and screen" (p. 9).

Historically, the mammy was depicted as an asexual, dark-skinned Black woman of robust physical size and stature who took great pleasure in caring for White individuals and/or families at the expense of herself and her family (Anderson, 1997; Collins, 2009). Committed and confined to servitude, a mammy is upheld as the ideal Black woman in the White imagination largely because she reflects a deep sense of loyalty to Whiteness – whether it be the White slave masters who owned her, the White children she lovingly reared, or the predominantly White owned and controlled institutions that employ her.

In contemporary U.S. American culture, caricatures including the mammy remain steadfast archetypes for representations of Black women but have been modernized to mirror societal changes (Chaney & Robertson, 2016; Washington & Harris, 2018; Harris-Perry, 2010; Jordan-Zachery, 2009). Although portrayals of Black women are no longer caged by legalized slavery or segregation, nor solely confined to White households, Black female characters are still replete with servitude, obedience, self-sacrifice, care-taking, domesticity, and an allegiance to White people, ideologies, and culture (Beauboeuf-Lafontant, 2009; Collins, 2005).

The widespread availability of mammy imagery signifies the omnipresence of the controlling image. Take for example, the continued use of Aunt Jemima in advertising, Nellie Ruth as Nell Harper in *Gimee a Break!* (1981–1987), Oprah on *The Oprah Winfrey Show* (1986–2011), S. Epatha Merkerson as Anita Van Buren on *Law & Order* (1990–2010), Jennifer Hudson in *Sex and the City* (2008), and Tyler Perry's Madea franchise (Collins, 2005; Harris-Perry, 2010; Merritt & Cummings, 2014; Smith-Shomade, 2002). More recently, and more explicitly, Viola Davis and Octavia Spencer were the help in *The Help* (2011), and Spencer earned an Oscar for her performance. The continued portrayal and celebration of Black women as mammies, alongside an equally disheartening parade of Black female characters as sapphires, jezebels, gold diggers, Black bitches, etc. (Allison, 2016; Collins, 2005, 2009; Goldman et al., 2014; Zook, 2010), indicates the regularity of Black women being stereotypically depicted which signifies our present absence. To clarify, Black women are present in accordance with the dominant imagination but oftentimes unrecognizable to ourselves amid the considerable absence of characters scripted to unapologetically defy systemic oppressions without concern for being palatable to White mainstream audiences. Since controlling imagery is readily available and dispensed with ease in U.S. American media and popular culture, negative caricatures and stereotypes maintain a stronghold on how Black femininity is scripted and understood – even in fiery and seemingly progressive shows such as *Scandal*.

SCANDAL AND OLIVIA POPE

Debuting in 2012 on ABC with a total of 124 episodes over seven seasons, *Scandal* depicts shocking storylines immersed in crisis, deceit, and secrets. Early on we learn that Olivia Pope is a fixer who manages the crises of powerful Washington D.C. elites with the help of her associates. Referred to as "gladiators in suits," each associate is indebted to Olivia as a beneficiary of her services. Initially, the gladiators are Harrison, Stephen, Abby, Huck, and Quinn. Narrating their role in relation to Olivia as their leader early on in the series, Harrison says, "Gladiators don't have feelings. We rush into battle. We're soldiers. We get hurt in the fight, we suck it up and hold it down. We don't question" (Rhimes, 2012–2018). Drawing upon their individual talents and flaws, Pope & Associates (OPA) is effective at eluding and controlling a broad range of crises including crime, infidelity, and disaster. Alongside Olivia's avid leadership of OPA and intermittent employment at the White House, a parallel storyline is her on again – off again affair with President Fitzgerald Grant (hereafter, Fitz).

Since Black women have long been scarcely represented among lead and reoccurring roles on primetime television series or within key crew positions such as producers and writers (Dates, 2005; Smith-Shomade, 2002), both Shonda Rhimes' production company, Shondaland, and *Scandal* are unique (Meyer & Griffin, 2018). Not only because the Black female lead character was created by Rhimes as a Black female executive producer; equally noteworthy, is that Rhimes' creation of Olivia was inspired by a Black woman named Judy Smith (Svetkey, 2013). Smith is a lawyer, crisis manager, and founder of Smith & Company, headquartered in Washington D.C. as a "full-service crisis management and communications firm" (Smith & Company, 2012). Though quite atypical in the media industry, Olivia's character is directly influenced by three Black women (i.e., Smith,

Rhimes, and Washington) from multiple angles of the creative process. Spurred by this sadly unique context, Black feminist thought and Black feminist spectatorship are positioned as theory and method to deconstruct the paradoxical representation of Olivia Pope.

U.S. AMERICAN BLACK FEMINIST THOUGHT AND BLACK FEMINIST SPECTATORSHIP

Primarily concerned with the oppressive forces of racism and sexism, "Black feminism is a social justice project advanced by African American women and their allies in defense of the interests of African American women" (Collins, 2013, p. 50; Collins, 2016). The overarching commitments of Black feminist thought (BFT) include: illuminating intersecting identities and systems of oppression, drawing upon individual and collective knowledge, challenging the imposition of inferiority, and exposing the prevalence of controlling imagery (Collins, 2009, 2013, 2016). As such, BFT offers a rich theoretical lens for Black women to engage with media and popular culture as Black feminist spectators interested in evaluating representations of Black femininity.

hooks (1992) defines a Black feminist spectator as a Black woman who leverages the "power in looking" (p. 115). To do so, Black feminist spectators engage with media and popular culture using an "oppositional" or "critical" gaze (hooks, 1992, p. 116) that pays "close attention to the intersections of identity, power of representation, and reproduction of domination" (Griffin, 2014, p. 172). Black feminist spectatorship not only fosters liberation from the confinement of controlling imagery, but also exposes how oppressive images continue to manifest despite "post-feminist" and "post-racial" fanfare that situates sexism and racism decisively in the past. To learn how historically situated, but modernly meaningful, controlling images continue to manifest, deconstructing shows like *Scandal,* meaning those that appear to be solely empowering and reformist – is essential. Therefore, as a biracial Black and White, cisgender female Black feminist spectator, I approach the show asking: How does Olivia Pope, at the intersections of race, gender, and class, paradoxically reproduce and challenge the mammy as a controlling image?

In response, I first deconstruct negative representations of Olivia that mammify her as a political fixer. Then, I analyze how the opposing force of de-mammification undermines Olivia being entirely collapsed into the mammy caricature, and subsequently accentuates her resistant embodiment of Black womanhood.

BLACK FEMINIST ANALYSIS: OLIVIA POPE
AS A MAMMIFIED POLITICAL FIXER

At first glance, Olivia Pope's economic status as an upper-class Black cisgender woman working alongside Washington D.C.'s elite ostensibly challenges the assertion that the mammy archetype shapes her career as a political fixer. On the contrary, "Irrespective of setting and job title, the mammy legacy continues to weave itself into the lives of nearly all Black women workers" (Omolade, 1994, p. 51). Echoing Omolade (1994), bell hooks reminds us that "the proverbial "mammy" cares for all the needs of others, particularly those most powerful" (hooks & West, 1991, p. 154). Cueing Olivia's mammification at the root of her character development is her character biography on ABC, which reads:

> What makes Olivia Pope the best is that she doesn't fix problems. She fixes clients. She fixes people. They come to her at their lowest moment. On the worst day of their lives. Covered in blood, on the verge of conviction. When rock bottom is in sight and there's nowhere left to turn they come to Olivia Pope for salvation. (ABC, n.d., http://abc.go.com/shows/scandal/cast/olivia-pope)

Read critically, ABC's framing of Olivia as a fixer who delivers "salvation" strongly aligns her with the societal expectation for Black women to serve as caretakers, which has been and remains a definitive feature of the mammy archetype. Building upon Olivia's mammified foundation, in the paragraphs that follow, I highlight how her relationship with her gladiators, profession as a fixer, interactions with White clientele, and confinement to her professional life serve as additional sites of mammification.

Reflecting on her team, Olivia is mammified via her role as their surrogate mother. Interpreting Olivia in this way is supported by her compassionate rescue of each gladiator from dire circumstances. Olivia rescued Harrison from a prison sentence; Abby from her abusive husband; Huck from desolate homelessness; and Quinn from being framed and convicted for the deadly Cytron explosion connected to rigged voting machines. In later seasons, Jake, Marcus, and Charlie become gladiators by association. Although they each travel different trajectories toward Olivia and OPA, their roles as gladiators are similar insofar as being rescued and finding a sense of belonging via a crisis management firm that Olivia founded. More often than not, her gladiators' secrets, struggles, and salvation are all beholden to Olivia's care. Exemplary of the pressure and responsibility Olivia feels to lead and care for her team, at the end of season two, she remorsefully tells Fitz that she took them too far into the peril of covering up his rigged presidential election. So far, that she is unsure of their individual and collective recovery, and therefore unwilling to disband OPA despite Fitz's desire to forgo a re-election campaign in order to ensure their future as a romantic couple. In this context, although Olivia deeply loves Fitz and is visibly pained by her choice, she chooses her team and his opportunity for presidential redemption over herself and their relationship, which reflects self-sacrificial mammification via the emphasis on others and work before herself and pleasure. Olivia's desire to protect her colleagues, defined in later seasons as family and friends, is threaded throughout the series. Even when Olivia leaves OPA behind, first to stand in the sun with Jake (season three) and then to serve as President Mellie Grant's Chief of Staff and Command of B613 (season six and seven), she still risks a prison sentence for herself in the hopes that others will not be punished.

Olivia embodying self-sacrificial responsibility does not singlehandedly beckon mammification. However, when paired with her role as a fixer who rescues those closest to her and her persistent refusal to accept their support in return, a relational imbalance emerges that is consistent with Black women serving as selfless mammies. Calling forth both the mammy and superwoman as controlling images, on multiple occasions in every season when Olivia communicates vulnerability via emotionally distraught facial expressions, she verbally insists upon her independence and declines the fixing that she prioritizes for others. For example, when First Lady Mellie Grant announces to the press that Fitz is having an affair but refrains from naming Olivia as his mistress, Harrison staunchly says, "The First Lady just put you on notice… You're not the fixer here, Liv. You're the problem. You're the client" (Rhimes, 2012). After a fleeting pause and despite the truths in Harrison's assertion, Olivia firmly denies his offer to help and indicates that she can and will take care of herself.

Intensifying the mammification of Olivia as a surrogate mother who refuses the support she delivers, she also protects members of her team from themselves, outsiders, and, at times, each other. For instance, Olivia orders her team to clean the murder scene of Quinn's romantic acquaintance to protect Quinn's true identity, and the underlying scandal of the Cytron explosion, from being discovered. Under Olivia's direction, they guide a grief stricken Quinn through removing her blood-spattered clothing, eliminate fingerprints and DNA, and remove everything with a connection to Quinn that cannot be wiped down. Unbeknownst to everyone except for Huck, Olivia's decision to help Quinn avoid being suspected of murder and exposed heightens Olivia's personal and professional risk. Thus, up to this point, Olivia has illegally helped Quinn evade being framed and falsely convicted for the Cytron explosion. However, once she gave the command, OPA destroyed evidence, mislead Assistant State Attorney David Rosen's murder investigation, and became implicated in election-rigging.

Olivia's mammification via the Cytron storyline is additionally solidified by her desire to protect Defiance, a code name used in reference to the election rigging that put Fitz in the White House. Although Fitz is unaware of Defiance throughout the first season and most of the second, and subsequently unaware of Olivia's tremendous risk-taking to protect his presidency; billionaire businessman Hollis Doyle, Supreme Court Justice Verna Thorton, Cyrus Beene as the White House Chief of Staff, and Mellie as the First Lady all benefit from Olivia's amplified risk-taking. All five, as members of Defiance, made the joint decision to rig Fitz's election, which led to the Cytron explosion as a cover up for Defiance. However, although Olivia reaps personal and professional benefits from using her skills as a fixer to keep Defiance a secret; as the main character of *Scandal*, her fixing becomes mammified given its' standing as an inherent characteristic and expectation of her role. This interpretation is bolstered by Olivia's presence as the only person and woman of color involved in Defiance. Also key to mammification, is Olivia feeling obligated to independently take the added risk of protecting a child-like (i.e., naïve and innocent) Quinn from Hollis' efforts to frame her.

In addition to Olivia's character biography, role as a surrogate mother, and token status as a naturalized fixer, her interactions with her predominantly White clientele also signify mammification, despite and via her many talents. A critical interpretation of *Scandal's* overarching plot reveals that Olivia spends the majority of her time rescuing and responding to her predominantly White clientele and protecting White interests. Notably, it is her parents Rowan and Maya Pope who consistently decry Olivia's professional endeavors as mammification throughout all six seasons in which they appear. While Maya is commonly upset that her daughter is, in essence, 'the help' in Washington D.C., Rowan is furious that Oliva is seemingly satisfied with the – in his view – minimal political power that she has access to as 'the help'.

Seemingly easy to dismiss given the indications that Olivia is handsomely compensated for her labor (i.e., she lives in a spacious apartment with posh décor, wears designer clothes, etc.), of importance to recognize is that her class status is usually dwarfed by that of her clients. This is not to dismiss the significance of Olivia's class privilege; instead, it is key to underscore that privileged class status does not function as a barrier to mammification. hooks reminds us that while "Black women are no longer forced by racist exploitive labor practices to "serve" solely in jobs deemed menial, they are still expected to clean up everyone's mess" (hooks & West, 1991, p. 154). With hooks' guidance, I interpret Olivia as an upper-class Black woman – privileged by class and simultaneously marginalized by race and gender – who is mammified via her sharp flair for cleaning up after people with more money, status, and power than she has. Even as Command of B613, a clandestine division of the U.S. government that secretly runs the country, Oliva remains mammified despite her colossal power. The audience watches as Olivia privately struggles as Command – she is emotionally forlorn by the decisions she makes yet effectively masks her pain publicly. So much so that she repeatedly encourages and orders others to rely on her despite her struggles. For instance, when President Mellie Grant discovers that Olivia ordered an assassination without her knowledge, Olivia says "I carry the burden so you don't have to" (Rhimes, 2012–2018).

More explicitly exemplary of Olivia being a well-paid yet mammified fixer is when she is called upon by millionaire CEO Sandra Harding to find her son Travis when he is late for his rape trial. Interactions between Sandra and Olivia reveal that Sandra feels Olivia can help Travis in ways that she cannot, which is strongly reminiscent of Black women stepping in to care for White women's children when they are unable and/or unwilling to do so themselves. Signaling the magnitude of the mess Olivia has to clean up, when she arrives to 27-year-old Travis' hotel room, he is naked, in bed with a random woman, and groggily hung over from the night before. Faithful to her client, Olivia sneaks Travis out the back to avoid the press.

Conveying mammification further, beyond being hired to in effect babysit a 27-year-old White male, we watch and listen throughout the episode as Olivia clues Sandra in to Travis' depravity. Although he did not sexually violate the woman he is on trial for raping, Harrison brings to light that Travis did pay off a past victim who eventually committed suicide. As Sandra dismally comes to grips with her son's depraved and unpunished behavior, it is Olivia who offers loyal counsel and comfort in response.

Additionally, for Sandra and Travis both, Olivia exudes the tough love expected from mammified Black women employed to take care of White children and their parents. This is particularly clear when Olivia shows up on Sandra's doorstep to tell her the hard truth about her role in her son's depravity. Soon after Olivia's grim insight that Sandra has spoiled Travis and continually let him evade responsibility for his mistakes, we watch as Sandra insists that he turn himself in for rape with Olivia, stern and satisfied, nearby. Here, Olivia's fixing falls even further in alignment with oppressive roles reserved for Black women when we understand her as the conduit through which Sandra effectively mothers her son.

Lastly, it is important to realize that our knowledge about Olivia's life is typically limited to the myriad ways she is useful to the White House, symbolically and factually an echelon of domination, and White people. More specifically, not only is Olivia's career largely in service to "White supremacist capitalist patriarchy" (hooks, 1995, p. 29) given her labor on behalf of D.C.'s elite and on again/off again employment at the White House, but this "matrix of domination" (Collins, 2009, p. 21) is also the lens through which Olivia's visibility, value, and status are secured. In alignment with the mammified role the dominant imagination bestows upon Black women, Olivia unswervingly puts the needs and interests of her clients, gladiators, colleagues, lover, and eventually the entire republic once she becomes Command far above her own, as mammies are expected to do. Fueling her ability to do so is the rarity of storylines that center her personal life, beyond her love interests. Olivia's work is her life, but her work overwhelmingly centers Whiteness leaving little room for anything or anyone else including Oliva herself. Arguably, the most personal information that the audience learns about Olivia – over all seven seasons – that is entirely disconnected from her work life is that her go-to snack is popcorn and wine.

The absence of Olivia's life beyond work fortifies her mammification via the reduction of who she is to the work that she does. Of great significance is that Olivia rarely stops working, or allows time for relaxation or rest despite the monumental stressors of her profession. Even when we are introduced to her home in season one, it is in service to her work since she brings her White female client, Amanda Tanner, home with her to keep her safely hidden. This is, again, where the mammy and superwoman archetypes merge in that Olivia's perpetual labor as a fixer is rooted in a seemingly endless supply of "self-sacrificial strength" (Harris-Perry, 2011, p. 21) that functions to her clients and colleagues benefit, but her detriment in that even her home is repeatedly invaded by her work. However, we are offered a rare glimpse into Olivia's home as respite when she unravels during season two; we watch as she protectively folds herself into bed, where she stays for two days until Huck arrives. Although Huck is sincerely concerned for Olivia's well-being, of importance to note is that she gets out of bed not because she has allowed others to care for her, or because she is ready to emerge from the layered crises linked to Defiance, a marriage proposal, and the attempted assassination of the president, whom she loves. Rather, outwardly unconcerned for her own emotional, mental, or physical health, Olivia gets up to, once again, be consumed by her work.

Overall, a Black feminist analysis of the series reveals that Oliva is consistently mammified through her role as a fixer. Tellingly, the nature of Olivia's mammified fixing changes minimally even when she professionally transitions from, for example, OPA to the White House to Command of B613. In the section that follows the paradoxical nature of *Scandal* is exposed via a discussion of how Olivia also personifies de-mammification.

OLIVIA POPE AS A DE-MAMMIFIED POLITICAL FIXER

Despite mammification, Olivia also destabilizes the mammy as an all-encompassing, controlling image of Black womanhood. From a Black feminist perspective, this does not nullify how Olivia is mammified; rather, de-mammification importantly humanizes her character beyond the confines of the dominant imagination. To illuminate Olivia's resistance to being fully encased by the mammy, I center her: authentic and reciprocal relationships with her gladiators; secrets as a means to secure agency and empowerment; embodiment of keen intellect opposed to automated deference; desirability as an intelligent and beautiful Black woman; and rise to power as B613's Command. Notably, mammification does steadily lessen as *Scandal* progresses to the series finale; however, Olivia never fully escapes the controlling image.

To begin, while Olivia did in fact rescue each gladiator, concern and protection are sometimes mutually exchanged. Thus, although Olivia habitually rebuffs fixing on her behalf, her team often safeguards her – without her request or permission. Early on Huck and Harrison in particular serve as examples of how Olivia is de-mammified as a recipient of genuine, unconditional support followed by Abby and Marcus in later seasons. Signifying the reciprocity between Olivia and Huck that fosters de-mammification, when Huck faces the danger of being named as a member of B613, a top secret group of Central Intelligence Agency (CIA) operatives, Olivia convinces him to let her help. Granting her 24 hours to do so before he takes deadly action, it is clear that Olivia genuinely cares for Huck and he genuinely respects her in return. Additional indications of the strength and sincerity of their relationship include Olivia facilitating Huck's release after being framed for the assassination attempt on Fitz; Huck's weekly security scans of her apartment to make certain it is not bugged; Olivia ensuring that the team cares for Huck's post-traumatic stress in her absence; Huck's ever-present willingness to kill to ensure Olivia's safety and protect her interests; and, finally, Huck's decision not to kill Olivia after she risks Quinn's life.

A pinnacle scene in which Olivia and Huck's relationship is authenticated is when she is able to disrupt his catatonic state prompted by B613 flashbacks. Prior to her arrival, Quinn, Harrison, and Abby unsuccessfully try to do so – it is Olivia's presence that renders Huck quiet and slows his rocking. Revisiting why she was drawn to rescue him, Olivia narrates to Huck the sadness and loneliness that they each live within and implores him to come back to her. In desperation, she says, "[Y]ou have to come back to me. I need you... I didn't save you in that Metro station. You saved me" (Rhimes, 2012–2018). Olivia feeling saved by Huck, alongside her articulation of their interdependence, communicates the existence of a concrete friendship between them; a relationship distanced from mammification by mutual vulnerability and respect. Also meaningful is that Huck's care is never just Olivia's responsibility alone. Not only did each gladiator aid him during his catatonic crisis, but just prior when Huck returns to the office badly beaten, he is warmly welcomed by everyone and sits among them at dinner. In this context, Olivia is depicted as a Black woman who not only shares the weight and responsibilities of caretaking but is also deeply cared for by others. This is incredibly apparent in season seven when the gladiators and Fitz stage an intervention because they think Olivia has crossed too far into the dark side of D.C. politics as Command. Pleading with Olivia through a closed door, Abby says, "You saved us all from something... Let us save you" (Rhimes, 2012–2018).

Similarly characterized by authenticity and reciprocity, Olivia's relationship with Harrison de-mammifies her in different but equally important ways. While Huck de-mammifies Olivia via devoted amity most often expressed privately between them, Harrison fosters de-mammification by guarding Olivia's reputation in public contexts – not for his own benefit, but rather out of profound respect for her. Harrison consistently undermines the mammifying forces of racism and sexism by reminding the gladiators that Olivia is a remarkable Black woman who is deserving of trust, esteem, and loyalty. For instance, he highlights her commendable performance as a fixer when anyone dares question her leadership and/or decision-making. He also rationalizes the difficult decisions that Olivia makes, many of which can be easily written off as immoral and/or devious, and defends her need for secrecy. When Quinn is troubled by not knowing how or why Olivia fixed her, Harrison says, "Liv's a good person and if a good person has to do something bad for the right reasons, I am down with that... I don't want to know the hows. I don't want to know the whys" (Rhimes, 2012–2018). Interpreting Harrison's advocacy on Olivia's behalf as de-mammification; he challenges the patronizing gleam of racist and sexist caricatures by drawing attention to Olivia's incessant pursuit of the "white hat" (Rhimes, 2012–2018), which signifies her devotion to justice, integrity, and patriotism.

Overall, members of Olivia's team make profound sacrifices to help and protect her, despite her shortcomings and, in some instances, manipulation of their lives. Drawing upon the links between Olivia, Harrison, and Abby, when Abby learns that Olivia had Harrison falsify a story about David to end their relationship, she is furious and does not want to help Olivia retrieve the Cytron memory card that proves Defiance happened. Once again defending Olivia and her authority, Harrison abrasively indicates that he did so simply because Olivia asked him to as a gladiator, and he tells Abby that she should do the same in reference to the Cytron card. Despite scoffing at Harrison's indignation, Abby chooses to manipulate David's rekindled love for her by stealing the Cytron card to keep Defiance a secret. When David rightly accuses her of stealing, Abby evenly denies it but then sobs because she realizes that he truly loved her. Although genuinely sorry for Abby's pain, Olivia is also relieved at the sight of the Cytron card as a symbol of the magnitude of her team's commitment to her. Yet it is Harrison who eventually makes the ultimate sacrifice as a gladiator when Olivia's father Rowan (as Command) murders him because he is too loyal to Olivia to keep Rowan's involvement in a horrendous crime a secret from OPA.

Indicative of the mutual exchange of risk, protection, sacrifice, and salvation among OPA, the gladiators' collective allegiance to Olivia de-mammifies her because it averts her perpetual isolation as a self-sacrificial caretaker, risk-taker, and problem solver. Even when Olivia is ostracized from the team in later seasons, Marcus remains a close friend, which prevents her from being entirely disowned by everyone she deems family. When Olivia asks him why he is still willing to befriend her, he offers a reason that is strikingly impervious to her work. Marcus says, "We're Black. Which means I'll always be here for you and I'll always root for you. It's how we do" (Rhimes, 2012–2018).

Given that secrets, keeping, leaking, or destroying them, serve as the crux of *Scandal*, the role that secrets play in Olivia's professional and personal lives serves as a key example of how her embodiment of Black womanhood is de-mammified. Historically, mammies who worked in White households as domestics were privy to the private lives of their employers (Thurber, 1992), subsequently their livelihood and safety was dependent upon their silence which mitigated their access to agency. The central difference in *Scandal* is that Olivia utilizes her agency and power to keep her gladiators', clients', and the White House's secrets while occasionally reaping benefits from doing so. Take for example, the backstory behind Quinn's arrival to OPA. Although unknown to Quinn during season one and most of season two, it was Huck who drugged her, relocated her to Washington D.C., and provided her with a new identity to evade being falsely framed for the Cytron explosion. Of importance to note is that Huck, despite working closely alongside Quinn as a gladiator, never exposed Olivia's role in Quinn's rescue. Therefore, the audience can interpret Olivia as someone who keeps secrets, benefits from the secrets kept, and has secrets kept on her behalf – all of which symbolize a heightened level of access to agency and power historically denied to Black women fully reduced to mammy archetypes.

The role of secrets in *Scandal* also functions as a form of valuable currency that Olivia can draw upon to de-mammify herself. Although her use of secrets as currency functions similarly to that of mammies, Olivia's calculated audacity often works against mammification. When Grayden Osborne, Director of the CIA, shows up unannounced to her home, Olivia sensibly pauses to gather herself before she opens her door to Osborne barging in and demanding to know who hired her to have him followed. In response, Olivia boldly ignores his questions, reminds him how powerful her clients are, and orders him to leave. Reading this scene critically, Olivia de-mammifies herself by keeping her secrets and disregarding Osborne's demands despite his power. In comparison, mammification necessitates Black female inferiority and exhorts "Black women to assume a status-reassuring deference to Whites, particularly in workplaces" (Beauboeuf-Lafontant, 2009, p. 30). While Olivia and Osborne's interaction occurs in her home, Beauboeuf-Lafontant's (2009) insight is useful because Olivia's refusal to cave to Osborne's threatening disposition is directly linked to their professional roles. Therefore, Osborne's unsatisfied, resentful exit renders Olivia's power undeniable and prevents her foreclosure into a mammified temperament that would have conceded to him as a White male authority figure.

Olivia's relationship with President Mellie Grant, a White woman, also confirms this de-mammified interpretation when Olivia offers Mellie a hard/harsh correction to remind her that Command, not the president, runs the world. Calling the shots, B613 facilitates the assassination of Bashrani President Rashad in the best interest of the republic – despite his intimate relationship with Mellie. Not only does Olivia make decisions without the president's knowledge, she also fails to abide by Mellie's wishes. When

Mellie asks Olivia to use B613 to murder Cyrus, now the Vice President, she almost kills him but ultimately cannot hand him a glass of poisoned wine. In a revealing scene that differentiates between Olivia's integrity and profession, Mellie genially says, "It's not who you are" (Rhimes, 2012–2018). Choosing not to kill Cyrus coupled with Mellie's respect for her choice underscores Olivia's agency and self-preservation. Although she hides it well, Olivia's obligations as Command are causing her to slowly unravel. Had she murdered Cyrus – a friend and colleague – and once again prioritized the republic at her own expense, it is feasible that she would have crossed over to the dark side permanently thereby rendering a return to the white hat pursuit of justice impossible.

Mirroring her confrontation with Osborne and relationship with President Mellie Grant, Olivia repeatedly draws upon her razor sharp intellect and brisk communication style which furthers her de-mammification. Traditionally, the intelligence of Black women as mammies is overlooked if not deemed impossible. However, Olivia's intelligence and mastery of semantics is on full display in every episode. Absent the obedient and demure temperament of mammies, Olivia never recedes in a moment of professional crises and always publicly radiates palpable confidence. This is not to imply that Olivia is reduced to the binary of being either emotionless or emotion ridden, which signals the underdevelopment of characters that is common to the roles Black women are cast in. Instead, indicative of Rhimes, Smith, and Washington's artistry, Olivia embodies a broad range of emotions including fear, angst, and vulnerability alongside her staples of courage, composure, and invincibility, but typically does so in private moments that preserve her professionalism.

Ultimately, rendering *Scandal's* progressive undertones quite audible, the series finale punctuates Oliva's emotional growth and challenges mammification by allowing us to witness the gravity of her choices and emotions. Deeply troubled that destroying B613 requires implicating herself, the gladiators, and both Grant administrations because criminality entangles them all, we watch as she comes to a decision in an extremely significant cultural space – the Smithsonian's National Museum of African American History and Culture. In the end, although Olivia attempts to sacrifice only herself for the greater good of the republic, which is surely a mammified choice, she is de-mammified by Huck, Abby, and Quinn. Out of respect and love, they embody the gladiators' steadfast "over a cliff" (Rhimes, 2012–2018). Mantra and form a united front by testifying as witnesses to B613's criminal reign. Their joint testimony protects Olivia and results in Jake serving a prison sentence.

A final illustration of Olivia's failure to fully embody the mammy is her enviable beauty, physique, and wardrobe. Harshly juxtaposed against White women as paragons of female virtue and beauty, Black women as mammies are stereotypically cast as sexually and romantically undesirable (Beauboeuf-Lafontant, 2009; Collins, 2009). However, Olivia offers a sharp contrast as a beautiful Black woman confidently dressed in a parade of elite designers including but not limited to: Michael Kors, Ralph Lauren, Escada, Dior, Ferragamo, Armani, and Gucci (Galanes, 2013; Mitchell, 2013). Importantly, her wardrobe serves as a testament to her poise, persona, and chic style rather than her being clad in a drab wardrobe or impersonal maid's uniform typical of mammified characters. Commenting on the empowering significance of Olivia's intelligence, beauty, style, and sex appeal, in combination with her professional success, Elisa (2013) says,

> We're not accustomed to being wanted. Lusted after, yes. Fantasized about, no doubt. Objectified, without question. But wanted, loved, dreamed for? Not so much… This, is why Black women love *Scandal*. Everything about it is against how we're usually depicted on TV and in movies. Pope is the star of the show. She has not one, but *two* (and occasionally three) successful and fine men in love with her. She runs her own business. She's well known for her work and not just her body.

CONCLUDING THOUGHTS: OLIVIA POPE AS PROGRESSIVE RATHER THAN "POST-"

From a Black feminist perspective, the wide performative range of Kerry Washington as Olivia Pope reveals steadfast opposition to confinement within the mammy caricature, despite the mammification of her career as a political fixer.

Importantly, Olivia also fails to be fully confined by additional controlling images including the superwoman, sapphire, and jezebel. For instance, her vulnerability incites care (opposed to dismissing her as a superwoman), her stern poise in the face of chaos incites respect (opposed to dismissing her as a sapphire), and her love for Fitz and Jake incites compassion (opposed to dismissing her as a jezebel). In essence, Olivia paradoxically oscillates among myriad interpretations – none of which fully reduce and confine her to one fixed interpretation. This is the dazzling gift of Rhimes storytelling via Shondaland shows – she consistently undermines caricatures and stereotypes by creating characters that illustrate the complexity of Black women in the real world.

When *Scandal* began in 2012, Olivia Pope was the only Black female character to lead a network drama in my lifetime. Surely the stark absence of women who look like me cast in fierce, diverse, and leading roles on television, signals the impossibility of being a "post-racial" or "post-feminist" society. However, the impracticality of "post-" logics and the glacial pace of societal change do not undermine the cultural significance of Olivia Pope's influential existence in our mediated lives. Personally, when I watch Olivia snap into decisive action in response to any given crises, I want to be like her because I see a real, really complex Black woman. Given the distance between popular culture and reality, more accurately, I want to be like Washington – a gifted Black woman who determinedly chases her professional dreams amid and despite her struggles. Consistently regarded as kind, gracious, passionate, driven, and humble (Galanes, 2013; Powell, 2013), Washington is accomplished far beyond the roles she has played. She earned a liberal arts degree from George Washington University, spoke at the 2012 Democratic Convention, served on President Obama's Committee on Arts and Humanities, accepted the 2013 NAACP's President's Award in honor of her public service, and earned rave reviews on Broadway after *Scandal* ended (Associated Press, 2013; Green, 2018; Mitchell, 2013; Powell, 2013).

Coupled with Washington's on and off screen triumphs, *Scandal's* (2012–2018) success and legacy surely signals progress; yet it remains key to distinguish progress from "post-" logics that antiquate racist and sexist oppression as past phenomena that contemporary society has effectively transcended. Distancing the show from such logics, Rhimes says, "I don't think the show is post-racial. I'm referring to race every time you see Kerry Washington being the person in charge and solving the crime and kissing the guy" (Svetkey, 2013). Building upon Rhimes understanding of *Scandal* and representational politics, I interpret the lessening of mammification throughout the series as an indication of Rhimes' earned agency as a showrunner increasingly able to script characters that appeal more to critical consciousness than caricatures. Allowing Kerry Washington to have the last word, she notes, "The fact that the show could be a success with a Black woman at the center of it says a lot about the kind of world we've become" (Leive, 2013).

DISCUSSION QUESTIONS

1. Do you agree and/or disagree with the assertion that Olivia Pope is mammified? Connecting popular culture to reality, can you think of real-life powerful Black women who have been mammified?

2. From your perspective, how does Olivia positively and/or negatively represent Black womanhood?
3. From a Black feminist perspective, how do Olivia's privileged identities as cisgender and upper-class impact her lived experiences as a Black woman in U.S. American society?
4. Beyond the mammy, are there additional controlling images that you think strongly shape Olivia's character?

ADDITIONAL READINGS

Coleman, R. R. M. (2011). "ROLL UP YOUR SLEEVES!": Black women, black feminism in feminist media studies. *Feminist Media Studies, 11*(1), 35–41.

Collins, P. H. (2009). *Black feminist thought: Knowledge, consciousness, and the politics of empowerment* (3rd ed.). New York, NY: Routledge.

Collins, P. H. (2013). *On intellectual activism*. Philadelphia, PA: Temple Press.

Griffin, R. A., & Meyer, M. D. (Eds.). (2018). *Adventures in Shondaland: Identity politics and the power of representation.* New Brunswick, NJ: Rutgers University Press.

hooks, b. (1981). *Ain't I a Woman: Black women and feminism.* Boston, MA: South End Press.

Puff, S., Moffitt, K., & Jackson, R. L. (Eds.). (in press). *Gladiators in suits: Race, gender, and the politics of representation in Scandal.* New York, NY: Syracuse University Press.

Squires, C. R. (2014). *The post-racial mystique: Media and race in the twenty-first century.* New York, NY: NYU Press.

REFERENCES

ABC. (n.d.). *Olivia Pope: Played by Kerry Washington.* Retrieved from http://abc.go.com/shows/scandal/cast/olivia-pope

Allison, D. C. (Ed.). (2016). *Black women's portrayals on reality television: The new sapphire.* Lanham, MD: Lexington.

Anderson, L. M. (1997). *Mammies no more: The changing image of Black women on stage and screen.* Lanham, MD: Rowman & Littlefield Publishers.

Associated Press. (2013, February 2). Kerry Washington wins 3 trophies at NAACP Image Awards. *USA Today.* Retrieved from http://www.usatoday.com/story/life/people/2013/02/02/washington-scandal-naacp-awards/1885461/

Beauboeuf-Lafontant, T. (2009). *Behind the mask of the strong Black woman: Voice and the embodiment of a costly performance.* Philadelphia, PA: Temple University Press.

Chaney, C., & Robertson, R. V. (2016). Chains of psychological enslavement: Olivia Pope and the celebration of the Black mistress in ABC's *Scandal. Africology: The Journal of Pan African Studies, 9*(3), 126–153.

Coleman, R. R. M. (2000). *African American viewers and the Black situation comedy: Situating racial humor.* New York, NY: Garland Publishing, Inc.

Collins, P. H. (2005). *Black sexual politics: African Americans, gender, and the new racism.* New York, NY: Routledge.

Collins, P. H. (2009). *Black feminist thought: Knowledge, consciousness, and the politics of empowerment* (3rd ed.). New York, NY: Routledge.

Collins, P. H. (2013). *On intellectual activism*. Philadelphia, PA: Temple Press.

Collins, P. H. (2016). Black feminist thought as oppositional knowledge. *Departures in Critical Qualitative Research, 5*(3), 133–144.

Dates, J. L. (2005). Movin' on up: Black women decision makers in entertainment television. *Journal of Popular Film and Television, 33*(2), 68–79.

Elisa, T. (2013). Why Black women love Scandal. *The Huffington Post*. Retrieved from http://www.huffingtonpost.com/tulani-elisa/why-black-women-love-scan_b_4179258.html

Galanes, P. (2013, September 26). For Cicely Tyson and Kerry Washington, roles of a lifetime. *The New York Times*. Retrieved from http://www.nytimes.com/2013/09/29/fashion/for-cicely-tyson-and-kerry-washington-roles-of-a-lifetime.html?_r=0

Goldman, A. Y., Ford, V. S. Harris, A. A., & Howard, N. R. (Eds.). (2014). *Black women and popular culture: The conversation continues*. Lanham, MD: Lexington.

Green, J. (2018, November 4). Review: 'American Son' puts Kerry Washington in a maternal nightmare. *The New York Times*. Retrieved from https://www.nytimes.com/2018/11/04/theater/american-son-review.html

Griffin, R. A. (2012). I AM an angry Black woman: Black feminist autoethnography, voice, and resistance. *Women's Studies in Communication, 35*(2), 138–157.

Griffin, R. A. (2014). Black women and gender violence in for colored girls: Black feminist reflections on the power and politics of representation. In J. S. C. Bell & R. L. Jackson (Eds.), *Interpreting Tyler Perry: Perspectives on race, class, gender, and sexuality* (pp. 169–186). New York, NY: Routledge.

Harris-Perry, M. V. (2011). *Sister citizen: Shame, stereotypes, and Black women in America*. New Haven, CT: Yale University Press.

hooks, b. (1992). *Black looks: Race and representation*. Boston, MA: South End Press.

hooks, b. (1995). *Killing rage: Ending racism*. New York, NY: Henry Holt, LLC.

hooks, b., & West, C. (1991). *Breaking bread: Insurgent Black intellectual life*. Cambridge, MA: South End Press.

IMDb. (1990–2014). *Scandal*. Retrieved from http://www.imdb.com/title/tt1837576/fullcredits?ref_=tt_ov_st_sm

Jordan-Zachery, J. S. (2009). *Black women, cultural images, and social policy*. New York, NY: Routledge.

Leive, C. (2013, October). Kerry takes off! *Glamour*, 254–261.

Merritt, B. D., & Cummings, M. S. (2014). The African American woman on film: The Tyler Perry image. In J. S. C. Bell & R. L. Jackson (Eds.), *Interpreting Tyler Perry: Perspectives on race, class, gender, and sexuality* (pp. 187–195). New York, NY: Routledge.

Mitchell, H. (2013, December). Sitting pretty. *Lucky Magazine*, 138–142.

Mullings, L. (1997). *On our own terms: Race, class, and gender in the lives of African American women*. New York, NY: Routledge.

Obell, S. (2018, April). In creating "Scandal" and Olivia Pope, Shonda Rhimes changed the TV landscape. *Buzzfeed*. Retrieved from https://www.buzzfeednews.com/article/sylviaobell/scandal-series-finale-legacy

Omolade, B. (1994). *The rising song of African American women*. New York, NY: Routledge.

Powell, K. (2013, March). Woman on top. *Ebony*, 112–117.

Rhimes, S. (Producer). (2012–2018). *Scandal* [Television series]. Burbank, CA: ABC Studios Production, Shondaland.

Smith & Company. (2012). *Professionals*. Retrieved from http://www.smithandcompany.com/professionals/judy-smith-president-and-ceo/

Smith-Shomade, B. E. (2002). *SHADED LIVES: African-American women and television.* New Brunswick, NJ: Rutgers University Press.

Squires, C. (2009). *African Americans and the media.* Malden, MA: Polity Press.

Svetkey, B. (2013, May). Kerry Washington's Scandal role breaks rules, makes history. *Parade.* Retrieved from http://parade.condenast.com/11185/benjaminsvetkey/kerry-washingtons-scandal-role-breaks-rules-makes-history/

Thurber, C. (1992). The development of the mammy image and mythology. In V. Bernhard, B. Brandon, E. Fox-Genovese, & T. Perdue (Eds.), *Southern women: Histories and identities* (pp. 87–108). Columbia, MO: University of Missouri Press.

Washington, M., & Harris, T. (2018). Interracial intimacies: From Shondaland to the postracial promised land. In R. A. Griffin & M. D. E. Meyers (Eds.), *Adventures in Shondaland: Identity politics and the power of representation* (pp. 156–175). New Brunswick, NJ: Rutgers University Press.

Wright, J. K. (2014). Scandalous: Olivia Pope and Black women in primetime history. In A. Y. Goldman, V. S. Ford, A. A. Harris, & N. R. Howard (Eds.), *Black women and popular culture: The conversation continues* (pp. 15–32). Lanham, MD: Lexington.

Zook, K. B. (2010). Has reality TV become Black women's enemy? *The Root.com.* Retrieved from http://www.theroot.com/articles/culture/2010/05/has_reality_tv_become_the_enemy_of_black_women.html

MELVIN L. WILLIAMS AND TIA C. M. TYREE

4. THE "UN-QUIET QUEEN"

An Analysis of Rapper Nicki Minaj in the Fame Comic Book

INTRODUCTION

Comic books are popular texts that facilitate a reflexive discussion on different aspects of culture. According to comic book scholar Scott McCloud, comic books serve a deeper purpose. As juxtaposed pictorial and other images in deliberate sequence, they intend to convey information and produce an aesthetic response in the viewer (McCloud, 1994). Female superheroes are not as often represented as male superheroes, and when superheroines are represented, many scholars and critics are quick to criticize the problems within their representations. Beyond the often-overt sexual representations, lie more complex issues regarding race, ethnicity, class and sexual orientation in superheroine portrayals.

Similarly, in Hip Hop, Black female rappers are often downplayed and stereotyped as the primary focus of misogynistic lyrics and images, despite their integral roles in the evolution of Hip Hop culture. Male rappers have outnumbered female rappers and male industry leaders have outnumbered female industry operatives, resulting in a system of domination that has perpetuated a greater visibility of men's prerogatives, masculine scripts for female rappers and little sustainability for the careers of female rappers (Phillips, Reddick-Morgan, & Stephens, 2005). Like Black superheroines, many female rappers have been reduced to sexual scripts that reflect misogynistic characterizations of women as predatory, sexual deviants who will fulfill sexual fantasies. Therefore, when female rapper, Onika "Nicki Minaj" Maraj was chosen in 2013 by Blue Water Comics to be featured in its *Fame* comic book series, a greater question emerged: Would the first Black female Rap superheroine in a comic book further propagate the misogynistic stereotypes and sexual scripts present in the history of comic books and Hip Hop culture, or would she offer a positive counter-stereotype?

This current study draws on phenomenology commonly associated with the social construction of reality theory as well as the concept of sexual

© KONINKLIJKE BRILL NV, LEIDEN, 2019 | DOI:10.1163/9789004414259_004

scripting (with a heightened emphasis on Stephens and Phillips' (2003) sexual scripts for Black women). Additionally, Saini's (2009) Black superheroine stereotypes were explored. In essence, Nicki Minaj's *Fame* comic book was analyzed to determine the presence of Stephens and Phillip's (2003) sexual scripts and Saini's (2009) Black superheroine stereotypes.

SOCIAL CONSTRUCTION OF REALITY THEORY

The social construction of reality theory asserts the sociology of knowledge rests on the presumption that knowledge is a cultural product shaped by social context and history. The reasonableness of knowledge in everyday life presents itself as a reality interpreted by individuals and is subjectively meaningful to them as a rational and coherent perspective (Heath, 2005). From this orientation, Peter Berger and Thomas Luckmann (1967) described reality as a "quality appertaining to phenomena that we recognized as having been independent of our own volition" and knowledge as "the certainty that phenomena are real and they possess specific characteristics" (p. 1). Individuals conceive their own distinctive social reality through contact and interaction with others and the media-generated images around them.

Gamson, Croteau, Hoynes, and Sasson (1992) asserted that media-generated images of the world are used to construct meaning about political and social issues. As a result, the lens through which one receives these images is not neutral but evinces the power and point of view of the political and economic elites who operate and focus it (Gamson et al., 1992, p. 374). Under this prism, readers perceive the social construction of reality as invisible, while the process of constructing meaning from such media-generated images is deemed natural and normal. The "reader" is privileged over "audience" under Gamson et al.'s (1992) perspective, because of his or her heavy emphases on those who decode such messages through sights and sounds as well as printed text.

As a social group, Rap artists describe and sell their realities to their audiences (Tyree, 2007, p. 49). Rap lyrics are first-person narratives that retell what the artists (allegedly) saw or did and recount events that happened personally or specifically to them (Light, 1992; Steaman, 1992; Rose 1994; Kelley, 1996; Barrett, 1999; Snoop Dogg, 1999; Armstrong, 2001). For rappers and their fans, Rap music is an opportunity to tell or hear their realities, respectively.

LITERATURE REVIEW: NICKI MINAJ IN POPULAR CULTURE

Nicki Minaj is a Trinidadian-born American rapper, singer, songwriter, actress and television personality whose musical career began in 2007 with a mixtape called *Playtime is Over* (Butler, 2013). After success with three mixtapes between 2007 and 2009, Nicki Minaj signed a recording contract with Young Money Entertainment, which was a critical move in her rise to global celebrity. Released in 2010, Nicki Minaj's debut studio album *Pink Friday* peaked at number one on the *Billboard 200* and was certified platinum by the Recording Industry Association of America. During this time, Nicki Minaj also became the first female solo artist to have seven singles simultaneously charting on the *Billboard* Hot 100 (Trust, 2012).

Two years later, her second album, *Pink Friday: Roman Reloaded* debuted at number 1 on iTunes, making her one of the best-selling female solo artists of all time (Butler, 2013). Following *Roman Reloaded*, Nicki Minaj released two additional albums entitled, *The Pinkpriint* (2014) and *Queen* (2018), which were both certified platinum. As of 2018, Nicki Minaj sold over five million albums globally (Embley, 2018). Additionally, she accumulated 102 chart entries on the *Billboard* Hot 100 Songs chart, a feat which broke Aretha Franklin's previous record as the female artist with the most entries among all genres (Trust, 2017). To date, Nicki Minaj is the only female to appear on Forbes list of the top earners in Hip Hop currently holding the number four position on the countdown with $29 million. *Forbes* referred to Nicki Minaj as "the female Jay-Z and Diddy" (Robehmed, 2013). Given her level of success, Nicki Minaj has become a figurehead for female rappers and much-discussed topic of critical debates on gender politics in contemporary Hip Hop.

As an artist, Nicki Minaj has adopted several alter egos in her journey to becoming a global celebrity, ranging from the Japanese-inspired "Harajuku Barbie" figure to the evil (and male) "Roman Zolanski" (Butler, 2013). Her Rap style includes wacky voices, foreign accents, grunt-barks, horror-movie screams and a doll squeaks (Zimmerman, 2010). The rapper embodies a wide range of characters that both align with prior female rappers' enactments of White female beauty ideals and negotiate the ways in which she is racialized in popular culture. For example, in "Stupid Hoe," the second single from *Pink Friday: Roman Reloaded,* the rapper appears as a pink-haired Barbie, a caged jungle cat, a blue-lipped "native," and a freckled "White girl" (Butler, 2013, p. 36).

Nicki Minaj has not escaped the commodification of sexuality, gender, and race that is a part of any neoliberal celebrity construction and has been accused of producing these multiple personas as a shallow ploy to sell records (Butler, 2013). On the contrary, Nicki Minaj is arguably one of the most sexually charged female rappers in existence. She often is compared to oversexualized rapper Lil' Kim, even mimicking her once controversial squat-positioned bikini clad album cover. Similar to Nicki Minaj's portrayal in "Stupid Hoe," female rapper Kimberly "Lil Kim" Jones appears as a Barbie-type doll in the video for the song "How Many Licks" whose body parts are bonded together in a factory. Both videos ultimately serve as apt metaphors for both artists' self-commodification and use of female beauty ideals.

Nicki Minaj has used her beauty and body as central part of her career. She is often seen onstage and offstage in tightfitting clothing, nipple pasties and even half naked. Her performances include lap dances, grinding and other erotic moves. Her discography is ripe with sexual references and content. For example, Nicki Minaj continued her sexually charged career with the release of "Anaconda." The song, inspired by Sir Mix A Lot's "Baby Got Back," was promoted by a snippet of Nicki Minaj twerkin' from the official video and album cover art with the female rapper baring her entire buttocks in a G-String. Comparably, Nicki Minaj released "Barbie Dreams," a lead single from her most recent album *Queen*, in which she lyrically details her sexual fantasies of having sex with famous rappers like 50 Cent, Dave East, Lil' Wayne, and Meek Mill.

With a supercharged, commercial, marketing image contingent on sex, it is important to investigate other places in which Nicki Minaj might be represented. It cannot be overlooked that Nicki Minaj's participation in *Fame* is groundbreaking and exposes both Hip Hop culture and a young Black female to a new audience. As of early 2019, she still remained the only Black female rapper to be the subject of a *Fame* comic book, despite the notable international stardom of some other rappers like Lil' Kim, Belcalis "Cardi B" Almánzar and Dana "Queen Latifah" Owens. The commodification of her sexual recording industry image might be clear, but the question becomes will it move into the genre of comics?

BLACK WOMEN IN COMIC STRIPS

Comic books were first introduced in American culture in the 1930s, and as a pop culture artifact, the texts and pictures provided a worldview to a large segment of the American culture that did not have one (Savage, 1990). Bringing together pictures and words is complex in nature and gives much flexibility on the part of the creators to manipulate meaning in a rather constrained space, which has implications for both representation and interpretation of ideological images and meaning (McAllister, Sewell, & Gordon, 2001). Further, these devices (pictures and words) are said to "encourage the form to occasionally create a closed ideological text, imposing on the reader preferred meanings" (McAllister et al., p. 3), and the results of this constrained space and relationships between the comic creators and story is said to potentially lure creators to use stereotypes to quickly provide information (Walker, 1994). In the case of Blacks, especially Black females, this has historically been documented in mass media, as Black female stereotypes date back decades and Americans have long been exposed to and digested negative images of Black females (Tyree, 2013).

Males largely control the comic book industry, except in this case it is White males. Akili (2013) asserts they are "largely inept in writing, crafting and celebrating complex superheroines," and what, too, complicates the presence of females in comics is society's struggle with the concept of women and power. Even more complex is White males' historic inability to write Black superheroine scripts that are not racial stereotypes or make the superheroines victims of the White male sexual imagination (Akili, 2013). There are a few Black superheroines, but their presence and analysis in scholarship is minimal. Some examples of Black superheroines include X-Men's Storm, Dark Horse comic's Martha Washington, Milestone comic's Rocket, DC comic's Vixen, Crimson Avenger, Michonne from the graphic novel The Walking Dead, Marvel's Photon/Captain Marvel, Misty Knight, DC's Thunder, Onyx and Bumble Bee; Melody Rich from Brotherman Comics, and independent Black comic characters Oya, Prodigy, Amazula just to name a few (Brown, 2013). In 2018, the Marvel Comics' Blank Panther was released to critical acclaim and earned six Oscar nominations and three Oscars wins, including Best Costume Design. Earning over 1.3 billion dollars worldwide (Rubin, 2018), several Black female comic book superheroines only formally known in print, including Shuri and Okoye, were brought to life on the movie screen and introduced to new fans across the globe.

Recently, only a few specific studies of Black females in comic books exist. Brown (2013) put the existence of Black females in this genre into perspective by noting, "Just as superhero comics have always relied on gender stereotypes of the most extreme sort, ethnicity in the comics has

63

predominately been portrayed according to racial stereotypes." Saini (2009) notes the presence of three Black superheroines, which are "The Quiet Queen," "The Dominant Diva" and "The Scandalous Sojourner."

According to Saini (2009), the superficial depictions of the Black superheroine contradict the ones offered at a deeper level of analysis. At first glance, it might appear they, with their breasts and booties, "kick an awful lot of butt," but overall, these characters are "doomed to navigate the confines of poverty and war with infinite resolve or, failing that, risk descending into madness, drug abuse or other social ills" (Saini, 2009, p. 96). She posed the following question: "What would I know about Black women if everything I learned came from comic books?" Her analysis uncovered the existence of three common images, which were the Quiet Queen, Dominant Diva and the Scandalous Sojourner.

The Quiet Queen holds the foundation of one of Stephens and Phillips' (2003) sexual scripts of the Earth Mother. Yet, the earth connection tends to be with "voodoo" or some type of "mystical spiritual presence." The soft-spoken heroine ascends to power after overcoming an adversity often associated with communities of color and encompasses an "inhumane resilience" escaping war or poverty. The Dominant Diva is emotional and willing to "stir things up," which could mean she assumes an antagonistic and abrasive role. In this case, their powers might be leveraged for the sake of personal revenge and as a response to anger, rather than in response to a genuine need to champion their causes. The Scandalous Sojourner image is one set against what is often the cautionary tale of drug abuse and promiscuity. These over sexualized superheroines must defeat their "inner demons" or fall victim to their mental illness.

IMPORTANCE AND IMPACT OF SEXUAL SCRIPTING OF BLACK WOMEN IN HIP HOP

Sexuality undoubtedly constitutes a significant feature of identity in Western society. Since the eighteenth century, there has been a discursive explosion concerning sex and sexuality in Western societies establishing a wide network of methods for listening to, recording, tracking and regulating the sexuality of individuals and populations (Fouclaut, 1978). In *The History of Sexuality: Volume 1,* Foucault (1978) defines sexuality not as an uncontrolled urge that must be dominated or as a hidden domain that must be illuminated, but rather as a socially constructed instrument of power (Butler, 2013). Individuals, to a great degree, are defined both socially and morally in terms of their sexuality (Foucault, 1978; Giddens, 1992; Plummer, 1995; Weeks, 1985). Consequently, recognizing this fact, human sexuality scholars have referred to such sexual identity frameworks as sexual scripts.

Sexual scripts are "schemas used to organize ideas about appropriate sexual experiences" (Stephens & Few, 2007, p. 49). Sexual scripts are the blueprints and guidelines for what we define as our role in sexual expression, sexual orientation, sexual behaviors, sexual desires and the sexual component of our self-definition. These scripts influence norms for sexual behavior, and they are primarily expressed and maintained through their usage (Simon & Gagnon, 1987). The power of sexual scripting lies with the internalization of its discourse by society. When internalized, sexual scripting becomes instrumental in the creation of belief systems. With these belief systems, a set of attitudes develops about one's sexual being that outlines meanings and prescriptions for behaviors (Simon & Gagnon, 1987). These meanings, however, do not remain stagnant, but become part of continually changing cultural and social contexts.

There is a body of literature that provides a foundation for examining sexual scripts in the African American community, which is too dense and complicated to properly address in this chapter. More is offered in the complex presentation of African American women in both visual and lyrical representations in Hip Hop culture and Rap music. It, too, is rich literature worthy of presentation in this chapter. Yet, space does not allow for it.

With this said, there is need to situate Black female scripting and representations in Hip Hop and Rap. The public views Hip Hop culture and Rap music through a racist lens (Sullivan, 2003), and scholars have strong views about why Rap became popularized and commodified. Peoples (2008) asserts mainstream Rap music was commodified "because it represents ideas of [B]lackness that are in line with dominant racist and sexist ideologies; it has economic potential only because it works hand-in-hand with long established ideas about the sexual, social, and moral nature of [B]lack people" (p. 24). Hill Collins (2004) argues the hegemonic ideas about Blacks sexuality play a critical role in the creation of interlocking systems of social inequality, such as racism, sexism, classism, and capitalism. Lena (2008) also argues, "the voyeuristic gaze is a learned mode of apperception that draws upon stereotypic notions of the 'other.'…The presumption is that members of the dominant group utilize the voyeuristic gaze to consume, understand, or authenticate images" (p. 266).

From the start, Hip Hop has been dominated by men, but women's voices have been actively silenced through sex, limiting their artistic persona to that in which the male figure often forces them to confirm to racial and hypersexual stereotypes (Rebollo-Gil & Moras, 2012). Phillips, Reddick-Morgan, and Stephens (2005) observed that while women have played an integral role in the evolution of Hip Hop culture, including Rap, historical accounts and critical analyses have minimized women's contributions, including their pivotal roles as artists, writers, performers, producers, and industry executives as well as their influence style and technique. With the multiple female rappers who shaped and are shaping Hip Hop culture, there is a need for female rappers to be both socially accepted and marketable, thus fitting multiple identities (Morgan, 2005). Some voice frustration that Black female rappers and video performers participate in the degradation of Black femininity (Byrd & Soloman, 2005). Phillips et al. acknowledge Black female rappers are not always "uniformly opposed" to the sexism present in the male voices in Hip Hop and Rap and could be criticized for "underutilizing their feminist/womanist potential," but it is necessary to recognize the complexities in which women are situated, for they must maintain a dually oppositional stance allowing them to retain their ability to generate and maintain relationships of identification and transformation with a wide variety of people (2005, pp. 254, 273).

Stephens and Phillips' (2003) seminal study is keenly relevant to the current discussion on Nicki Minaj and her feature in the *Fame* comic book series. Stephens and Phillips (2003) identified eight sexual scripts through an analysis of racial and ethnic specific messages about sexuality evident in media forums, namely Hip Hop media and music genres. From within Hip Hop, the Diva, Gold Digger, Freak, Dyke, Gangster Bitch, Sister Savior, Earth Mother, and Baby Mama have emerged as unique sexual scripts for African American women (Stephens et al., 2003). Using Stephens and Phillips' (2003) descriptions, the following scripts were examined:

1. The Diva: This script was represented by images of a woman who had material items, which she obtained herself without the assistance of man.
2. The Gold-Digger: This script was represented in situations where the depicted woman specifically talked about looking for men based on what financial and material goods they could provide.
3. The Freak: Images where women were covertly accentuating and calling attention to the their sexuality represented the Freak. This also included scenes that implied sexual intercourse.
4. The Dyke: This term, often used as a negative slur for lesbians, refers to images or lyrics where the artist expresses desire for or mention of sexual interactions with other women.

5. The Gangster Bitch: This script refers to images or lyrics in which women were performing illegal acts, particularly situations where they may have done so in partnership with men.
6. The Sister Savior: Images associated with this script were those in which women either directly stated or were depicted in situations where they expressed moral or religious reasons for not being sexually active.
7. The Earth Mother: This script includes images of women who did not have straightened hair and instead wore hairstyles considered to be Afrocentric, such as dreadlocks, short-shaved hairstyles, braids, or Afros.
8. The Baby Mama: This script encompasses images where the mothers of children born of out wedlock were depicted arguing with the child's father in front of the child in such a way that the child seemed to be used in the argument.

In many ways, these scripts serve as contemporary manifestations of historic stereotypes of Black womanhood (i.e. the Jezebel, Sapphire, Welfare Mama, and the Matriarch), possessing only slight amendments that illustrate the hypersexual and misogynistic culture of Hip Hop. Black women are the primary focus of misogynistic Rap lyrics, and Black female rappers have worked both within and against the dominant sexual and racial narratives in the genre (Tyree, 2009; Rose, 1994). As a result, it is critical to investigate the presence (or lack thereof) of Stephens and Phillips (2003) eight African American female sexual scripts when analyzing the comic book portrayal of Nicki Minaj in *Fame*.

The sexual scripts posed by Stephens and Phillips (2003) as well as those of the Black superheroine by Saini (2009) are critical to analyzing how Nicki Minaj is being presented in the *Fame* comic series. Will her representation conform to the Black female sexual scripts present in Rap or those of Black superheroines? Will she be highlighted as a "token" Black Barbie? Or, will she offer a counter stereotype that resists both Black female stereotypes in mass media, especially within Rap and comic books?

METHODOLOGY

A textual analysis was conducted to analyze the *Fame* comic book published in 2013 of Nicki Minaj. Bluewater Productions, Inc., an independent production studio of comic books and graphic novels, launched the *Fame* series in 2010 as a companion piece to the successful *Female Force* and *Political Power* biographical comic strips. Biographical comics pioneer new grounds in comics, extending past the traditional "gag writing" associated with mainstream commercial comics and pioneering new ground – using the comic strip as therapy, social commentary and storytelling (McAdams, 2000). As a biographical comic, *Fame* explores celebrity culture and attempts to understand how a person rises to fame, achieves success in the public eye and deals with newfound celebrity status (Bluewater Productions, 2014, January 20). The comic also utilizes the power of celebrity to broaden comic distribution featuring actors, sports figures, recording artists and royals. Since its inception in 2010, *Fame* has featured two Black women (Beyonce and Nicki Minaj) and two rappers (50 Cent and Nicki Minaj).

Textual analysis is a useful methodology for mass communications and media studies researchers, and they use it is a data gathering process by which to understand who individuals within various cultures and subcultures are and how they fit into the world (McKee, 2003). Within a textual analysis, researchers focus on meanings by interpreting narrative elements and evaluating how they act as examples of the larger stories or broader systems that exist (Potter, 1996). As a medium intended for mass consumption, Bongco (2000) asserts analyzing comic books emphasizes the connections between them and the society that supports them, but this medium is also said to cater to the popular demands and wishes of society.

During the analysis, the plot, setting, clothing and characteristics – both physical and behavioral – of Nicki Minaj's character were analyzed. The researchers analyzed the dialogue as well as actions of not only Nicki Minaj's character but others to identify if they placed her within any of Stephens and Phillips' (2003) sexual scripts, which are Diva, Gold Digger, Freak, Dyke, Earth Mother, Baby Mama, Gangsta Bitch and Sister Savior. In addition, researchers sought to uncover whether Nicki Minaj's character fit within the characteristics of Sainai's three Black superheroines: Quiet Queen, Dominant Diva and Scandalous Sojourner.

FINDINGS

In examining Nicki Minaj's portrayal in *Fame*, a number of findings revealed themes that both aligned with and challenged prior stereotypes associated with Black female rappers and superheroines. Consistent with the histories of Rap and Black superheroines, Nicki Minaj was depicted in the comic as hypersexual and dressed scantily clad, while enacting a variety of erotic poses. The rapper was seen as a curvy superheroine who wore tightly fitted, costumes commonly affiliated with historic superheroines, including lingerie, body suits, short skirts, bustier and panty combinations with utility belts, and other cleavage-baring clothing.

While Nicki Minaj's sexual depiction in *Fame* aligned with prior stereotypes attached to Black female rappers and superheroines, Nicki Minaj countered the ideal of Black rappers and superheroines being subordinate to their male counterparts. In the comic book, Nicki Minaj's independence and self-determination to become a successful Rap artist was highlighted. For example, the comic emphasized that Nicki Minaj "paid her dues" and earned the opportunity to gain her recording deal with Young Money Entertainment. *Fame* consistently acknowledged Nicki Minaj's ownership of her hypersexualized image and how her multiple personalities and looks were used for commercial gain. These findings, among others, allowed Nicki Minaj to strongly meet several criteria for Rap sexual scripts and Black superheroine stereotypes.

LOCATING NICKI MINAJ AS A SUPERHEROINE IN FAME

As a superheroine, Nicki Minaj was portrayed as a Trinidadian immigrant within the United States who navigated through hardships and archenemies to achieve success in the entertainment industry. The comic began with a candid discussion about the rapper's childhood, stating Nicki Minaj was born in Saint James (a suburban of Trinidad) and traveled to the United States after her "parents didn't get along too well." Nicki Minaj's mother was also described as being integral in leading Nicki Minaj "on a path that would begin a new journey" to the Queens borough of New York City. This fresh start for Nicki Minaj ignited the rapper's first entre into music and, ultimately, resulted in Nicki auditioning to attend the prestigious LaGuardia High School of Visual and Performing Arts in an attempt to become a singer.

It was during this scene in the comic that Nicki Minaj's trajectory drastically shifted. Nicki Minaj lost her voice during an audition for the visual and performing arts high school, forcing her to enter the school's drama department. The comic chronicled a series of other failures, including being declined for acting roles and fired from 15 jobs, encountered by Nicki Minaj, before she ultimately decided to become a Rap artist. For Nicki Minaj, rapping was her superpower, and it helped her overcome the multiple oppressions affiliated with being a Trinidadian, female immigrant raised in a poverty-laden community in the United States and achieve mainstream success. *Fame* acknowledged Nicki Minaj's superpower of Rap by stating, "With great (Rap) powers comes great endorsement deals." According to the comic, Nicki Minaj's Rap superpowers enabled her to "pay her dues" by appearing on different Rap artists' and her own mixtapes, which led to her record deal and successful solo albums.

As a superpower, it is important to note that Nicki Minaj's rapping ability was not manifested simply by lyrical content. The distinguishing factor of Nicki Minaj's Rap superpower lied with one element: Her use of multiple voices and personas that were fueled in the comic by the Dungeon Dragon. In Hip Hop, the Dungeon Dragon was first introduced by Busta Rhymes in one of his classic lines off of Tribe Called Quest's "Scenario." Metaphorically, Rhymes conceptualized the Dungeon Dragon as an embodiment and energy that ignited fire hot lyrics by a fierce MC (Blair, 2012).

Connecting Rhymes and Nicki Minaj's uses of Dungeon Dragon to the depictions of dragons in the fantasy genre, dragons have historically possessed magic and supernatural powers that are evidenced through multiple personas and tongues, wisdom, and longevity (Halovsmarvel, 2014). Halovsmarvel also noted in some fantasy genres, dragons are said to be wiser than humans and are capable of human speech. When incorporating the history of dragons and Rhymes and Nicki Minaj's use of Dungeon Dragon in Rap and Hip Hop to her *Fame* superheroine portrayal, there are important connections that must be emphasized.

In Nicki Minaj's *Fame,* her "Ruh Ruh…Like a Dungeon Dragon" lyric was emphasized and coupled with her development of a signature style in her rhymes. The Dungeon Dragon was discussed and later revealed in two scenes in the comic's plot that preceded major challenges in Nicki Minaj's career: (1) Nicki Minaj's rejection from the LaGuardia High School's music program and (2) her Twitter and Rap beefs with established artists. "Beef" is Hip Hop that refers to conflict with (Rose, 2008) or resentment toward (Tyson, 2002) another individual. Highlighted during these critical turning points in the comic's plot, the Dungeon Dragon served as a guardian force for Nicki Minaj who equipped her with the power to ignite her Rap superpower. Nicki Minaj was also shown traveling through space on top on a rocket in the beginning and the end of the comic book. Additionally, the backgrounds of spread of the book itself contained visual imagery that suggested a connection with a mystical land or outer space. Nicki Minaj's powers were also evidenced verbally by the rapper's use of lyrical content from her hit single "Fly" to narrate her constant travel in space throughout the comic.

Recognizing these factors along with other verbal and physical confirmations, Nicki Minaj's *Fame* portrayal strongly met the criteria for and complicated two of Saini's (2009) Black superheroine stereotypes. Nicki Minaj incorporated familiar themes associated with the Quiet Queen and Scandalous Sojourner stereotypes. Consistent with the Quiet Queen stereotype, Nicki Minaj ascended to power after overcoming adversities associated with a rough upbringing, failed acting career and multiple beefs in the entertainment industry. Nonetheless, Nicki Minaj showcased a resilience to escape poverty and achieve mainstream success through her Rap superpower.

While the Quiet Queen is often a soft-spoken heroine, Nicki Minaj complicated this stereotype through her embodiment of multiple personas in *Fame*. In the comic book, Nicki Minaj took on a variety of identities including, but not limited to, the Harajuku Barbie, Roman Zolanski and Onika Tanya Maraj. These multiple personalities made her not quiet as a superheroine and aligned with the history of other popular superheroes, such as Clark Kent and Superman and Bruce Wayne and Batman, who embraced multiple identities in their pursuits to "save the day" while living a normal life. It is important to note that Nicki Minaj's use of these multiple personas also encompassed multiple moods, including pleasant, angry, somber, that created inner conflicts.

Particularly, these inner conflicts resulted in a series of setbacks initiated by Nicki Minaj in the comic book and met the criteria for the Scandalous Sojourner. For instance, Nicki Minaj got into a disagreement with a fan over a music leak, and in anger, she deleted her Twitter account and lost a considerable number of followers. Similarly, Nicki Minaj lost 15 jobs in the comic, because of her disagreeable manner. She was forced to do acting after losing her voice due to nerves in a school audition. Despite the massive success accumulated by Nicki Minaj in *Fame*, the rapper was always at risk of falling victim to her own inner demons and cynical behavior, strongly qualifying her for the Scandalous Sojourner superheroine stereotype.

Despite the complexity of Nicki Minaj's storyline as a superheroine, the rapper's depiction still aligned with Brown's (2013) and prior research that categorized superheroines as "scantily clad and erotically posed fetish objects." For Nicki Minaj, her breasts and butt were significant aspects of her advertisement and packaging as a Black superheroine in the comic. In the comic, Nicki Minaj was shown posed in sexually suggestive ways, including licking her lips, placing her hands in her mouth, and other sexually suggestive poses. These sexually suggestive poses invited the viewers into a voyeuristic space, where Nicki Minaj was a fetish object ready to be consumed by a larger public. In addition to these gender stereotypes, there was a noticeable shift in Nicki Minaj's skin tone throughout the comic that prompted the researcher to investigate further.

Her skin tone deviated from dark brown to light brown to nearly white, containing explicit skin tone differences between *Fame's* regular comic book cover for Nicki Minaj and the rapper's "Superheroine Edition" cover. On the regular comic book, Nicki Minaj was depicted with Black hair and a significantly browner skin tone than the "Superheroine Edition" *Fame* cover. On this specialty edition cover, the rapper was wearing a blonde wig, a more traditional superheroine costume with a utility belt, and had a nearly white skin tone. Such occurrences were pervasive in the comic. For example, when Nicki Minaj was rapping or in social situations with Black artists, her skin tone was significantly darker than her social situations with Madonna, Mariah Carey, and Keith Urban. These findings support prior findings on Black superheroines in comics and highlighted how *Fame* relied heavily on racial and gender stereotypes to position Nicki Minaj as an over-sexualized, fetish object for the male sexual imagination.

DEPICTIONS OF SEXUAL SCRIPTS IN *FAME*

While Nicki Minaj's depiction in *Fame* gave the researchers an array of material to locate her as a superheroine, there was not much to substantiate her placement into many of the categories of Stephens and Phillips' (2003) sexual scripts in Rap. However, based on the verbal and physical confirmations in the comic, Nicki Minaj incorporated themes that aligned with the Diva and The Freak sexual scripts. In *Fame,* the rapper was verbally confirmed as a Diva twice, as the comic labeled her as a "Future Diva" and "Bickering Diva." Aligning with Stephens and Phillips' (2003) conceptualization of a Diva, Nicki Minaj's physical image also aligned with Eurocentric standards of beauty, such as long straightened hair and lighter complexion skin tone. Additionally, the comic emphasized how Nicki Minaj attained success on her own and without the success of anyone else. For these reasons, the researchers determined that it was appropriate to situate Nicki Minaj as Diva given the comic book's explicit verbal confirmations of her behavior.

While verbal confirmations played a significant role in Nicki Minaj's enactment of the Diva sexual script, her physical confirmations – facial expression and body imagery – strongly aligned with The Freak sexual script. As showcased in *Fame*, Nicki Minaj was depicted as a symbol for sexual arousal and called great attention to her sexuality through her cleavage, tight clothing and erotic poses. For example, the rapper was shown straddling a rocket in a sexually suggestive way. Despite the possibility of sitting inside of the rocket to travel to a mystical space, the comic book depicted Nicki Minaj on top of the rocket, further making her a sexual object. Throughout the comic, Nicki Minaj's breasts, butt, and mouth are emphasized with the rapper even touching these body parts to illustrate her sexual prowess.

While these actions and images corroborated the presence of Stephens and Phillips' (2003) sexual scripts in Rap music, they also directly spoke to the history of Black superheroines in comics and the fantasy genre that reduce Black women to longstanding sexist and racist stereotypes. When taking into the consideration the racism and sexism that undergird Black superheroine portrayals, the hypersexual representation of Nicki Minaj as a superheroine in *Fame* was quite typical. For such reasons, Stephens and Phillips' (2003) sexual scripts were present in Nicki Minaj's superheroine portrayal in *Fame*, but they were not deeply rooted.

CONCLUSION

Similar to the multilayered and complicated depictions of women in Hip Hop, Nicki Minaj's portrayal in *Fame* offered a complex reading of her life and rise to success in the entertainment industry within a comic book. Her selection as a *Fame* subject is worthy of acknowledgement. As the only Black female rapper highlighted in the series, her comic book helps raise the profile of women in Hip Hop and the comic book industry as well as shows they are worthy of attention and celebration. Yet, Nicki Minaj was portrayed in ways that both supported and ran counter to longstanding Hip Hop and comic sexual scripts, including the freak, Quiet Queen and Scandalous Sojourner.

Like the historical sexual scripts of women in Hip Hop, Nicki Minaj was visually hypersexual. She was repeatedly seen wearing tightly fitted clothing and posed in sexually suggestive manners, and while she did not engage in any sexual behaviors with men or say anything sexual in the comic book, her portrayal supports the enduring practice of women being portrayed as sexual objects both within Hip Hop culture and the comic book industry. What does complicate her imagery is that some costumes were duplications of or based upon her real-life wardrobe. Therefore, her reading as a sexual object must be understood through the context that it is based on the image Nicki Minaj crafts within the Hip Hop industry. Nicki Minaj's image is one she takes both ownership and pride in having developed herself.

Her sexual objectification mirrors historic images of females in comic books, but Nicki Minaj complicated the Quiet Queen and Scandalous

Sojourner Black superheroine stereotypes by not completely fitting into either one. She was a complex, take-charge, self-motivated, successful character who often prompted her failures or setbacks. Nicki Minaj was a superheroine in charge of her own destiny; one able to seek out partnerships and opportunities utilized her powers – rapping.

While Nicki Minaj's sexual depiction in *Fame* aligned with prior stereotypes of women being "scantily clad and erotically posed fetish objects" (Brown, 2013), she complicated many of the principles of Black superheroine stereotypes. Aligning with the Quiet Queen stereotype, Nicki Minaj came to power after overcoming obstacles by exhibiting a high level of strength and persistence that allowed her to persevere. This is a powerful message to those reading, especially young women or aspiring female rappers, that setbacks and failures do not have to define whether success is achieved. Nicki Minaj is seen as the one who paved her own way in the music business and plays an active role in establishing her own style and utilizing her "powers" for commercial gain.

Yet, Nicki Minaj is far from quiet. Instead, part of what secured her labeling as the Scandalous Sojourner was the many voices and personalities she cultivated and utilized as an artist. While these researchers could not deny multiple personalities is connected to mental illness, which is a key attribute of the Scandalous Sojourner, she also was seen as having personalities issues that caused her to lose several jobs and delete her Twitter account. These were important aspects of the storyline and showed how her "inner demons" often hurt her. Nonetheless, as a superheroine, Nicki Minaj's *Fame* portrayal did not have her fighting crime, stopping the bad guys or saving those in need. In fact, it is not the purpose of the *Fame* series to showcase celebrities in this manner. Instead, the portrayal was one that, despite its historical siding with both Hip Hop and comic book sexual objectifications, did portray a young woman who was able to go from an immigrant to elite celebrity by taking control of her own career and talents. Her Rap superpower allowed her to escape poverty, obtain mainstream success and do so with no overbearing male lead superhero or sidekick. She was a true self-emPOWERed superheroine.

DISCUSSION QUESTIONS

1. Butler (2013) argues that Nicki Minaj "has not escaped the commodification of sexuality, gender, and race that is a part of any neoliberal celebrity

construction." Provide three examples from the reading that illustrates Nicki Minaj's use of hypersexual and racial tropes to position herself as a successful rapper.

2. In what ways, does racism and sexism undergird Nicki Minaj's representation in the *Fame* comic book?

3. Describe the role of the Dungeon Dragon in unlocking Nicki Minaj's Rap superpower in the comic book. How does her use of the Dungeon Dragon connect to past depictions of dragons in the fantasy genre?

4. How are the findings regarding Nicki Minaj's representation in the *Fame* comic book similar or different from current images of Black women in popular culture?

ADDITIONAL READING

Brown, J. A. (2013). Panthers and vixens: Black superheroines, sexuality, and stereotypes in contemporary comic books. In S. C. Howard & R. L. Jackson (Eds.), *Black comics: Politics of race and representation* (pp. 133–150). New York, NY: Bloomsbury Academic.

Butler, J. (2013). For White girls only? Postfeminism and the politics of inclusion. *Feminist Formations, 25*(1), 35–38.

McAllister, M. P., Sewell, E. H., & Gordon, I. (2001). *Introducing comics and ideology.* New York, NY: Peter Lang.

Perry, I. (2003). Who(se) am I?: The identity and image of women in Hip Hop. In G. Dines & J. Humez (Eds.), *Gender, race, and class in media: A critical reader* (pp. 136–148). Thousand Oaks, CA: Sage Publications.

Rebollo-Gil, G., & Moras, A. (2012). Black women and black men in hip hop music: Misogyny, violence and the negotiation of (white-owned) space. *Journal of Popular Culture, 45*(1), 118–132.

Rose, T. (2008). *The Hip Hop wars: what we talk about when we talk about Hip Hop-and why it matters.* New York, NY: Basic Civitas Books.

Saini, A. (2009). Annals of the black superheroine. *Bitch: Feminist Response to Popular Culture, 45*, 35–41.

REFERENCES

Akili, Y. (2013). Black, female and super powered: An interview with grace gipson on black comic book super heroines. *Huffington Post.* Retrieved from http://www.huffingtonpost.com/yolo-akili/black-female-super-powered_b_2659118.html

Armstrong, E. (2001). Gangsta misogyny: A content analysis of the portrayals of violence against women in Rap music, 1987–1993. *Journal of Criminal Justice and Popular Culture, 8*(2), 96–126.

Barrett, L. (1999). Dead men printed: Tupac shakur, biggie smalls, and hip hop eulogy. *Callaloo, 22*(2), 306–322.

Berger, P. L., & Luckmann, T. (1967). *The social construction of reality: A treatise in the sociology of knowledge* (p. 1). New York, NY: Anchor Books.

Bluewater Productions. (2014, January 20). *Fame*. Retrieved from http://www.bluewaterprod.com/comics/fame.php

Bongco, M. (2000). *Reading comics: Language, culture, and the concept of the superhero in comic books*. New York, NY: Garland Publishing, Inc.

Brown, J. A. (2013). Panthers and vixens: Black superheroines, sexuality, and stereotypes in contemporary comic books. In S. C. Howard & R. L. Jackson (Eds.), *Black comics: Politics of race and representation* (pp. 133–150). New York, NY: Bloomsbury Academic.

Brown, S. (1995, March). *Unwrapping Rap: A literacy of lived experience*. Paper presented at the Annual Meeting of the Conference on College Composition and Communication, Washington, DC.

Butler, J. (2013). For White girls only? Postfeminism and the politics of inclusion. *Feminist Formations, 25*(1), 35–38.

Byrd, A., & Soloman, A. (2005). What's really going on? *Essence, 35*(9), 82–86.

Embley, J. (2018). *From Nas to Drake, the most influential Hip Hop artists of all time*. Retrieved from https://www.standard.co.uk/go/london/music/the-most-influential-hip-hop-artists-of-all-time-a3863356.html

Foucault, M. (1978). *The history of sexuality* (Vol. I). New York, NY: Random House.

Gamson, W. A., Croteau, D., Hoynes, W., & Sasson, T. (1992). Media images and the social construction of reality. *Annual Review of Sociology, 18*, 373–393.

Giddens, A. (1991). *Modernity and self-identity: Self and society in the late modern age*. Palo Alto, CA: Stanford University Press.

Halovsmarvel. (2014, January 14). *Dragons*. Retrieved from http://www.comicvine.com/dragons/4060-57602/

Heath, R. L. (2005). *Encyclopedia of public relations*. Thousand Oaks, CA: Sage Publications.

Hill Collins, P. (2004). *Black sexual politics: African Americans, gender, and the new racism*. New York, NY: Routledge.

Kelley, R. D. (1996). *Kickin' reality, kickin' ballistics: Gangsta Rap and postindustrial Los Angeles*. In W. Perkins (Ed.), *In droppin' science* (pp. 117–158). Philadelphia, PA: Temple University Press.

Lena, J. C. (2008). Voyeurism and resistance in Rap music videos. *Communication and Critical/Cultural Studies, 5*(3), 264–279.

Light, A. (1992). Rappers sounded warning. *Rolling Stone, 15*(7).

McAdams, H. (2000). *Autobiographical comic strips*. Retrieved from http://www.uic.edu/classes/ad/ad382/sites/Projects/P009/P009_first.html

McAllister, M. P., Sewell, E. H., & Gordon, I. (2001). *Introducing comics and ideology in comics and ideology*. New York, NY: Peter Lang.

McCloud, S. (1994). *Understanding comics: The invisible art*. New York, NY: Harper Perennial.

Morgan, M. (2005). Hip Hop women shredding the veil: Race and class in popular feminist identity. *The South Atlantic Quarterly, 104*(3), 424–444.

Peoples, W. A. (2008). Under construction: Identifying foundations of Hip Hop feminism and exploring bridges between second-wave and Hip Hop feminisms. *Meridians, 8*(1), 19–52.

Plummer, K. (1995). *Telling sexual stories*. London, UK: Routledge.

Rebollo-Gil, G., & Moras, A. (2012). Black women and black men in hip hop music: Misogyny, violence and the negotiation of (white-owned) space. *Journal of Popular Culture, 45*(1), 118–132.

Robehmed, N. (2013, April 24). Why Nicki Minaj is the only lady on the cash kings list. *Forbes.* Retrieved from http://www.forbes.com/sites/natalierobehmed/2013/09/24/why-nicki-minaj-is-the-only-lady-on-the-cash-kings-list/

Rose, T. (1994). *Black noise: Rap music and black culture in contemporary America.* Hanover, NH & Middletown, CO: Wesleyan University Press.

Rose, T. (2008). *The hip hop wars: What we talk about when we talk about hip hop-and why it matters.* New York, NY: Basic Civitas Books.

Rubin, R. (2008). Box Office by the Numbers: 5 Game Changers for 2018. *Variety.* Retrieved from https://variety.com/2018/film/news/box-office-2018-records-black-panther-1203095795/

Saini, A. (2009). Annals of the Black superheroine. *Bitch: Feminist Response to Popular Culture, 45,* 35–41.

Savage, W. W. (1990). *Commies, cowboys, and jungle queens: Comic books and America, 1945–954.* Middletown, CT: Wesleyan University Press.

Scott, J. C. (1985). *Weapons of the weak: Everyday forms of peasant resistance.* New Haven, CT: Yale University Press.

Simon, W., & Gagnon, J. H. (1987). A sexual scripts approach. In J. H. Greer & W. T. O'Donohue (Eds.), *Theories of human sexuality* (pp. 363–383). New York, NY: Plenum.

Snoop, D. (1999). *Tha Doggfather.* New York, NY: William Morrow and Company.

Steaman, I. (1992). Gangsta Rap runs risk of becoming passé. *Billboard, 10.*

Stephens, D. P., & Few, A. (2007). Hip Hop honey or video ho: African American preadolescents' understanding of female sexual scripts in Hip Hop culture. *Sex Cult, 11,* 48–69.

Stephens, D. P., & Phillips, L. D. (2003). Freaks, gold differs, divas and dykes: The socio-historical development of African American female adolescent scripts. *Sexuality and Culture, 7,* 3–47.

Sullivan, R. E. (2003). Rap and race: It's got a nice beat, but what about the message? *Journal of Black Studies, 33*(5), 605–622.

Trust, G. (2012). Carley Rae Jepsen still no. 1, Nicki Minaj makes history on hot 100 chart. *Billboard.* Retrieved from http://www.billboard.com/biz/articles/news/1084732/carly-rae-jepsen-still-no-1-nicki-minaj-makes-history-on-hot-100-chart

Trust, G. (2017). Nicki Minaj passes Aretha Franklin for most Billboard Hot 100 hits of any female artist. *Billboard.* Retrieved from https://www.billboard.com/articles/columns/chart-beat/7728788/nicki-minaj-passes-aretha-franklin-for-most-billboard-hot-100

Tyree, T. C. (2007). *The pursuit of movie money: A textual analysis of Rap artists as actors in Hollywood films* (Unpublished doctoral dissertation). Howard University, Washington, DC.

Tyree, T. C. (2013). Contemporary representations of Black females in newspaper comic strips. In S. C. Howard & R. L. Jackson (Eds.), *Black comics: Politics of race and representation* (pp. 45–64). New York, NY: Bloomsbury Academic.

Tyson, E. (2002). Hip Hop therapy: An exploratory study of a Rap music intervention with at-risk and delinquent youth. *Journal of Poetry Therapy, 15*(3), 131–144.

Walker, L. (1994). The feminine condition: Cartoon images of women in The New Yorker. *Inks, 1*(3), 8–17.

Weeks, J. (1985). *Sexuality and its discontents.* London: Routledge.

Zimmerman, E. (2010). Who is Nicki Minaj? *The Hairpin.* Retrieved from http://thehairpin.com/2010/11/who-is-nicki-minaj/

LAUREN J. DECARVALHO AND NICOLE B. COX

5. QUEERNESS (UN)SHACKLED

Theorizing Orange Is the New Black

As one of the most talked about series today, *Orange Is the New Black* (*OITNB*) has garnered praise and criticism in its depiction of women inmates at a fictional federal prison in Litchfield, New York. Based on Piper Kerman's memoir, *Orange Is the New Black: My Year in a Women's Prison*, the series focuses on the trials and tribulations of Piper Chapman (played by Taylor Schilling), an upper-middle-class, white, bisexual woman who was sentenced to 15 months for illegally transporting drugs ten years prior, for her then-partner Alex Vause (played by Laura Prepon). Written and created by Jenji Kohan, who is no stranger to creating women-centric series – as evidenced by her Showtime dramedy *Weeds* (2005–2012) – *OITNB* debuted as Netflix's fifth original series on July 11, 2013. While it is more difficult to determine viewership for a series outside the traditional television platform, it has been speculated that *OITNB* brings in between 8–15 million viewers per episode (Obenson, 2013); by its sixth season premiere in 2018, the series was reported to bring in more viewers in the target 18–49 age demographic than any other program airing on broadcast TV at the time (Lynch, 2018). Obenson points to the first season's success: "[*Orange Is the New Black*] will end the year as our most watched original series ever and, as with each of our other previously launched originals, enjoys an audience comparable with successful shows on cable and broadcast TV" (para. 1). *OITNB*'s second season debuted on June 6, 2014, and before that airdate Netflix announced that the series was renewed for a third season.

Regarding its success, the Netflix series garnered 12 Emmy nominations for its first season – and won three. Some of *OITNB*'s other recognition include the 2014 Television Critics Association Award for "Outstanding New Program," the 2014 Gay and Lesbian Entertainment Critics Association (GALECA)'s Dorian Award for both "TV Drama of the Year" and "LGBT TV Show of the Year," and the 2014 AFI Award for "TV Program of the Year." In 2015, Uzo Aduba – the actor who plays the character of Suzanne "Crazy

© KONINKLIJKE BRILL NV, LEIDEN, 2019 | DOI:10.1163/9789004414259_005

Eyes" Warren – also won an Emmy for Outstanding Supporting Actress in a Drama Series ("Orange," 2019). More recently in 2017, *OITNB* won a Screen Actors Guild Award for Outstanding Performance by an Ensemble in a Comedy Series. Thus, both its cultural prominence and critical success make *OITNB* a cultural text worthy of examination.

To date, much has been written on the series – both praise and criticism. *OITNB* has garnered much applause for featuring a mostly female cast, including multiple characters of color, highlighting female friendships, and depicting transgender issues. The latter has been achieved particularly through its portrayal of trans inmate Sophia Burset (played by real-life trans woman, Laverne Cox). Evidence of this praise was reified in July 2014, when Cox became the first trans individual to receive an Emmy nomination for her role in the series. Just a month earlier (in June 2014), Cox became the first transgender person to grace the cover of *Time* magazine. However, just as the series has received much applause, it has also received criticism. In September 2014, a former inmate who served time at Danbury Federal Prison – the same prison that *OITNB* is based on, and where author Kerman served time – wrote an Op-Ed critiquing the series' depiction of prison life. As Codianni (2014) wrote, "I spent 15 years in the federal prison system, mostly at the Danbury Federal Prison Institution...Unfortunately, I know what 'real' prison is like. It sure isn't what non-incarcerated viewers were led to believe by their weekly diet of Netflix's prison caricature" (para. 3). Codianni discusses the series' inaccuracies in portraying its visiting room scenes, the repercussions of same-sex relationships in prison, and the "real-life collateral consequences" of women losing custody of their children for mostly nonviolent, low-level drug offenses (para. 6). Some criticisms by others, which were explicitly aimed at the first season, were addressed by episodes in the second season. For instance, some argue that the first season's storytelling needed to be tightened and by the second season, Kohan had done just that (Nussbaum, 2014). More recently, when season four of the series aired, it contained a number of touchpoints that spoke to the current cultural tensions regarding violence against those in the black community. As Brinkhurst-Cuff (2017) writes, the series was seen by some as "exploiting black struggles for white audiences" (para. 7).

Most of the discussions around *OITNB* have stemmed from mainstream and popular press. Given this, our analysis aims to contribute to academic scholarship through the examination of gender performativity and compulsory heterosexuality as illustrated throughout the Netflix series. Applying theories from Judith Butler and Adrienne Rich, we examine *OITNB*'s depictions of queerness, including the intersections of race and body type that affect how queer narratives play out onscreen. We also deconstruct the shift that takes place in the symbolic punishment of queerness from the first season to the second. Through narrative and character analysis, we interrogate how queerness (as embodied by lesbian, bisexual, or transgender characters) is showcased, circumscribed, and even punished at times on the series.

This chapter argues that *OITNB* challenges gender performances and compulsory heterosexuality, while simultaneously privileging mostly white-on-white female sexual relations as well as reinforcing the gazing of women who reify idealized body types (or in this case, thin figures). Starting with our theoretical framework, we look at how two key conversations in queer theory are crucial in unpacking queerness in *OITNB*. Next, we examine *OITNB*'s queer narratives and how they often function as tales of morality for viewers. Our analysis stems from a textual reading of the 26 episodes that comprised seasons one and two of the series; or all the episodes aired to date at the original time of writing. We close with our discussion section, which offers readers some final thoughts on the series, as well as important factors to consider regarding queer narratives.

QUEERING CONVERSATIONS: GENDER PERFORMANCE AND COMPULSORY HETEROSEXUALITY

For feminist and media studies scholars, questions concerning the intersections among gender, sex, and sexual orientation have been longstanding. While the biological determinism of sex and the social constructedness of gender have long been theorized by feminist scholars, it was the groundbreaking work of scholars such as Butler (1990), de Lauretis (1991), Sedgwick (1990; 1994), and Rich (1980) that gave rise to queer theory as we know it today. The goal, as Butler (1990) writes, is to:

> think through the possibility of subverting and displacing those naturalized and reified notions of gender that support masculine hegemony and heterosexist power, to make gender trouble, not through the strategies that figure a utopian bond, but through mobilization, subversive confusion, and proliferation of precisely those constitutive categories that seek to keep gender in its place by posturing as the foundational illusions of identity. (p. 34)

Linking the centrality of gender to personal identity, Butler (1990) posits that it is only when we both recognize the constructedness of gender and disassociate it from sex and sexual orientation are we able to understand it for the performance that it is.

GENDER PERFORMATIVITY

While queer theory takes to task discursive constructs and the ways in which we understand sex, gender, and sexual desire, another key component relevant to understanding *OITNB* is Butler's (1990) theory of gender performativity. Butler explains that gender is only understood as a result of the performances we enact every day. Contending that gender is not something we are, but rather something that we do, Butler argues that gender does not precede from one's sex as a biological determinant. Instead, sex is an equally gendered construct.

In advocating for understanding gender as a performance, Butler (1990) writes, "there is no gender identity behind the expressions of gender; that identity is performatively constituted by the very 'expressions' that are said to be its results" (p. 25). Critiquing the gender binary of male or female, Butler contends that to suggest that chromosomal, biological sex precedes gender, which then precedes sexual desire (i.e., heterosexuality), is inherently flawed. She argues that because all parts of this "heterosexual matrix" (p. 151) are socially constructed, we must understand that they all are open to interpretation and resignification. Sex does not determine gender, and gender does not determine sexual desire.

But this gender performativity is not an active choice that one makes (Butler, 1993). Rather, "gender is performative insofar as it is the *effect* of a regulatory regime of gender differences in which genders are divided and hierarchized *under constraint*" (p. 21, emphasis in original). We act in accordance with the gendered norms, rules, and understandings of our culture(s); we seldom create them for ourselves. But one's gender performativity is also inextricably linked with the ways in which one becomes "eligible for recognition" (Butler, 2009). In order to be recognized as a sexed and gendered being, one must first adopt at least some of the norms relating to gender identity. It is through performances of gender that the subject is made recognizable.

As Wright (2011) explains, "to be understood as a person means that there is a social recognition of a gendered person and that the gender must also be socially recognizable" (p. 75). In order for gender to be successfully performed, the "correct" gender identity must be understood by others. Gender, in this vein, is a continual process and is marked by repeated occurrences and constant (re) negotiations. We never "become" masculine or feminine in our own right, as Butler (1990) writes, gender is a construct that "cannot rightfully be said to originate or to end" (p. 33).

COMPULSORY HETEROSEXUALITY

More than just gender performativity, any examination into *OITNB* must also take into consideration Rich's (1980) groundbreaking essay, "Compulsory Heterosexuality and Lesbian Existence." Rich addresses the ways in which cultural understandings of sex, gender, and sexual desire have resulted in a "compulsory heterosexuality." Rich (1980) writes

> I am concerned here with two matters… first, how and why women's choice of women as passionate comrades, life partners, co-workers, lovers, tribe, has been crushed, invalidated, forced into hiding and disguise; and second, the virtual or total neglect of lesbian existence in a wide range of writings, including feminist scholarship. (p. 632)

In examining these questions, Rich (1980) argues that heterosexuality is "presumed as a 'sexual preference' of 'most women'" (p. 633). Rich examines the cultural bias toward compulsory heterosexuality, and conceptualizes it as a "political institution." Drawing on Gough's (1975) work, Rich suggests that male power is maintained and works to convince women that "marriage, and sexual orientation toward men, are inevitable, even in unsatisfying and oppressive components of their lives" (p. 640).

Butler (1990) argues, "The institution of a compulsory and naturalized heterosexuality requires and regulates gender as a binary relation… and this differentiation is accomplished through practices of heterosexual desire" (pp. 22–23). Butler discusses how this "heterosexual matrix" keeps intact hegemonic models of sex, gender, and sexual desire (p. 151), as well as how it functions by repressing homosexual desires. Compulsory heterosexuality is enacted and embraced by dominant discourses, while lesbian homosexuality is denounced and erased from social consciousness (Rich, 1980). According to Rich (1980), the "erasure of lesbian existence" emerged as a response to threats against compulsory heterosexuality, because to acknowledge that, for women, heterosexuality may not be a 'preference' at all but something that has had to be imposed, managed, organized, propagandized, and maintained by force, is an immense step to take if you consider yourself freely and 'innately' heterosexual (p. 648).

Similarly, Wittig (1992) notes how a refusal to enact prescribed heterosexual relations can influence gendered understandings. She writes, the refusal to become (or remain) heterosexual always meant to refuse to become a man or a woman, consciously or not. For a lesbian this goes further than the refusal of the *role* 'woman.' It is the refusal of the economic, ideological, and political power of a man. (p. 13, emphasis in original)

Thus, lesbian existence encompasses a wide range of women's experiences (both homosexual and homosocial) that conflict with compulsory heterosexuality. Indeed, it is because of this conflict that lesbian existence is often erased from the workings of popular culture (e.g., Rich, 1980). When lesbian existence is incorporated, it is often treated as "less than" heterosexuality and in need of explanation.

Ultimately, Rich (1980) argues that the lie of compulsory heterosexuality is problematic and crippling for hetero- and homosexual women alike. While heterosexual women are encouraged to embrace compulsory heterosexuality, it is lesbian women who are likewise circumscribed into a very limited, if not completely absent, existence. Women are repeatedly denied the fluidity to explore alternative combinations of sex, gender, and sexual desire, as a result of compulsory heterosexuality.

IF THE PUNISHMENT FITS THE CRIME: A LOOK AT QUEER NARRATIVES AND CHARACTERS IN *OITNB*

Over the course of two seasons, viewers have witnessed the backstories of the Litchfield inmates, most of whom have had trouble fitting into society in some way. For instance, one character (Alex Vause) was teased as a young girl due to her lower socioeconomic status; a different character (Tasha "Taystee" Jefferson) spent most of her life being tossed around foster care; and yet another (Sister Jane Ingalls) never quite felt like she belonged in a congregation because God did not "speak" to her. Multiple characters have experienced hardship from the lack of belonging and acceptance – hardship that stems from transgressing heterosexuality and instead attempting to move fluidly outside of societal norms. These characters include: Piper Chapman, Sophia Burset, and Suzanne "Crazy Eyes" Warren. The storylines around these particular characters, we argue, work two-fold for audience members: first, they allow viewers to see the daily struggles of individuals who do not fit neatly (or at all) within society's heterosexist framework; and second, they also serve as tales of morality on a symbolic level. While the former is more obvious, this chapter focuses on the latter and highlights the various narratives and character relationships. Due to space constraints, it should be noted that our analysis does not include all characters who are members of the LGBTQ community at Litchfield. Instead, we focus on the characters who were given more programming time to divulge their hardships experienced, as a result of transgressing heterosexuality. Because of this, we omitted analysis of Nicole "Nicky" Nichols, Poussey Washington, Carrie "Big Boo" Black, Tricia Miller, and more recent characters such as Dominga "Daddy" Duarte (season six).

PIPER CHAPMAN'S ON-AND-OFF AGAIN RELATIONSHIP WITH ALEX VAUSE

In the opening montage of the series' pilot, viewers see flashbacks of Piper first in the shower with Alex and later in the tub with Larry. Both shots are quickly juxtaposed with a shot of Piper in a prison shower, hating her current living conditions. Interestingly, it wasn't her relationship with Larry that landed her in prison. Even though Piper never labels herself as bisexual, gay, or straight, viewers are reminded throughout the series that it was her romantic relationship – with Alex, specifically – that landed her in Litchfield.

In season one, episode eight (henceforth S#-E#), Piper begins to open up again to Alex, but only after having Alex tell her that she wasn't the one who ratted her out (in S1-E3) and having this "confirmed" by Larry (in S1-E5). In S1-E9, Piper and Alex are shown dancing close together, at the celebration for Tasha "Taystee" Jefferson's impending prison release. The dancing is cut short, however, when Tiffany "Pennsatucky" Doggett (an inmate known for her extreme religious conviction) tells Sam Healy, the prison's counselor, of Piper and Alex's intimate behavior. As a result, Piper is thrown in the Secure Housing Unit (SHU) for what Healy claims is attempted rape. Viewers are privy to the fact that because of Piper's intersectional identity as a white, middle-to-upper class, "straight" woman, Healy holds Piper to a different standard than the other inmates, and has difficulty accepting Piper's romantic relationship with Alex. (It is important to point out that, throughout the series, Healy symbolizes a white, straight, conservative, patriarchal society that intervenes to preserve the dominance of compulsory heterosexuality.) When Healy comes to visit her briefly, Piper calls him out on his heterosexist mentality and his obsession with her in particular; Healy leaves, having the last word since he controls her continued stay in solitary confinement. After being in the SHU for quite some time, Piper commits herself to behaving and avoiding Alex at all costs, if that is what it takes to never be in solitary confinement again. However, this "lesson learned" is short lived, as Piper has sex with Alex in the Chapel immediately upon being released to her regular bunk area. Instances like these – as well as when Piper and Alex eventually get married later in season six – are ones where *OITNB* challenges compulsory heterosexuality.

In S1-E11, Piper lays with Alex and they kiss, as both of them admit to being in love with the other. They are once again interrupted, but this time by Nicky Nichols, who tells them that it is 11AM and Larry's radio interview about Piper's imprisonment is airing live on public radio. During his air time, Larry is passive aggressive in letting Piper know that he is aware that she and Alex are growing close again in prison. Piper later confronts Larry about his on-air stunt, which results in serious consequences for her prison life. Piper learns the truth about Alex; she was indeed the rat who landed her in prison. By now, viewers are used to the same old pattern – Piper and Alex grow close, only to have Piper punished (both figuratively and literally) shortly after. Compulsory heterosexuality is repeatedly reaffirmed as the "correct" route for women through the punishment of Piper.

In S1-E12, Piper tries to maintain her distance from Alex, but eventually they end up holding hands again. At the end of the episode, she is "punished" when Larry visits her and gives her an ultimatum – either they get married while she is in prison, or their engagement/relationship is over. However, after meeting Alex for the first time during visitation, Larry is informed that it was Piper, not Alex, who re-initiated their intimacy while in prison. This leads Larry to end his relationship with Piper. The tale of morality does not stop there though, but instead is solidified in the season two opener: Piper is transferred to a prison in Chicago and learns that she must testify at the trial of Kubra Balik, the man whom Alex worked for in the drug trafficking ring. Piper is reunited with Alex, who has also been temporarily transferred to the same prison. Alex begs Piper to lie under oath and say that she never met Kubra, otherwise their lives could be in danger. Piper initially refuses, but later changes her mind (despite her lawyer, who is also Larry's father, advising her not to lie at all). Piper lies under oath for the woman she loves, while Alex tells the truth in court and ends up being released. Piper is left alone in a Chicago prison, as a result of her commitment to Alex.

While most of season one shows Piper being punished time and again for caring and showing affection toward Alex, viewers are left with a change of tone at the end of the second season when Piper finally takes matters into her own hands. In S2-E13, Alex visits Piper in prison (Piper was transferred back to Litchfield in S2-E3). She lets Piper know that she is skipping town because she fears for her life now that a mistrial was declared for Kubra, who also walked. This would have typically meant that Piper was once again paying the price alone for her feelings toward Alex. However, Piper guilts her best friend, Polly, into calling Alex's parole officer and notifying him of her plans to leave town. Piper's plan is two-fold: to reunite Alex with her in prison but also to keep her love safe from Kubra's men on the outside.

SOPHIA BURSET'S MALE-TO-FEMALE TRANSITION

In S1-E3, viewers first learn the backstory to Sophia Burset, an African-American woman and the series' only transgender inmate. Once a firefighter, Sophia struggled internally with keeping up with her gendered performance. While on duty, Sophia (whose masculine name was Marcus) would play the part of the masculine firefighter wearing the uniform and heavy equipment. However, as soon as his shift was over, Marcus would change out of his uniform only to reveal that he was wearing pink lace undergarments. Sophia was hiding her true identity. This internal struggle is reified for viewers through the juxtaposition of two shots: Marcus washing and analyzing his face after his work shift, versus Sophia washing her face and applying makeup while in prison. These shots are immediately followed by Sophia stepping back to check herself out in the prison restroom mirror, where viewers see her exposed breasts (enhanced through implants) as she wears nothing but a white thong and some homemade sandals.

However, Sophia's struggles do not stop there. In the same episode, she learns that, due to the prison's budgetary problems, she is being forced to switch to the generic, lower dose brand of her hormone pills. Within the show's diegesis, Sophia had undergone gender affirmation surgery where Marcus' penis was inverted and his testes were surgically removed. After being denied permission to see a doctor (Healy didn't consider her health concerns an "emergency"), Sophia takes matters into her own hands and swallows a small figurine from Healy's desk. This prompts her to finally see a doctor, who informs her that she will be taken off hormones altogether until her elevated levels return to normal. As a result, the option to provide sexual favors to correctional officer George "Pornstache" Mendez is offered in return for hormone pills, but Sophia outright refuses.

Over the course of the series, Sophia often acts as a sympathetic ear for other inmates. While cutting hair in the prison's salon, she is often seen encouraging and empowering her clients. Viewers might read her encouragement and empowerment of fellow inmates as her way of compensating for the pain that she feels daily, especially regarding her strained relationship with her son,

Michael. It also may relate to her awareness of the pain that she unintentionally brought to her wife, Crystal, who stayed with Sophia after her transition and is now raising their son alone. When Sophia's desperate need of hormone treatment sets in (S1-E5), Sophia befriends Sister Jane Ingalls in hopes of getting some of her estrogen pills. Sister Jane, in response, tells Sophia that she will not be getting any of her estrogen supply. It is then when Sister Jane speaks about the pain that Sophia is going through with her family. Viewers are reminded of the hardship that Sophia faces in balancing who she is versus who society (and family) want and expect her to be. Similar to the outcome for Piper at the end of season two, Sophia also finds peace with herself when her son, Michael, comes to visit her in prison for the very first time. This relationship with her son builds traction over latter seasons, of the series, and by season six becomes a focal point of Sophia's storyline.

SUZANNE "CRAZY EYES" WARREN'S OBSESSION WITH PIPER CHAPMAN

In S1-E2, viewers first meet Suzanne "Crazy Eyes" Warren. Suzanne is a lesbian African-American inmate, who is first introduced to viewers when she is shown eyeing Piper in the cafeteria. Suzanne enthusiastically moves over to give Piper a seat near her at the table, before Piper is pulled away by another inmate Lorna Morello and instructed not to sit with Suzanne. Viewers quickly gather from her nickname alone that the character may have mental health issues. Despite her stares toward Piper in this episode, viewers see that Suzanne (who goes by "Sue" herself) goes out of her way to help Piper and even gives her spicy peppers (to aid in Piper's attempts to make a smoothing lotion for another inmate). The tale of morality sets in at the end of this episode when Piper realizes her mistake in accepting the peppers: Suzanne sits next to Piper during movie night and shares her headphones, only to then rub Piper's thigh and reach for her hand. The problem is solidified through the facial expressions of both characters: Piper looks shocked while Suzanne looks content.

This marks the beginning of what becomes Suzanne's obsession with Piper, whom she calls "Dandelion." In the subsequent episode (S1-E3), Suzanne tries to peek in on Piper while she is using the toilet, sniffs at Piper as she runs around the outside track, recites a poem that she wrote for Piper (despite Piper not wanting to hear it), and sings a song that describes their relationship whereby Piper is "vanilla" and she is "chocolate." When Piper tries to distance herself from Alex, Suzanne steps in, threatens to cut Alex, and then throws pie at her. In the process, viewers see Suzanne slap herself in the head – a gesture that becomes common for her character. Piper later breaks the news to Suzanne that she is not her "wife" and never will be. In retaliation of Piper's rejection, Suzanne stops by Piper's bunk in the middle of the night and pees on the floor as Piper watches in horror. The song that plays during this episode's closing credits only serves to reify Suzanne's attitude toward the situation, with lyrics such as "one crazed bitch" and "not giving a f**k about none of you."

What makes Suzanne a particularly complicated character in the eyes of viewers is seeing her backstory and learning that she has always been deemed the Other, while also witnessing her asking Piper (in S1-E11) why everyone calls her "Crazy Eyes." Suzanne has a look of genuine hurt on her face. This is problematized in that manner that Suzanne also has mental health issues and a history of violence. Throughout the series, she is prone to anger and retaliation. Through all of this, the pathologization of homosexuality is again reified on *OITNB*, as Suzanne's character is shown to be both gay and mentally unfit.

DISCUSSION

In this chapter, we examined some of the more prominent queer narratives and characters that stem from Netflix's *OITNB*. Focusing on the narratives around Piper Chapman, Sophia Burset, and Suzanne "Crazy Eyes" Warren, we grounded our analysis in the application of theories from both Judith Butler and Adrienne Rich. In particular, we demonstrate not only the representations but also the implications of the latest manifestations of queer narratives in popular culture. Litchfield prison, which is mostly operated by men with a limited number of women as authority figures, works to preserve compulsory heterosexuality and keep threats against it to a minimum. Through careful monitoring and punishment, such as Healy punishing Piper time and again, the prison offers viewers a microcosm of white, heterosexist patriarchal society where any sign of "rebellion" or transgression must be dealt with. In many cases, the inmates are sent to the SHU (which the show suggests is the second worst place they can go, after the psych ward). More so, Rich (1980), who quotes and expands upon the work of Gough (1975), would argue that this exemplifies not only men denying women of their own sexuality, but also "confin[ing] them physically and prevent[ing] their movement" – both of which are what Rich and Gough describe as characteristics of compulsory heterosexuality (pp. 638–639).

While the first season of the series often symbolically (but many times literally) punished inmates who strayed away from traditional gender performances and compulsory heterosexuality, there seemed to be a shift in the second season where more control and agency were given to characters. And, as the series continued to progress through season six, viewers continued to see changing dynamics, struggles, and questions raised related to heterosexist conformity, gender, and the Other through the characters themselves. Piper took matters into her own hands, Sophia found comfort in her ability to help others, and Suzanne prompts us to think further about the relationship between mental health issues and violence. In this way, *OITNB* tends to challenge compulsory heterosexuality as a whole by offering viewers multiple portrayals of LBT women – from Piper to Alex to Sophia to Suzanne to Nicky to Big Boo to Tricia to Mercy to Poussey. It also offers a rare glimpse into the hardships faced by trans women. *OITNB* reminds viewers that injustices are often carried out as means to preserve compulsory heterosexuality – such as when Healy makes his best efforts to punish Piper, respectively, for not abiding by societal norms of sexual orientation. Consideration should also be made around the fact that only male, and never female, correctional officers are seen engaging in sexual acts with female inmates. More so, Rich (1980) would argue that this would be reflective of "the power of men…to force it [male sexuality] upon [women]," due to the power dynamics between inmates and correctional officers. As *OITNB* alludes to, under New York penal law, inmates are not legally in the position to give consent and therefore even consensual sex between an inmate and a guard is defined as rape in the third degree.

Thinking further about the displays of sexuality seen onscreen, we would be remiss if we did not discuss how intersectionality impacted precisely whose actions and bodies were made visible to audiences. For the most part, when viewers see two naked women having sex within the series, they are white, thin women – such as Piper and Alex, but also Nicky and Lorna. Two exceptions to this are the following: in S2-E4, the relatively new inmate, Brook Soso, who is half white and half Japanese, has sex with Nicky, who is white; and in S2-E6, viewers watch in a flashback as Poussey, who is black, has sex with her German partner, who is white. While Brook and Poussey would fall under the "thin" category, Poussey's German love interest would be the exception in that she is of "average" weight. It is worth noting that when women's bodies were exposed (outside of having sex), the majority of them belonged to the "thin" category. However, there was a transgression of race, as viewers saw white, black, and Latina bodies.

As such, while notions of gender performativity and compulsory heterosexuality are often challenged on *OITNB*, the series is not without its drawbacks. As previously noted, onscreen sexual relations between two women are typically reserved for thin, white women while the only requirement for gazing at the female body outside of sexual relations is that she must still be slender. In this sense, gender performances remain at work in the manner that only thin characters whose performances reaffirm white, heterosexist, patriarchal patrolling of women's bodies are desired. Although the series has received much praise for the ways in which it has exposed viewers to a variety of sexual and gendered performances, it continues to keep certain expectations related to sex, gender, and sexual desire intact.

DISCUSSION QUESTIONS

1. Based on what was discussed in this chapter, what is meant by "gender performativity" and how is this notion reified onscreen in *OITNB*?
2. Similarly, what is "compulsory heterosexuality" and how is it perpetuated or challenged in *OITNB*?
3. How does the intersection of gender, race and ethnicity, sexual orientation, and class impact the storylines of characters from the Netflix series?
4. Reflecting on the series in general, which character most resonated with you? Thinking further about this, why might this be the case? How might the way the series presented this character's backstory have contributed to this resonation?
5. Considering what was discussed in this chapter, can you think of any examples of other entertainment programs that employ similar representations of gender, sexuality, and race? How are they similar (or different) from *OITNB*? Why do you think that is?
6. Given that four additional seasons have aired since we wrote and published this chapter, how do you see the queer narratives and patterns discussed here change, if at all, over time?

REFERENCES

Brinkhurst-Cuff, C. (2017, June 5). Orange is the new black stars: 'I couldn't look. I had to turn away.' *The Guardian*. Retrieved from https://www.theguardian.com/tv-and-radio/2017/jun/05/orange-is-the-new-black-stars-taystee-crazy-eyes-sophia

Butler, J. (1990). *Gender trouble: Feminism and the subversion of identity*. New York, NY: Routledge.

Butler, J. (1993). Critically queer. *GLQ: A Journal of Lesbian & Gay Studies, 1*, 17–32.

Butler, J. (2009). Performativity, precarity, and sexual politics. *Journal of Iberoamerican Anthropology, 4*(3), i–xiii.

Codianni, B. (2014, September 3). Former prisoner: 'Orange is the new black' is not funny. *Truthout*. Retrieved from http://www.truth-out.org/opinion/item/25957-former-inmate-orange-is-the-new-black-is-not-funny

De Lauretis, T. (1991). Queer theory: Lesbian and gay sexualities. *Differences: A Feminist Journal of Cultural Studies, 3*(2), iii–xviii.

Gough, K. (1975). The origin of the family. In R. Reiter (Ed.), *Toward an anthropology of women* (pp. 69–70). New York, NY: Monthly Review Press.

Kerman, P. (2011). *Orange is the new black: My year in a women's prison*. New York, NY: Spiegel & Grau.

Kohan, J. (Producer). (2013–2015). Orange is the new black [streaming video]. *Netflix*. Retrieved from http://www.netflix.com

Lynch, J. (2018, July 7). Orange is the new black scored more viewers in TV's most coveted demo than anything on broadcast. *AdWeek*. Retrieved from https://www.adweek.com/tv-video/orange-is-the-new-black-scored-more-viewers-in-tvs-most-coveted-demo-than-anything-on-broadcast/

McCormick, J. P. (2014, January 9). Trans actress Laverne Cox: 'A preoccupation with transition and surgery objectifies trans people.' *Pink News*. Retrieved from http://www.pinknews.co.uk/2014/01/09/trans-actress-laverne-cox-a-preoccupation-with-transition-and-surgery-objectifies-trans-people/

Nussbaum, E. (2014, July 7). Lockdown: The lessons of 'Orange is the New Black' and 'Louie.' *The New Yorker*. Retrieved from http://www.newyorker.com/magazine/2014/07/07/lockdown-2

Obenson, T. A. (2013, October 21). 'Orange is the new black' is Netflix's most-watched original series ever – likely thanks to you. *Indiewire*. Retrieved from http://blogs.indiewire.com/shadowandact/orange-is-the-new-black-is-netflixs-most-watched-original-series-ever-likely-thanks-to-you

Orange Is the New Black: Awards and Nominations. (2019). *Television academy*. Retrieved from: https://www.emmys.com/shows/orange-new-black

Rich, A. (1980). Compulsory heterosexuality and lesbian existence. *Signs, 5*(4), 631–660.

Sedgwick, E. (1990). *Epistemology of the closet*. Berkeley, CA: University of California Press.

Sedgwick, E. (1994). *Tendencies*. London: Routledge.

Wittig, M. (1992). One is not born a woman. In M. Wittig (Ed.), *The straight mind: And other essays* (pp. 9–20). Boston, MA: Beacon Press.

Wright, J. (2011). Facing gender performativity: How transgender performance and performativity trouble facework research. *Kaleidoscope, 10*, 73–90.

CARRIE L. BUIST AND JEAN-ANNE SUTHERLAND

6. WARNING! SOCIAL CONSTRUCTION ZONE

Exploring Masculinities, Femininities, and Gender Roles in Cop Shows

We saw our first feminist perspectives develop during the age of enlightenment, and in a general sense these theories share similarities, but they also vary regarding the root causes of oppression experienced by women. For instance, the most basic explanation of liberal feminist theory might note that the root cause of oppression is institutional inequality, focusing primarily on legislative equity. Conversely, radical feminism might indicate that the root cause of oppression is male domination, thus the patriarchy. It could be argued that different theories have developed in response to something missing in another. Thus, returning to liberal feminist theory and radical feminist theory, the radical feminist would purport that even if equitable legislation develops and is implemented, there will still be discrimination in the form of sex and gender inequality. Another example of the development of new theories can be highlighted in the genesis of Black feminist theory which was a response to the White middle class standards of the theories that came before. Or further still, feminist theories of intersectionality that focus on class, race, gender, and sexuality, characteristics that identify the "matrix of domination/oppression" (Collins, 2000).

In this chapter, we will provide examples of performance/expectations/ stereotypes relating to masculinity, femininity, and gender roles as evidenced in television crime dramas and reality shows by highlighting three television shows (*Chicago P.D.*, *The Shield*, and *Rookies*). Our intention is to explore how masculinity is not only performed but interpreted. We have chosen to relate these depictions via crime programming for two reasons, the first being that they allow us to address masculinities and in doing so, femininities through criminological and sociological lenses. Next, it is often in television programs such as these that hyper-versions of performances are detailed. In observing these performances it will be important for the audience to identify behaviors and apply theory to the societal assumptions of gender performance and identity.

© KONINKLIJKE BRILL NV, LEIDEN, 2019 | DOI:10.1163/9789004414259_006

MASCULINITIES AND FEMINIST THEORY

Second-wave feminism "assumed an antagonism" with masculinity (Gardiner, 2002, p. 2). Radical feminists of this era, often the ones most vocal, cast men as "oppressors," wielding power and domination over women. More liberal feminists did not hold men, as individuals, responsible for women's oppression but rather elaborated on the social structures that held women in subordinate realms. In addition, feminists of color demonstrated the ways in which race, social class and, gender were intersecting systems of oppression. As these feminists observed, not all women were oppressed in the same way just as not all men were oppressors (see Wiegman, 2002).

In the early years of masculinity studies, feminist thinking and masculinity were both incompatible *and* complementary. As Gardiner (2002) notes, even as masculinity studies entered the academy via gender and women's studies programs, there were still those who saw masculinity as representative of "institutional practices, attitudes, and personality traits of men – like aggression and competitiveness…" (p. 3). At the same time, the "masculinist" men's movements (think: Robert Bly's *Iron John*) were highly critical of feminist arguments of men's power and oppression and, instead, blamed feminism for men's declining, essential masculinity. On the other end of the spectrum were pro-feminist men who "sought gender equality by changing men, reeducating the abusive, and seeking to dismantle the male privileges enjoyed by dominate men" (Gardiner, 2002, p. 4). The pro-feminist writings in academia began to flourish in the 1980's while "masculinist" men's movements began to lose their attractiveness.

In 1985, Carrigan, Connell and Lee published "Toward a New Sociology of Masculinity." While this was not Connell's first work in the field of gender, it heralded in a new and invigorating approach to the study of masculinity. Unlike much of the 1970's work on masculinity, this piece took a distinctly feminist tone. (For more on the impact of Connell's work, see Wedgwood, 2009.) Another important aspect of this work was the manner in which it deconstructed the sex-role essentialism that had governed gender studies to date. Sex-role theorists depicted gender in terms of strict binary roles for men and women as if there was a "natural" quality to them. Rather than studying men as a homogenous group, Carrigan et al argued for a more nuanced study of "historically specific masculini*ties*" (Wedwood, 2009, p. 332).

Connell's influential book, *Gender and Power* (1987) detailed the notion of hegemonic masculinity, a form of masculinity which is dominant in a society. Erving Goffman (1963) described this hegemonic male as "young, married, White, urban, northern, heterosexual, Protestant, father, of college education, fully employed, of good complexion, weight, and height, and a recent record in sports" (p. 23). According to Connell (1987), the notion of hegemony is not intended to mean that masculinity in this manner is adopted by all men (as sex-role theorists would imply). Hegemonic masculinity, according to Connell, was not an identity or a set of specific role expectations. Instead he depicted hegemonic masculinity as a set of practices; practices that become normative. It leads toward a sense of entitlement and allows for aggression towards women (Gardiner, 2002).

In the 1980's and into the 90's, a feminist study that centered on men and masculinity was considered suspect by feminists. Wiegman (2002) notes that feminists of this time saw the inclusion of men into gender studies as a movement away from the politics of justice for women. The focus on men and masculinity results in "a theoretically driven appropriation, if not displacement, of feminist political struggle" (Weigman, 2002, p. 37). Modleski (1991) wanted to keep the focus on "differences" among women, a shift in analysis that had occurred post 1970's, especially among feminists of color. For feminism to be political, and thus effective, women needed to be the center of critical analysis rather than a "politically neutralized 'gender studies'" (Thomas, 2002, p. 61).

Not all of the feminist community, during the period of the 1980's and the 90's, considered the inclusion of men and masculinity to be antithetical to feminist studies. In fact, some key work from this period brought to light the relationships between heterosexism and homophobia and, the mission of feminism. Gay studies (later queer theory) was considered a vital and welcomed direction for masculinities studies (Wiegman, 2002). Writers of this period noted the symmetry of considerations of men and homosexuality and feminist deliberations on the interconnectedness of discriminatory practices under patriarchy.

During the late 80's a burgeoning body of scholarship began to examine men and power, employing Marxist, feminist standpoint epistemologies and postmodern critiques. These include Kaufman's (1993) *Cracking the Armour: Power, Pain, and the Lives of Men*; Kimmel's (ed) (1987) *Changing Men: New Directions in Research on Men and Masculinity* and Kimmel and Messner's (1989) *Men's Lives*. Coltrane (1994), regarding the "masculinist men's movement" versus the academic scholarship of masculinity studies, noted that "One celebrates male bonding and tells men they are OK, and the other focuses on issues of power using academic feminist interpretive frameworks" (p. 42). Certainly it was the latter that began to be embraced by feminists as more profeminist men explored gender and power, institutional power, inequality and "the ways that men create and sustain gendered selves..." (Coltrane, 1994, p. 44).

Feminist criminology, developed in the late 1960s and 1970s, emerged as a response to women being ignored in the criminological research and literature. This timeframe coincides with second-wave feminism, where more politically charged feminism began to emerge, the most notable being radical and socialist feminism (Messerschmidt, 1993). These theories moved beyond the egalitarian focus of liberal feminist theory that, as previously mentioned, focused simply on equal rights, rather than the influence or impact of gender and the patriarchy.

Indeed, radical feminism highlights both sex-role, and gender role differences, viewing "gender [as] an elaborate system of male domination" (Jaggar, 1983, p. 85). Additionally, radical feminism indicates the biological differences between women and men first by indicating women's innate qualities regarding nurturance and passivity therefore, men were seen by some radical feminists as being innately more aggressive than their female counterparts and therefore this aggression led to rape, abuse, and the need to control women (Daly, 1978; Jaggar, 1983; MacKinnon, 1989).

Socialist feminism's priority is to analyze women's oppression through both capitalism and patriarchy. Further, socialist feminism is concerned with gender construction and contend that our "inner" and "outer" lives; mind and body are influenced and structured by gender. Unlike radical feminism's exploration of the importance of biological influence, socialist feminism is more apt to apply our behavior to social constructionism based on both capitalism (division of labor, more women in the home) and a patriarchal society.

GENDER, CRIME, AND POLICING

This section will highlight how the aforementioned feminist theories relate to gender, crime, and policing. Moreover, how they are closely associated not only with masculinity but femininity as well. Some have argued that the percentage of women offenders would increase upon their liberation from the home (Adler, 1975) positing that the increase in the female crime rate was simply attributed to the increased opportunities that women were encountering as they left the private sphere and entered the public sphere (a topic salient to both radical and socialist feminism). This theory of criminal behavior has been highly scrutinized within criminological research, mostly because it "ignores how the intersecting inequalities of sexism, racism, and classism affect not only criminal offending, but also the policies and practices of the criminal justice system" (Renzetti, 2013).

As mentioned, women who were traditionally left out of research were beginning to have their behaviors scrutinized and studied by scholars, wanting to know why a woman would offend, or even more salacious, why a women would kill. However, in addition to the research on why women and men commit crime, there was an increased effort to explore male-centered and dominated professions within the criminal justice system where women were slow to gain entrance or equality upon entrance such as policing. Reasons for this have been attributed to gender role assumptions that speak directly to our discussion of masculinities and femininities. Constructs of gender, masculinity, and femininity are often realized in policing because there has been a focus on characteristics that are commonly attributed to men such as physical strength, agility, and aggression; in general those thoughts and behaviors deemed rational. However characteristics that have commonly been associated with women, such as communication skills, empathy, and in general more relational characteristics are given less weight on the job.

It should be noted that research has found women perform their police duties just as successfully as men and may prove even more successful in community aspects of the job that require more effective communication skills (Miller, 1998; Lonsway, 2003). Further, while a gender role stereotype is that women possess greater communication skills and relational traits, it would be remiss to assume that all women police officers succeed in verbal communication. Another gender stereotype that is highlighted in policing is the importance of physical strength, something that we stereotype men as possessing. What we do know is that communication skills are key to policing (whether a male or female officer is utilizing that skill), that policing is not as physically demanding and does not require the physical strength and agility that many often assume it does, especially in today's policing where both male and female officers have a variety of tools to utilize such as batons, tasers, pepper spray, and their vehicles or their handguns (see Corsianos, 2009).

These stereotypes are gender constructions that are formed and found at the societal level and reappear in subsets of society and culture that are applied to certain careers and the individuals who work in those careers. For instance, it is still assumed that medical doctors are men and the nurses who assist them are women. The aforementioned stereotypes will be addressed ahead.

MASCULINITIES IN PRIMETIME

One way to draw attention to examples of masculinities (and femininities) and how those identities are performed is by highlighting examples in popular culture. Here we have selected three programs (two dramas and one reality show) that focus on police officers. We watched two episodes of each of the dramas and four episodes from the reality program (6 hours total). While we contend that a more detailed content analysis would be beneficial, we narrowed the focus. While we took detailed notes for each episode we only focused our coding and themes on representations of masculinities, femininities, or gender roles. The shows selected for viewing were *Chicago P.D.* (NBC 2014–ongoing), *The Shield* (FX 2002–2008), and *Rookies* (A&E 2008–2009).

Chicago P.D., whose tagline is "Don't Fuck With My City" is a recent addition to the NBC line-up, spinning off from the popular drama, *Chicago Fire*. For this analysis, the first two episodes from the inaugural season of the show were selected. The show follows a special unit within the police department responsible for different tasks including but not limited to the introduction of gangs, drugs, and internal corruption. The team is led by Sgt. Hank Voight and the seven to eight person unit contains two women officers, although one of them, Julie Willhite is murdered in the second episode. Secondary characters featured in the series include female desk Sgt. Platt, female frontline (uniformed) officer, Burgess and her male partner, officer Atwater. In *Chicago P.D.*'s first year on the air it delivered a 2.5 ratings share and nearly 9 million viewers (Bibel, 2014).

The Shield was a controversial, yet popular show that ran on the cable network, FX from 2002–2008 which followed the corrupt police unit run by Det. Vic Mackey. Mackey's team is all male, however the show does highlight female officers such as Det. Wyms, and frontline officer Sofer, who like on *Chicago P.D.*, has a male partner, officer Lowe. *The Shield* was a critically acclaimed drama that won some of the most prestigious awards in the industry including a Golden Globe for best drama and best actor as well as an Emmy for best actor to Michael Chiklis for his portrayal of Vic Mackey. Indeed, Lafayette (2008) noted that *The Shield* changed cable television forever by opening the door for more current popular FX dramas such as the top 10 rated *Sons of Anarchy*.

Finally, *Rookies* ran for one season on the cable channel, A&E and follows the first time experiences of patrol officers in various police departments. While we were unable to ascertain the official ratings from the show, it is safe to assume that they were low as the series only lasted one year. However, the viewer ratings for the show on websites such as IMDB.com, TV.com, and Amazon.com are all high, in the 8/10 range.

When viewing the episodes of the dramas the male characters often represented a textbook example of hegemonic masculinity which as noted, "involves practices characterizing dominance, control, and independence" (Messerschmidt, 1993, p. 93). We saw much less of this in the reality show, *Rookies* as these "fish out of water" officers were much more open regarding their fears and worries, both male and female alike. In the following we will highlight examples of masculinities, femininities, and gender role constructions through the use of a contextual analysis of the programs and the episodes that we watched.

CHICAGO P.D.

Stepping Stone

The first two episodes of the first season were watched and coded for behavior that is traditionally viewed as masculine, feminine, and for societal expectations of gender role performance. It is clear at the onset that the main character, Sgt. Voight plays the traditional role of the patriarch in his intelligence unit. Voight uses physical aggression and violence in order to obtain a confession from a male suspect and in general there is an ongoing antagonistic relationship between Voight and other male officers outside of his unit; these men often exchange threats both professionally and personally, verbally and physically.

Other examples of physical aggression and gender role stereotypes include a woman officer taking on the role of nurturer/caregiver when questioning a young male suspect as opposed to the aggressive techniques used by the male officers – these techniques are clearly favored over communication, a characteristic that is more often attributed to women officers (Miller, 1998; Lonsway, 2003). For instance, when one of the seasoned officers goes to the academy to recruit a new member for the team, the training officer tells him to observe his "ball breaker" recruit in action. The particular scenario the recruits are practicing is a negotiation scene where the person playing the suspect has a gun and is threatening to commit suicide. The overall goal of the scenario is for the officer to get the gun away from the suspect. However, the means through which the officer should achieve this is through calm, thoughtful, clear communication (all traditionally female characteristics). Instead of taking this approach the recruit takes the suspect down using physical force and takes the gun. The training officer is unhappy to which the recruit states sarcastically, "you said get the gun out of this hand."

According to radical feminism, the prevailing systems of oppression both privately and publicly stem from male domination, men are the oppressors and women are the oppressed (Jaggar, 1983; Messerschmidt, 1993). These prevailing systems of domination can be highlighted both in the public and private spheres. Beginning with the private sphere, radical feminism notes that women are often subjected to their sex-role expectations by becoming sexual servants to their husbands and through the expectation that they are not only to produce children but to be the sole caretakers of the children once they are born (Jaggar, 1983; Firestone, 1970; Millet, 1970). Thus far in this episode women have been seen as valued when needed to take on a nurturing role with a young suspect, yet their characteristics are devalued when searching for a new member of the unit.

In a later example of masculinities, femininities, and gender role construction, one of the female members of the unit, Lindsay, drives herself and her male partner, Halstead to an investigation, and while in the car, Halstead expresses his displeasure that she always drives when they go on calls, telling her that it makes him feel like a "house husband." Later during the investigation some bystanders catcall Lindsay. She ignores their sexually charged comments, but Halstead hands his gun and badge to Lindsay and proceeds to physically attack the young male who has made the comments to his partner. After beating the man, Halstead helps him up and walks away. When heading towards the vehicle, Lindsay comments, "my hero, but I'm still driving."

In a surprising turn that highlights a departure from traditional gender roles as viewed in relation to masculinity, Voight speaks with the earlier suspect, a young African American boy who is being released from jail. He takes him aside and tells him that one day when the boy decides to get out of his situation he can contact him for assistance. Voight gives the young man his card and tells him to go. Later, the young man is beaten and calls Voight for help. Voight goes to the boy and calms his fears (the boy fears he will be considered a snitch). This exchange shows a clear example of the nurturing side of an otherwise hyper-masculine character.

Wrong Side of the Bars

Overall, this episode focuses on the physical aggression that the male officers use in order to retrieve Dawson's kidnapped son. There are several instances during this episode of brutality, threats, and overall violence. Other notable moments during this second episode include officer Burgess telling her partner that "Sometimes my temper inhibits my ability to communicate." This is a brief, yet important scene because it expresses to the astute viewer that it's not only the men in the unit who have tempers or who find communication difficult. It allows us to view or at least entertain the idea that it's the specific position one holds within the institutional structure of the police department and not the individual characteristics of the officer. Finally, the characteristics of strength and courage that men so often are constructed to value are highlighted when upon recovering his 10 year old son, the first thing that Dawson does as he holds him in an embrace is to tell him that he was brave.

THE SHIELD

The Quick Fix

Season two, episode one begins with male gang members setting another gang member on fire. Soon we see that Det. Vic Mackey is looking for his wife who has taken their children and left him. Much like *Chicago, P.D.*, *The Shield* fulfills all the assumptions of hegemonic masculinity previously mentioned. The program is a tour-de-force of control, dominance, and independence, exemplified by Mackey's character as the leader of his corrupt police unit, there is no doubt, in these episodes, at least, that Mackey is the alpha male not only in his department but in his life. We see this displayed as he tells his private investigator to find his wife and children because it "can't be hard to find a housewife."

While all of the male characters are stereotypically masculine, the women officers display the same stereotypical traits of the nurturer/caregiver as one of the prominent women officers yells at a male officer for interviewing a child, telling him that "if you had kids you'd know." One of the more notable scenes highlights a departure from gender role expectations in that the female officer who Mackey is having an affair with tells him that she doesn't want their sexual relationship to turn into a "thing." Mackey seems to agree with this, but also takes a momentary beat – perhaps he was surprised that officer Sofer was so straight-forward, or that she wasn't emotionally connected with him but instead only interested in him for sex.

Dead Soldiers

In the second episode of the second season there is a push and pull between Mackey and the female Det. Wyms as they are investigating arson and are in a disagreement over whom they suspect should be interviewed for the crime. Mainly, Mackey is contentious with her because the person who he has identified to her as confidential informant is actually a drug dealer who Mackey and the members of his corrupt unit are working with. Throughout the entire episode Wyms is assertive and aggressive, even tenacious in pursuing her case. It's clear within the storyline that Wyms is suspicious of Mackey's behavior in regards to his "C.O." as she suspects he is trying to keep her from interviewing him and voices her opinion about the investigation loudly to the captain and Mackey.

The episode culminates with Mackey's "C.O." being murdered to which Mackey responds with almost unimaginable violence towards the suspect. Mackey and his partners illegally bust into the suspects home and Mackey begins to viciously beat the suspect, drawing blood and knocking out the suspect's teeth. In the kitchen, Mackey turns on the oven's stovetop and grabs the suspect ordering him to confess as he presses the man's face closer and closer to the range. The suspect continues to refuse to comply and Mackey in turn presses his face to the hot irons of the stovetop and burns his face. Mackey's character is consistently asserting his masculinity by fighting anyone and anything to maintain his control, dominance, and independence throughout these episodes. These images of physical aggression displayed by the character contribute to our social constructions of masculinity, control and power.

ROOKIES

Tampa: Class Begins

Part of the first episode of this reality show follows rookie officer, A.J. who physically displays characteristics that have been favored and valued in policing – he is a physically fit, White, male, even as he has fears about the dangers of his job. A.J. is ribbed by his fellow officers and while he mentions the importance of having compassion in the field he follows that by noting that it should not interfere with the importance of safety. It's ironic that he mentions the importance of safety when it is clear to his female training officer and his sergeant that he requires more training. A.J. admits this when he tells his training officer that "I'm completely lost, I have no idea." The producers note that after a week on the job, A.J. quit.

Size Doesn't Matter

The second episode in season one is titled as such because the focus is on two dramatically different officers: one physically small female officer and one large male officer. Here there is attention given to verbal communication, but soon we see the female officer and her female training officer using their physicality, not to fight off criminals, but rather to employ their social work duties and push a disabled vehicle out of traffic.

When the male rookie and his male training officer are on the road the F.T.O. (field training officer) asks the rookie what he likes to do. As he begins to answer, "watch football…" one might suspect that he is another example of the stereotypical male. However, as he continues, the viewer would no doubt be surprised at what else the officer states, "… lift weights, and write poetry." Comments like this, that would most likely leave the viewer feeling as though something is askew is an example of just how our social constructions of men's likes and dislikes are constructed through myriad representations, not least of which the media.

Additional observations that were made during this episode include the female F.T.O. instructing the female rookie officer to work on lowering her voice when she speaks in order to appear more authoritative. In a secondary highlight from the show, the male officers were referred to as "ladies" by the leader of the tactical unit. By calling these men ladies, the goal is to use the word to discredit them or insult then in some way (e.g. it would be insulting for any man to be referred to as a woman). This is another example of how devalued women are in policing and it speaks to the general commentary of devaluing the strength of women.

What we have seen with regards to gender and crime is that women are the outliers who are performing against their perceived roles, and men are either expected to be aggressive and perhaps manifest that aggression through criminal behavior, or they are pressured into proving their masculinity and in doing so may commit crime in order to prove that they are a "real man" (Messerschmidt, 1993). Further, while West and Zimmerman (1987) introduced the concept of "doing gender" we mustn't forget Butler's (1990) related concept of performativity which indicates that we perform our gender based on societal constructs where we act in certain ways in relation to our sex. Gender, masculinities, and femininities are all constructions and they only exist because "we, as a collective have decided that men should be physically and emotionally strong [and] [w]e, as a collective have decided that women should be physically and emotionally weak" (Buist, 2011, p. 13). We see these performances of gender displayed in the third and fourth episodes of *Rookies*, especially regarding Levine's reaction to being scolded by her FTO in the final episode.

Tampa: A Deer in Headlights

In the fourth episode, the story of the male rookie Johnson is told. His story provided few examples of masculinities, beyond what his F.T.O. described as a problem with "over confidence." However, Levine, the female rookie's story highlights gender role stereotypes related not specifically to policing but more universal stereotypes about women. First, her F.T.O. tells her that she cannot carry her pink gym bag with her on the job and that he would not allow that bag to be placed in his car. Levine then follows orders and unloads her pink bag as to not embarrass her F.T.O. In her interview segment, Levine is clear when she states that she is not nervous, nor scared of anything on the job. This may be because she has come from a family of officers, her father the chief of police in a neighboring area. However after her first day on the job, her F.T.O. takes her aside and tells her that she needs to "get more gumption" which leads her to break down in tears when she is interviewed by the camera crew. By the second day, however, her F.T.O. comments that she has improved, but then ends by saying, "now you know why we don't carry pink bags." Pink bags, of course, are assumed to be antithetical to the masculinity that police officers must possess; even female ones.

DISCUSSION

The police dramas, *Chicago P.D.*, *The Shield*, and the reality program, *Rookies*, were used to exemplify masculinities and femininities in action – since the occupation of policing is still male-centered we utilized these programs to present you various ways in which masculinity, especially hegemonic masculinity, are present and achieved. Further, while these behaviors are indeed dramatized in *Chicago P.D.* and *The Shield* (some could also argue that just because a program is defined as "reality" there are still story editors and producers) these dramatizations come from real life scenarios as television both creates *and* reflects culture.

The male characters on these shows (*Chicago P.D.* and *The Shield*), behaved in ways that displayed their need to dominate, control, and either gain or maintain independence (Messerschmidt, 1993). Again, we must note, that even though masculinities were central to this discussion, these programs highlight the segregation that women often experience on the job that has been traditionally or historically deemed male, such as policing. We continue to see women either completely shut out of the profession, or overtly or covertly denied access to the "brotherhood" of policing (Martin, 1999;

Westmarland, 2001; Freedman, 2002; Corsianos, 2009). These programs highlighted the importance placed on men protecting women, by strength, bravery, courage, and the embodiment of the father figure.

A more in-depth content analysis would further highlight the representation of masculinities and femininities in television crime shows. In addition to other types of media, we find in television, for the most part, depictions of binary gender scripts (men as aggressors, women as nurtures). Certainly media, as one agent of socialization, helps us to construct expected gendered behaviors both as they are embedded in institutions like the police force and in individual actors who perform gender on the job and at home.

DISCUSSION QUESTIONS

1. Thinking of the characteristics of hegemonic masculinity, describe some examples of how hegemonic masculinity is highlighted in popular media.
2. As indicated in the chapter, research has found that women police officers perform their duties just as effectively and successfully as male officers. Why then are women officers still de-valued in policing? Use examples from the chapter to support your answer.
3. Using examples from the television programs in the chapter provide some instances of how male officers asserted their authority.
4. How do the television programs highlighted in this chapter depict the working relationships between the male and female characters?

ADDITIONAL READINGS

Gardiner, J. K. (Ed.). (2002). *Masculinity studies & feminist theory: New directions*. New York, NY: Columbia University Press.

Kimmel, M. (1987). *Changing men: New directions in research on men and masculinity*. Newbury Park, CA: Sage Publications.

Kimmel, M., & Messner, M. (1989). *Men's lives*. New York, NY: Macmillan Publishing.

Westmarland, L. (2001). *Gender and policing: Sex, power, and police culture*. Portland, OR: Willan Publishing.

Wiegman, R. (2002). Unmaking: Men and masculinity in feminist theory. In J. K. Gardiner (Ed.), *Masculinity studies & feminist theory: New directions* (pp. 31–59). New York, NY: Columbia University Press.

REFERENCES

Adler, F. (1975). *Sisters in crime*. New York, NY: McGraw-Hill.

Bibel, S. (2014). Chicago fire, Chicago P.D. & Grimm renewed. *TV by the numbers*. Retrieved May 22, 2014.

Buist, C. L. (2011). *"Don't let the job change you, you change the job:" The lived experiences of women in policing* (Doctoral dissertation). Western Michigan University, Department of Sociology, Michigan, MI. Retrieved from Proquest Dissertations and Thesis. (Accession Order No. AAI3492975)

Butler, J. (1990). *Gender trouble*. New York, NY: Routledge.

Carrigan, T., Connell, B., & Lee, J. (1985). Toward a new sociology of masculinity. *Theory & Society, 14*, 551–604.

Collins, P. H. (2000). *Black feminist thought*. New York, NY: Routledge.

Coltrane, S. (1994). Theorizing masculinities in contemporary social science. In H. Brod & M. Kaufman (Eds.), *Theorizing masculinities* (pp. 39–60). Thousand Oaks, CA: Sage Publications.

Connell, R. W. (1987). *Gender and power: Society, the person, and sexual politics*. Stanford, CA: Stanford University Press.

Corsianos, M. (2009). *Policing and gendered justice: Examining the possibilities*. Toronto: University of Toronto Press.

Daly, M. (1978). *Gyn/Ecology: The meta-ethics of radical feminism*. New York, NY: Beacon Press.

Firestone, S. (1970). *The dialectic of sex*. New York, NY: Farrar, Straus, and Giroux.

Freedman, E. (2002). *No turning back: The history of feminism and the future of women*. New York, NY: Random House Publishing.

Gardiner, J. K. (Ed.). (2002). *Masculinity studies & feminist theory: New directions*. New York, NY: Columbia University Press.

Goffman, E. (1963). *Stigma*. Englewood Cliffs, NJ: Prentice Hall.

Jaggar, A. (1983). *Feminist politics and human nature: Philosophy and society*. Lanham, MD: Rowman and Littlefield.

Kaufman, M. (Ed.). (1993). *Cracking the armour: Power, pain, and the lives of men*. New York, NY: The Viking Press/Penguin.

Kimmel, M. (1987). *Changing men: New directions in research on men and masculinity*. Newbury Park, CA: Sage Publications.

Kimmel, M., & Messner, M. (1989). *Men's lives*. New York, NY: Macmillan Publishing.

Lafayette, J. (2008). How the shield changed cable T.V.: FX series starts last season after rocking cable, advertising. *TVWeek.com*. Retrieved May 22, 2014, from www.tvweek.com/news/2008/08/how_the_the_shield_changed_cable_t.php

Lonsway, K. (2003). Tearing sown the wall: Problems with consistency, validity, and adverse impact of physical agility testing in police selection. *Police Quarterly, 6*, 237–277.

MacKinnon, C. A. (1989). *Towards a feminist theory of the state*. Cambridge, MA: Harvard University Press.

Martin, S. E. (1997). Police force or police service? Gender and emotional labor. *Annals of the American Academy of Political & Social Science, 561*, 111–126.

Messerschmidt, J. (1993). *Masculinities and crime: Critique and reconceptualization of theory*. Lanham, MD: Rowan and Littlefield.

Messerschmidt, J. (2014). *Crime as structured action: Doing masculinities, race, class, sexuality, and crime*. Lanham, MD: Rowan and Littlefield.

Miller, S. (1998). Rocking the rank and file: Gender issues and community policing. *Journal of Contemporary Criminal Justice, 14*, 156–172.

Millet, K. (1970). *Sexual politics*. Urbana, IL: University of Illinois Press.

Modleski, T. (1991). *Feminism without women: Culture and criticism in the "post-feminist" age*. New York, NY: Routledge.

Renzetti, C. M. (2013). *Feminist criminology*. London: Routledge.

Thomas, C. (2002). Re-enfleshing the bright boys: Or, how male bodies matter to feminist thinking. In J. K. Gardiner (Ed.), *Masculinity studies & feminist theory: New directions*, (pp. 60–89). New York, NY: Columbia University Press.

Wedgwood, N. (2009). Connell's theory of masculinity: Its origins and influences on the study of gender. *Journal of Gender Studies, 18*, 329–339.

Westmarland, L. (2001). *Gender and policing: Sex, power, and police culture*. Portland, OR: Willan Publishing.

Wiegman, R. (2002). Unmaking: Men and masculinity in feminist theory. In J. K. Gardiner (Ed.), *Masculinity studies & feminist theory: New directions* (pp. 31–59). New York, NY: Columbia University Press.

EMILY BENT

7. *GIRL RISING* AND THE PROBLEMATIC OTHER

Celebritizing Third World Girlhoods

Over the last ten years, the plight of the third world girl has increasingly captured popular imagination. From the launch of Nike Foundation's Girl Effect campaign, to the United Nations' declaration of October 11th as the "International Day of the Girl Child," to the 2012 shooting of Pakistani girls' education activist Malala Yousafzai, to the recent #BringBackOurGirls marches and social media initiatives calling for the rescue of nearly 300 schoolgirls kidnapped in Northeastern Nigeria, girls' education and specifically, the directive to "invest in girls" remains prominent in mainstream western media. It is against this cultural backdrop that the documentary feature film *Girl Rising* emerges to tell "the story of nine extraordinary girls from nine countries" (*Girl Rising*, 2014, para. 1).

This chapter explores the film in tandem with feminist standpoint theory in order to understand how popular beliefs about third world girls' experiences shape humanitarian aid efforts for girls' education in the global south. It considers the function of celebrity in telling the story of *Girl Rising* and asks readers to problematize the ways in which experience, identity, and voice produce certain types of 'celebritized' knowledge about third world girls. The New York Times called *Girl Rising* "one of the hottest "cause" documentaries in years" (Barnes, 2013, para. 1) and the Huffington Post (2013) declared the film "the most powerful film you'll see this year" (Horansky, 2014, para. 1). But in this chapter, I challenge readers to move beyond the powerful emotive responses produced by the film to instead critically examine the stylistic utility of A-list actresses (re)telling nine girls' stories in nine different countries. Feminist standpoint theory provides the tools from which to theorize these concepts, and popular culture more broadly, with a grounded and intersectional lens. To start, I begin this analysis with an overview of the *Girl Rising* enterprise.

THE STORY OF GIRL RISING

Girl Rising is a "global social action campaign for girls' education created by Ten Times Ten" (Girl Rising, 2014, para. 1) which seeks to

© KONINKLIJKE BRILL NV, LEIDEN, 2019 | DOI:10.1163/9789004414259_007

"raise awareness about the issue, inspire action and drive resources" to organizations working to educate girls in the developing world (Girl Rising, 2014, para. 6). The philanthropic feature film, also titled *Girl Rising*, was produced by The Documentary Group and Vulcan Productions in association with CNN Films, Gathr, and Intel Corporation; it serves as the cornerstone feature of the larger Ten Times Ten initiative with the campaign more broadly including screening guides, advocacy and educational videos, and standards-aligned school curriculums to explore the issues raised by the film. *Girl Rising* was directed by Richard E. Robbins and released in March of 2013. It "spotlights nine unforgettable girls living in the developing world" (FAQ: What kind of stories do you tell, 2014, para. 2) who collectively share "this powerful truth: educating girls can transform families, communities, countries and eventually, the world" (FAQ: About the film, 2014, para. 2).

The structure of the film is such that A-list celebrities narrate each of the nine stories, while individual girls play themselves in creatively "re-imagined" accounts written by award winning female authors and storytellers from the girls' native countries (FAQ: Are the stories true, 2014, para. 1). Celebrities featured in the film include: Alicia Keys, Anne Hathaway, Kerry Washington, Meryl Streep, Selena Gomez, and Frieda Pinto among others. Spliced between the vignettes of Sokha in Cambodia, Wadley in Haiti, Suma in Nepal, Yasmin in Egypt, Asmera in Ethiopia, Ruksana in India, Senna in Peru, Mariama in Sierra Leone, and Amina in Afghanistan, viewers learn about the statistical vulnerabilities and violence experienced by girls in the developing world, but they also learn about the powerful potential of girls' education.

The film's compelling narration encourages viewers to understand that the solution to poverty, bonded labor, early and forced marriage, homelessness, sexual assault, war and conflict, HIV, trafficking, insufficient health care, maternal mortality, and natural disasters is to educate a girl. *Girl Rising* concludes with an appeal to viewers to get involved, make a difference, and donate to Ten Times Ten to support its' partner organizations "with proven girl-focused programs… that serve girls everyday" (FAQ: How did you decide on the countries, 2014, para. 2). The call to action reminds viewers of the humanitarian politics shaping the production of the *Girl Rising* venture. It is from this particular point of departure that feminist standpoint theory allows us to consider the function of these politics in the telling and (re) telling of the *Girl Rising* story.

WHAT IS FEMINIST STANDPOINT THEORY?

Feminist standpoint theory emerged in the 1970s and 1980s as a critical intervention and expansion of Marxian analyses of the subject, experience, knowledge production, and axes of power (Collins, 2004; Haraway, 1988; Harding, 2004; Hartsock, 2004; Scott, 1991). According to Harding (2004), feminist standpoint theory is "a kind of organic epistemology, methodology, philosophy of science, and social theory that can arise whenever oppressed peoples gain public voice" (p. 3). Standpoint theorists claim, "the social location of women and other oppressed groups [can] be the source of illuminating knowledge claims not only about themselves but also about the rest of nature and social relations" (Harding, 2004, p. 4). Because knowledge is bound within socio-cultural, geo-political and historical conditions of power, standpoint theorists suggest that those positioned in the margins (the marginalized, the oppressed, the other) have a better understanding of how power operates than those positioned closer to its' center. In this way, standpoint theorists consider how "social and political disadvantage can be turned into an epistemological, scientific, and political advantage" (Harding, 2004, p. 7). It is often theorists' claims to expedient knowledge that sparks controversy and debate in standpoint theory's application.

Feminist standpoint theorists however also look beyond discursive systems of power to prioritize the voices, knowledge, and experiences of the structurally marginalized. They begin at the intersections of material difference with the expressed goal of shifting the *other* from object to subject (Collins, 2004). Haraway (1988) resolves standpoint theory requires "the object of knowledge be pictured as an actor and agent, not... as a slave to the master who closes off... agency and authorship of 'objective' knowledge" (p. 592). This operational epistemology complicates "patterns of inequality and the underlying structural conditions of society" in such a way that it makes them "dynamic, complex, and contingent, but also amenable to explanation" and change (McCall, 2005, p. 1794). Mohanty (2003) therefore proposes, attending to the specific ways that the marginalized experience and understand their situatedness allows us to "explain the connections and border crossings" more completely and without dismissing the central role intersectionality, power, and agency play in this constructive process (p. 226).

The pivotal function of individual experience further compliments the central tenants of standpoint theory. Standpoint theorists claim that in privileging the experiences of the margins, one gains a better understanding of how power creates and inscribes hierarchies of domination and subordination.

111

Yet, because the margins are neither innocent nor unmarked by power, Scott (1991) comments, "we need to attend to the historical processes that, through discourse, position subjects and produce their experiences" (p. 83). Marginalized knowledge is not natural or automatic in other words, but rather systematically shaped and regulated by power. To avoid pluralist reductions or hierarchies of knowledge, standpoint theorists must situate experience within the confines of socio-material, historical, and intersectional difference.

This chapter uses feminist standpoint theory to investigate *Girl Rising* and the function of celebrity figures in the representation of third world girlhood. It considers how girls' experiences shape the message and knowledge produced in the film; the ways in which, girls' voices and stories of difference become 'celebritized'; and the role of the western viewer and Hollywood celebrity in movement for girls' education. In each of the subsequent sections, I explore concepts of experience, voice, and knowledge alongside a critical analysis of the film. Taken together, I suggest this study demonstrates the judicious applicability of feminist standpoint theory to contemporary popular culture sites, as well as examines the (im)possibilities of hearing girls' authentic voices and truth vis-à-vis *Girl Rising*.

"THIS IS A SIMPLE STORY AND IT DID NOT BEGIN HERE"
EXPERIENCE AS KNOWLEDGE

Feminist standpoint theorists argue all knowledge claims stem from the politics of experience; each socio-cultural and geo-political division "whether by gender or class, can be expected to have consequences for knowledge" (Hartsock, 2004, p. 38). The intersections of difference deeply impact and shape one's perspective and experience of that difference, or of oppression and injustice more broadly. Employing standpoint theory methodologies is thus about accessing otherwise invisible knowledge derived from marginalized experiences and positioning that experiential knowledge against the hegemonic norm. Because of this counter-hegemonic location, Harding (2004) argues standpoint theorists "study up" in order to gain "critical insight about how the dominant society thinks and is structured" (pp. 6–7). Standpoint theorists maintain that the vision which stems from one's marginality "can transform a source of oppression into a source of knowledge and potential liberation" within feminist resistance projects (Harding, 2004, p. 10).

Girl Rising taps into the experiences of third world girls to drive the narrative of girls' education. From the opening sequence of the film to its' conclusion, viewers witness the educational struggles and triumphs of nine individual girls from different locations (Cambodia, Haiti, Nepal, Egypt, Ethiopia, India, Peru, Sierra Leone, and Afghanistan). Their stories endeavor to "capture the things these girls and these writers want you to see" (*Girl Rising*, 2014, 6:48–6:52), drawing upon "the persuasive power of a great and well-told story… [to] change the way we see the world and our place in it" (FAQ: What kinds of stories, 2014, para.1). The film's opening scene sets the stage for the *Girl Rising* narrative; viewers watch Sokha perform a traditional Cambodian dance against a solid black backdrop with slow sorrowful music as the narrator reflects upon the devastating experiences of girls bound by the intersectional oppression and injustices of the developing world. Once viewers understand that her society sees her as "weak, submissive, property, obedient, silent, worthless," *Girl Rising* offers a different story – a story of personal empowerment and societal transformation for girls in the margins (*Girl Rising*, 2014, 0:05–0:20).

True to the central tenants of standpoint theory, *Girl Rising* converts the experiences of third world girls into a vision for social change. Throughout the film, viewers learn about the practice of kumlari (or bonded labor) in Nepal through the eyes of Suma, Yasmin's experience of sexual violence in Cairo, Ruksana's life on the streets of Kolkata, Amina's forced marriage and child birth in Afghanistan, Sokha's work in the trash dumps of Cambodia, Wadley's memories of the 2010 earthquake in Haiti, Senna's struggle for education in the mountains of LaRinconada, Peru, Mariama's experiences at the local radio station in Sierra Leone, and Asmera's resistance to early marriage in Ethiopia. *Girl Rising* shares these stories of violent injustice "to generate solidarity between the [viewer] and the suffering subject" driving the narrative solution of girls' education (Wells, 2013, p. 278). It is in this way, Wells (2013) contends, "the deployment of the melodramatic mode allows visceral identification with a subject whose life is radically different to that of the putative audience of the film… [The mode] invites an identification which might otherwise be withheld" (pp. 278–279). The viewer, upon learning about girls' personal experiences of trauma, is prompted by "the gut feeling that what [they] witnesse[d] is wrong" (Wells, 2013, p. 288); this feeling "forc[es] us to confront the question of what kind of world we want, and [with] whom we stand in solidarity" (Wells, 2013, p. 291). *Girl Rising* then not only highlights the continued violation of girls' human rights around the world, but it also puts a face and name to that violation; it is this shift from invisibility to visibility that lends to the transformative potential of the film itself.

On the other hand, because *Girl Rising* is part of a larger philanthropic initiative, viewers might also be skeptical of the experiential narratives and images of vulnerability projected in the film. Too often Jiwani (2006) states,

> Girls and women of color are seen as victims of infanticide, female genital mutilation, dowry deaths, honor killings and the like. Rarely are these forms of violence situated in comparison with the violence that girls and young women in the West endure. Instead, the focus on culture serves as the explanatory vehicle by which these practices are made sense of. (p. 73)

Narayan (2000) labels this practice the "package picture of culture" where certain practices or experiences singularly define *other* cultures and countries, specifically those outside of the West (p. 1084). This view "represents cultures as if they were entities that exist neatly distinct and separate in the world, independent of our projects of distinguishing among them" (Narayan, 2000, p. 1084). The package picture obscures how structural inequalities like poverty, gender-based violence, colonization, and globalization inform the cultural practices and experiences of those in both the developing *and* developed worlds (Bent, 2013b; Sensoy & Marshall, 2010). It moreover encourages Western viewers to 'save the third world girl' from her "cycle of backwardness… and the [cultural] conditions that do not recognize her potential" without giving consideration for similar acts of violence and injustice experienced in the West, or the role of international policies and politics which maintain structural divisions between the so-called 'west and the rest' in the first place (Sensoy & Marshall, 2010, p. 300; Jiwani, 2006; Mohanty, 2003).

Thus, in the telling of nine stories from nine countries, *Girl Rising* gives a fairly limited understanding of girlhood in their respective countries. For example, we learn that Sokha is a Cambodian orphan who picks through garbage to survive; and we watch her dream of going to school and building a better life. But we learn virtually nothing about her culture, family or community, or the organization that funds her education. The story of Sokha, and indeed the history of Cambodia itself, is instead collapsed into a narrative of singular marginalization – a package picture of culture. According to feminist writer Chimamanda Ngozi Adichie (2009), the danger of this collapse is that,

> It robs people of their dignity. It makes our common humanity difficult. It emphasizes how we are different, rather than how we are similar. (13:58–14:08)

... the single story creates stereotypes, and the problem with stereotypes is not that they are untrue, but that they are incomplete. They make one story become the only story. (13:14–13:24)

Girl Rising produces nine single stories, nine package pictures of culture, and nine limited visions of girlhood in the global south. It encourages viewers to see third world girls as distant *others* waiting for western funds and rescue (Bent, 2013b; Sensoy & Marshall, 2010); and it denies the socio-cultural, geo-political, and historical complexities of their daily lives. It lastly makes the story of poverty, sexual violence, and child marriage *the* singular story of third world girlhood, and in the process, problematically defines their lives against the backdrop of an ahistorical and apolitical message of Western investment.

THE POLITICS OF VOICE: CELEBRITY MEETS GIRL

Standpoint theorists propose to understand marginalized experiences, we must ask questions about the politics of voice: who has the ability to speak, who do they speak for, what do they say, and how is that voice heard? bell hooks (2004) furthermore contends "when the radical voice speaks about domination we are speaking to those who dominate. Their presence changes the nature and direction of our words. [Because] language is also a place of struggle" (p. 154). This struggle is pronounced in the telling and re-telling of girls' stories in mainstream culture. Girls' studies scholars have identified the problematic pathology and division of girls' lives across adult-defined interests (Bent, 2013a; Kirk et al., 2010; Taft, 2014). They note the importance of not only including girls in contemporary research projects, but also "finding ways to ensure that the voices of real girls become central to the project of mapping girlhood" (Kirk et al., 2010, p. 20). As discussed in the previous section, girls from the global south remain overly determined by their socio-cultural and material realities; their lived experiences are collapsed into narratives of universal vulnerability and spectacles of otherness (Projansky, 2014). Kirk et al. (2010) additionally note that despite increased international attention dedicated to the needs of girls living in the developing world,

She herself tends to be a silent figure. She has been photographed for the cover of attractive donor agency publications, been the subject of a number of meetings and conferences, and has been written about in numerous reports and policy briefs. Strategies to promote her educational opportunities, improve her health, and protect her from abuse, early marriage, and genital mutilation have been developed and implemented by a large number of well-intentioned individuals and organizations. Yet in most of these instances, the girl child remains voiceless. She is seen as a passive object suffering a series of interlocking oppressions and discriminations. (p. 21)

Her voice and story are instead coopted for philanthropic purposes (Kirk et al., 2010; Projansky, 2014; Sensoy & Marshall, 2010). Given this practice of silencing, we must examine the discursive function of Hollywood celebrity voices in *Girl Rising*.

The use of celebrities and their voices is not unique to humanitarian campaigns. Chouliaraki (2013) argues that in a relatively short time span the celebrity "has shifted from a 'powerless' elite to become the official communication strategy of the United Nations and global International Non-Governmental Organizations (INGOs), as well as the source of major private initiatives" (p. 78). Celebrity figures performs the moral discourse of humanitarianism, calling western publics to stand in solidarity with so-called "suffering others" through protest, petition or donation (Chouliaraki, 2013, p. 79). In this way, celebrities "use the spectacle of suffering... [to] command the necessary symbolic capital to articulate... the message of suffering as a moving moral plea" (Chouliaraki, 2013, p. 80). The viewer responds in turn to both the familiarity and commerciality of the celebrity brand, as well as the suffering figure in deciding whether to take action. Chouliaraki (2013) attests, "this 'multi-vocality' renders celebrity a complex communicative figure in the humanitarian imaginary" (p. 80); indeed, the celebrity is tasked with "bringing [humanitarian] organizations, sufferers and publics together" while always also maintaining separation between the sufferer and spectator (p. 80).

Girl Rising similarly endeavors to balance the relationship between the suffering other and celebrity in the (re)telling of third world girls' stories; however, I would argue that it problematically and (perhaps inadvertently) functions to silence the same girls it professes to speak on behalf of in the film. For example, the film's narrator (Liam Neeson) explains, the stories featured in the film are the result of several rounds of creative edits between the girl (in some cases several girls), a native writer, and the director of the film. The stories, *Girl Rising* claims "are all based on the lives of real girls whom we have met and spent time with. [They] all contain elements of truth and elements of imagination – both the girls' imagination and the writers'... we put just as much emphasis on emotional truth" (FAQ: Are the stories true, 2014, para. 1). *Girl Rising* tells stories that are not "literal, factual truth... but [the film] certainly isn't pure fiction, either" (FAQ: Is this a documentary, 2014, para. 1). It is this blurred line between fact and fiction which erases the authentic voice of the third world girl; her story and her voice have been likely filtered several times to fit the narrative of the *Girl Rising* campaign. The blurring and (re)telling of girls' stories, Baker (2013) comments, produces "a style of appeal [that] just doesn't sit right. It's well-meaning, but it feels exploitative" (para. 6). *Girl Rising* "turns [girls] into spectacle[s] – visual objects on display" absent and silent in the telling of their own stories (Projansky, 2014, p. 5).

In addition to the questionable authenticity of the film's stories, the use of A-list celebrity voices to tell the girls' stories raises concerns. *Girl Rising* defends the use of celebrities in the fil, stating, "we looked for actors who have great vocal impact, with voices that were appropriate for the stories" (FAQ: How did you choose the actresses, 2014, para. 1). Throughout the film, viewers listen to the likes of Alicia Keys, Anne Hathaway, Kerry Washington, Meryl Streep, Selena Gomez, and Frieda Pinto, but rarely, if ever, do we hear the real voices of girls themselves. *Girl Rising* instead relies on the power of celebrity figures to speak for third world girls and in doing so, "promotes an easy message of effortless efficiency" devoid of socio-cultural and geo-political complexity, yet filled with "the false promise of commodified individualism as a force of social change" (Chouliaraki, 2013, pp. 83–84). Despite the celebrity's ability to bring popular attention to the cause of girls' education, Chouliaraki (2013) warns, celebrities "may stifle the plurality of alternative voices, managing to defuse, drain or even suffocate more radical forms of protest and political mobilization" for girls' human rights (p. 83). Because *Girl Rising* employs celebrity voiccover throughout the film, producers deny viewers the opportunity to hear from the so-called 'suffering other' thereby reinforcing the *spectacularization* of third world girls in mainstream western media (Projansky, 2014).

THE PRODUCTION OF 'CELEBRITIZED' KNOWLEDGE ABOUT THIRD WORLD GIRLHOOD(S)

The purpose of feminist standpoint theory is to produce counter- hegemonic knowledge that resists dominant systems of power. In this space of resistance, standpoint theorists imagine the margins offer "the possibility of radical perspective from which to see and create, to imagine alternatives, [and] new worlds" (hooks, 2004, p. 157). The lived experience of intersectional oppression affords a different vision of hegemonic power. According to Collins (2004), it is the ability to "defin[e] and valu[e] one's consciousness and one's own self-defined standpoint in the face of images that foster a self-definition as the objectified "other" [that resists] the dehumanization essential to systems of domination" (p. 108). Proponents of standpoint theory counter the ways in which the dominant defines and speaks for the other; as hooks (2004) declares

> I am waiting for them to stop talking about the "Other," to stop even describing how important it is to be able to speak about difference... this speech... hid[es the] gaps [and] absences, that space where our words would be if we were speaking, if there were silence, if we were there. (p. 158)

Thus, standpoint theorists highlight not only the radical importance of self-produced knowledge, but they also stress the necessity of the marginalized (and not the dominant) to articulate counter-hegemonic knowledge. What does this expectation mean in the analysis of *Girl Rising* and in particular, in the knowledge produced about third world girls? How does the voice of the center, projected through celebrity narration, determine what we come to know about their lived experiences? And what is left out in the production of 'celebritized' knowledge? Previous sections have considered the package picture of culture and the function of celebrity figures in the (re) telling of girls' stories; this final section investigates the significance of these discursive practices in the production of knowledge about third world girls. I argue *Girl Rising* defines the parameters of third world girlhood against the backdrop of neoliberal girl power (Bent, 2013b; Koffman & Gill, 2013) and Western benevolence (Bent, 2013b; Sensoy & Marshall, 2013), whereas the celebrity concurrently works to make invisible the "complex political realities [that] may necessitate complex solutions" in the girls' education agenda (Chouliaraki, 2013, p. 83). In her analysis of humanitarian campaigns, Chouliaraki (2013) attests the celebrity allows viewers to remain ignorant of broad structural and political forces shaping issues of interest. This erasure of structural systems propels a narrative of Western benevolence, which in the case of *Girl Rising* drives the philanthropic agenda of the film and reinforces neoliberal paradigms based on individual girl power.

Girl Rising markets the power of girls' education in each of the film's vignettes; viewers witness girls' determination and passion to succeed, as well as experience their educational triumphs at the conclusion of the story.

Despite the absence of girls' *actual* voices, *Girl Rising* positions each girl at the center of her story. Girls perform their stories through gesture and facial expressions, and the occasional interaction with family, friends and the community. For the most part, the film follows a similar trajectory to other girls' education campaigns where "girls are 'lifted out' of history and politics to be recast as individual entrepreneurial subjects" (Koffman & Gill, 2013, p. 91). Indeed, whether viewers watch Wadley refuse to leave her Haitian classroom or witness Asmera's escape from forced and early marriage, the film promotes individual girl power in the classroom as *the* solution to global inequality.

According to Bent (2013b), the discourse of individual girl power "encourage[s] girls to take personal responsibility for their successes and their failures," and denies the necessity of girls' familial or communal support systems (p. 11). Switzer (2013) similarly contends "promoting institutional access to formal schooling for adolescent girls... serves neoliberal aims... [which] reify postfeminist female exceptionalism as the singular 'solution' to global poverty" (p. 347). The continued overreliance on individual girls picking themselves up by the bootstraps to change the world places an extraordinary burden on their shoulders. Cobbett (2014) contends moreover that the idea that investing in girls and not boys yields stronger economies legitimizes male irresponsibility and gender essentialism, as well as "take[s] the individual girl as a [singular] unit of analysis, failing to see that individual well-being is relationally constituted" (p. 313). While *Girl Rising* does a better job than other enterprises in including girls' families and communities as players in their stories, the film nevertheless fails to bring those critical relationships into play when promoting girls' education as *the* solution. The film mobilizes instead individual girl power rhetoric, which erases girls' structural support systems in favor of Western benevolent rescue.

Another critique of the girls' education narrative is the way that school is presumed to be a "gender-neutral public good" despite on-going evidence "schools are not always safe spaces for girls, particularly the most vulnerable among them" (Switzer, 2013, p. 355; Kirk et al., 2010; Koffman & Gill, 2013). Cobbett's (2014) research demonstrates "how the stories that are told about girls in order to promote the agenda of girls' schooling serve to silence the voices of girls who have different ambitions" or difficult experiences in schools (p. 314). *Girl Rising* likewise erases the challenges posed by formal schooling; as a result, viewers do not learn about the lack of sanitary facilities for girls at school, schooling expenses from books to uniforms, access to quality education and trained teachers, transportation concerns, or the prevalence of sexual violence and abuse inside the classroom, and on the way to school. The film rather summons an image of latent girl power waiting to be 'unleashed' by supporters 'like you.'

Because of the film's explicit fundraising agenda, the role of the Western viewer cannot be underestimated. The viewer not only witnesses the stories featured in *Girl Rising*, but they also participate actively in the relative success of the message. Operating within post-humanitarian terms, the Western viewer engages in the narcissistic performance of charitable giving through the *Girl Rising* brand; in the process of doing so, Chouliaraki (2013) argues the donor remains driven by self-interest as "the actor and spectator of its own performance" and not only the needs of third world girls (p. 18). The discursive logic of contemporary humanitarianism "ignores the systemic causes of global poverty and turns humanitarianism into a practice of depoliticized" benevolent rescue (Chouliaraki, 2013, p. 9). This practice problematically positions Western viewers as the *true* solution to the problem.

Postcolonial feminist theorists also argue popular representations of the third world tell us more about how the Western subject imagines themselves in the global landscape than it does anything about the third world 'other' (Mohanty, 2003; Narayan 2000; Sensoy & Marshall, 2010). *Girl Rising* "participate[s] in the process of racialization... [as it] seek[s] to save or emancipate 'other' girls" (Sensoy & Marshall, 2010, p. 207). Throughout the film, viewers are reminded of their central and necessary purpose; from the structure of the girls' stories to the use of recognizable Hollywood celebrity voices, and the inclusion of statistical information presented by uniformed schoolgirls representing mythical Western norms, the viewer sits front and center in the story about how they can save the third world girl.

This omnipresence is most clearly evidenced in the concluding sequence of the film where viewers meet Amina, a young Afghani child bride and mother. In her story, Amina struggles against "the embroidered cage" of her burka, which is historically an image of oppression to Western audiences, but at the conclusion of her story, she boldly states, "I will read. I will learn. I will study. I will return to school" as she and several other girls remove their burkas and headscarves, and climb to the top of a mountain as the musical crescendo concludes the film (Robbins et al., 2014, 1:32:51; 1:35:27–1:35:33). The moment illustrates colonial fantasies made real by the Western subject vis-à-vis the veiled woman/girl. In the end, *Girl Rising* appears to maintain that it is always the benevolent charity of the Western viewer that unveils and rescues the third world girl from her differential otherness. And of course, who better to symbolize the urgency of that Western rescue than the veiled Afghani girl waiting to unleash her potential in the global south.

CONCLUDING THOUGHTS

This chapter critically analyzed the feature film *Girl Rising* in the context of feminist standpoint theory. It asked readers to look past *Girl Rising's* feel good sentiment in order to (re)think the absence of socio-cultural, geo-political, and historical complexities, and the over-reliance on individual girl power scripts as *the* solution to global inequalities. It likewise explored the (im)possibilities of hearing the authentic voices of third world girls vis-à-vis celebrity culture, and considered some of the more problematic representations of third world girlhood singularly categorized as experiences of poverty, vulnerability, and violence, or contrastingly absolute individual empowerment. Using feminist standpoint theory, readers investigated the role of the benevolent Western viewer in shaping the film's content and message. The chapter lastly illustrated the limitations of celebrity paradigms for bringing forward girls' *real* voices and stories, calling for more complex representations of third world girlhood(s).

DISCUSSION QUESTIONS

1. According to feminist standpoint theory, how do the margins inform social justice projects?
2. Watch one of the vignettes from *Girl Rising* and consider the following: what is the story that is told? Who tells this story? What role does the girl play in the telling of this story? What are the gaps and absences? And what do we learn about third world girlhood as a result of this story?
3. How does celebrity culture assist and detract from the message of girls' education?
4. In what ways does *Girl Rising* (or other humanitarian campaigns), position third world girls against the image of empowered Western girlhood? What are the consequences of this oppositional positioning?
5. According to Mohanty (2003), global and intersectional analyses "allow us to explain the connections and border crossings better and more accurately; [because] specifying difference allows us to theorize universal concerns more fully" (p. 226). What would *Girl Rising* look like if it took on board the lived experiences of girls in the global south *and* north? What would happen to the message of girls' education?

REFERENCES

Adichie, C. (2009, October 7). *The danger of a single story* [Video file]. Retrieved from http://www.ted.com/talks/chimamanda_adichie_the_danger_of_a_single_story.html

Baker, N. X. (2013, March 21). Film "Girl Rising" has good intentions–But ends up as cinematic chivalry. *Bitch Magazine*. Retrieved from http://bitchmagazine.org/post/film-girl-rising-cinematic-chivalry- review-feminist

Barnes, B. (2013, January 23). Making a film a philanthropic event. *New York Times*. Retrieved from http://carpetbagger.blogs.nytimes.com/2013/01/23/making-a-film-a-philanthropic-event/

Bent, E. (2013a). The boundaries of girls' political participation: A critical exploration of girls' experiences as delegates to the United Nations Commission on the Status of Women (CSW). *Global Studies of Childhood, 3*(2), 173–182.

Bent, E. (2013b). A different girl effect: Producing political girlhoods in the "Invest in Girls" climate. *Sociological Studies of Children and Youth, 16*, 3–20.

Chouliaraki, L. (2013). *The ironic spectator: Solidarity in the age of post-humanitarianism*. Cambridge: Polity Press.

Cobbett, M. (2014). Beyond 'victims' and 'heroines': Constructing 'girlhood' in international development. *Progress in Development Studies, 14*(4), 309–320.

Collins, P. H. (2004). Learning from the outsider within: The sociological significance of Black feminist thought. In S. Harding (Ed.), *The feminist standpoint theory reader: Intellectual and political controversies* (pp. 103–126). New York, NY: Routledge.

Girl Rising. (2014). Retrieved from http://www.girlrising.com

FAQ. (2014). Retrieved from http://www.girlrising.com/faq/

Haraway, D. (1988). Situated knowledges: The science question in feminism and the privilege of partial perspective. *Feminist Studies, 14*(3), 575–599.

Harding, S. (2004). *The feminist standpoint theory reader: Intellectual and political controversies*. New York, NY: Routledge.

Hartsock, N. C. M. (2004). Comment on Hekman's "truth and method: Feminist standpoint theory revisited": Truth or justice? In S. Harding (Ed.), *The feminist standpoint theory reader: Intellectual and political controversies* (pp. 243–246). New York, NY: Routledge.

hooks, b. (2004). Choosing the margin as a space of radical openness. In S. Harding (Ed.), *The feminist standpoint theory reader: Intellectual and political controversies* (pp. 153–159). New York, NY: Routledge.

Horansky, C. (2014, March 14). The story behind Girl Rising, the most powerful film you'll see this year. *Huffington Post*. Retrieved from www.huffingtonpost.com/christine-horansky/the-story-behind-girl-ris_b_4967372.html

Jiwani, Y. (2006). Racialized violence and girls and young women of color. In Y. Jiwani, C. Steenbergen, & C. Mitchelle (Eds.), *Girlhood: Redefining the limits* (pp. 70–88). Montreal, Canada: Black Rose Books.

Kirk, J., Mitchell, C., & Reid-Walsh, J. (2010). Toward political agency for girls: Mapping the discourses of girlhood globally. In J. Helgren & C. A. Vasconcellos (Eds.), *Girlhood: A global history* (pp. 14–29). Piscataway, NJ: Rutgers University Press.

Koffman, O., & Gill, R. (2013). 'The revolution will be led by a 12-year-old-girl': Girl power and global biopolitics. *Feminist Review, 105*, 83–102.

McCall, L. (2005). The complexity of intersectionality. *Signs: Journal of Women in Culture and Society, 30*(3), 1771–1800.

Mohanty, C. T. (2003). *Feminism without borders: Decolonizing theory, practicing solidarity.* Durham, NC: Duke University Press.

Narayan, U. (2000). Undoing the 'Package Picture' of cultures. *Signs: Journal of Women in Culture and Society, 25*(4), 1083–1086.

Projansky, S. (2014). *Spectacular girls: Media fascination & celebrity culture.* New York, NY: New York University Press.

Robbins, R. E, Adams, M., & Yellin, T. (Producers), & Robbins, R. E. (Director). (2014). *Girl Rising.* USA: Cinedigm Entertainment.

Scott, J. (1991). The evidence of experience. *Critical Inquiry, 178*(3), 773–797.

Sensoy, O., & Marshall, E. (2010). Missionary girl power: Saving the 'third world' one girl at a time. *Gender & Education, 22*(3), 295–311.

Switzer, H. (2013). Post-feminist development fables: The girl effect and the production of sexual subjects. *Feminist Theory, 14*(3), 345–360.

Taft, J. K. (2014). The political lives of girls. *Sociology Compass, 8*(3), 259–267.

Wells, K. (2013). The melodrama of being a child: NGO representations of poverty. *Visual Communication, 12*(3), 277–293.

PATRICIA R. BOYD

8. PARADOXES OF POSTFEMINISM

Coercion and Consent in Fifty Shades of Grey

"What I think you fail to realize is that in Dom/sub relationships it is the sub who has all the power. That's you. I'll repeat this – *you* are the one with all the power. Not I" (James, 2011, p. 400). So writes Christian Grey in an email to Anastasia Steele in *Fifty Shades of Grey* (2011). In this email, he is responding to her reaction when he hit her, reassuring her that she is the one who in charge, even though he ties her up, beats her, spanks her, and blindfolds her. Throughout the now famous book written by E.L. James, the main female character, Anastasia, vacillates between feeling empowered by the relationship and afraid of what she sometimes perceives as the abusive, uber-controlling nature of the man she's fallen head-over-heels in love with. She feels empowered when he is overpowering her *and* when she's "in charge" of pleasing him. Throughout the relationship, Anastasia claims to not be submissive, yet gains her own sense of power – her identity as agent – through submitting to Christian's control. Thus, she is empowered by being disempowered through over-the-top renditions of traditional masculine/ feminine roles.

How do we make sense of the conflict that Anastasia feels? How can we interpret the paradox of Anastasia's participation in, identification with, and simultaneous resistance to the BDSM lifestyle that her relationship with Christian Grey demands? It is easy for critics – feminist and otherwise – to denigrate the novel for its representation of women as submissive to men's desires and as being forced into demeaning and uncomfortable roles as evidenced by Anastasia's feeling of being a high-paid prostitute. But this would be an over simplification of the reception and interpretation of the book. There is no easy agreement between critics about the book's impact on the day-to-day lives of the women who read it – and women in general (even ones who haven't read it). Anastasia's own conflicting feelings about the power relationship are echoed in the critics' confusion over how to interpret the book, with extreme voices offering knee-jerk reaction for/against with

© KONINKLIJKE BRILL NV, LEIDEN, 2019 | DOI:10.1163/9789004414259 008 corresponding moderate voices trying to understand *why* so many women readers are so attracted to the story.

The paradoxes found in *Fifty Shades of Grey* (2011) metaphorically represent the ones facing women – particularly young women – in our culture today. While certainly not all women are deciding whether to be in a BDSM relationship, the conflicts Anastasia feels and the critics' competing/contradictory responses to the book highlight the complicated choices that women now make as they navigate a terrain where even various types of feminists are conflicted and quite often opposed to one another. The book and critics' responses emphasize the tension found in a fairly new movement in feminism called postfeminism which is defined by Gill (2007) as a set of sensibilities in which "the notions of autonomy, choice and self-improvement sit side-by-side with surveillance, discipline and the vilification of those who make the 'wrong' choices (become too fat, too thin, or have the audacity or bad judgment to grow older)" (p. 163). Intimately tied to postfeminism is the concept of neoliberalism which highlights that the choices women must make today can easily turn them into consumerist objects who supposedly make "free-will" choices about how to represent themselves and their bodies through a makeover paradigm that encourages them to "buy" a singular yet supposedly unique identity. As Gill (2007) points out, neoliberalism "is understood increasingly as constructing individuals as entrepreneurial actors who are rational, calculating and self-regulating. The individual must bear full responsibility for their life biography, no matter how severe the constraints upon their action" (p. 163). Although there are competing definitions of postfeminism and its intersections with neoliberalism, I argue in this chapter that the most compelling and useful one comes from Gill (2007) who argues that postfeminism is less a body of theory or a reaction to feminisms of old and more a sensibility which emphasizes that through their individual choices and daily practices, women empower (and disempower) themselves, building identities linked to individualistic and consumerist culture. Gill (2007) points out that the key paradox is (as highlighted by Anastasia's character in the book) that women's perceived empowerment often resembles stereotypical behaviors and beliefs that have been ascribed as "appropriately" feminine. This paradox is, for Gill (2007) and others who share her critique, what makes postfeminism distinct from other types of feminism that co-exist with it and have come before it, making postfeminism useful in analyzing the negotiations in which women are currently engaged.

Gill (2007) and others (Brooks, 1997; McRobbie, 2004; Mann, 1994) argue that popular cultural texts are great places to look if we want to understand the material and rhetorical situations in which women find themselves. These texts help us see, through cultural representations, the myriad of material practices that women engage in today and the meaning given to these practices both by the women themselves and by others outside of them. Studying key works in popular culture, then, is an important postfeminist project that goes beyond an academic exercise. As the incredible sales, the ubiquitous hoopla around it, and its designation as a #1 New York Times Best Seller suggest, *Fifty Shades of Grey* (2011) is an important text *and* set of reading practices to study. I hope to show that Gill's (2007) lens of postfeminist sensibilities is the most helpful one use to understand the myriad of responses to the book and what these responses indicate about the choices facing women today.

In this chapter, then, I set out to elucidate the value of using postfeminism sensibilities and their inherent link to neo-liberal individualism to analyze this popular cultural text in order to illustrate the complexities of the choices and identities/agency women engage in/enact today. I use Gill's (2007) definition of postfeminist sensibilities to analyze *Fifty Shades of Grey's* (2011) representation of women's choices and the potential empowerment associated with them. Further, I analyze critics' and readers' responses to *Fifty Shades of Grey* (2011). Doing so helps us understand the importance of using postfeminism to study our current cultural moment in order to determine where to go from here so that women can create empowered identities within the paradoxes in which they are situated.

FIFTY SHADES AND POSTFEMINISM

In six months, *Fifty Shades of Grey* (2011), the first book in a trilogy by E. L. James (first created as a *Twilight* fan fiction blog), sold more copies than the phenomenally successful Harry Potter series. *Fifty Shades of Grey* (2011), which has been turned into a movie to be released in February 2015, has continued to sell quickly and to inspire other consumerist practices like sex shops' "Fifty Shades" packages which include handcuffs and bondage tape along with copies of the book (Martin, 2013). Women are rushing out to buy the book and then talk to their friends about what they have read (Felthouse, 2012, p. 32). The novel follows Anastasia Steele and multi-millionaire Christian Grey as their relationship moves through the typical trials and tribulations found in traditional romance genres – but with the huge difference that their relationship *also* includes significant elements of BDSM, including bondage, whipping, caning, and spanking.

Discussing the significance of the book, Christian (2012) argues that "*Fifty Shades* will, no doubt, be remembered as when *everything* changed" (p. 18). With the book being widely available at big box stores like Costco and Target, BDSM has become more public rather than relegated to sex shops (Fury, 2012), making BDSM practices and popular reading/discussion about them "more socially acceptable" (Felthouse, 2012, p. 32). Midori (2012) argues that "the book has brought the notion of sex toys, whips, bondage, and erotic roleplay into mainstream discourse" (p. 138). Commentators (Harrison & Holm, 2013; Hutcherson, 2012; Martin, 2013; Wright, 2012) are lauding the book precisely because it opens up new – and potentially productive – conversations about sex for both the women reading the book and critics commenting about it. As Wright (2012) argues, the book offers an important shift that suggests that "we need to grow up and be responsible for our own sexual choices, and this national discussion is a good step. Anything that gets people talking about sex – not just sensationalizing it or making fun of it – is a good thing for Americans" (p. 241). Those who value the book contend that people are using the book to explore their sexuality in new and more public ways that are challenging taboos.

Others continue this support for the book, arguing that it gives women "erotic empowerment" and "a new voice for sexual, political and financial choices" (Perkins, 2012, p. 3). Some of those advocates even position the book as a postfeminist treatise that helps women readers "embrace sexual power" which is important, it is argued, "for a woman who wants to be completely powerful" (Kenley, 2012, p. 39). Others have critiqued the book vehemently for what is perceived as an imbalanced power relationship in which physical abuse is seen as "romantic," some suggesting dramatically that the book represents "the end of civilization as we know it" (Perkins, 2012, p. 4). What is clear from the critics' responses and women readers' use/ perceptions of the book is that the book is stirring up discussions about sex.

What is not so clear is the impact the book has on real women's identities and sense of agency. As Midori (2012) argues, the discussions about *Fifty Shades of Grey* revolve around whether or not the books are being used as escapist fantasy or impact women's lived experiences (p. 137). Hutcherson (2012) argues that the book advocates abuse and presents a distorted vision of the BDSM lifestyle. Critics contend that book sets up negative expectations of women's sexual pleasure, suggesting that there is something wrong with a woman if she does not experience an orgasm purely through having her nipples kissed. Some say that the book makes it okay for women to be controlled and traps women (once again) in traditional heterosexual, heteronormative roles – all in the name of having a White Knight take care of them. Others, though, like Bussel (2012), contend that the book is fiction and needs to be treated that way: "*Fifty Shades of Grey* has clearly set the publishing industry on its head, but let's give it credit – or discredit – in concordance with its role as fiction, not as some grand manifesto being obeyed without question" (p. 150).

So, exactly what is the impact(s) of the book on women's lives and choices and how does a study of it help us understand the current state of women's lives in our culture? This is where Gill's (2007) arguments about/ definitions of postfeminism are the most salient in helping us understand the current material and rhetorical conditions that women face in their everyday lives and the contradictory nature of what it means to have agency in our current cultural moment. Gill (2007) writes: "postfeminism is understood best neither as an epistemological perspective nor as an historical shift, nor (simply) as a backlash in which its meanings are pre-specified. Rather, postfeminism should be conceived of as a sensibility" (p. 148). This sensibility "emphasizes the contradictory nature of postfeminist discourses and the entanglements of both feminist and anti-feminist themes within them" (Gill, 2007, p. 149). Thus, by approaching postfeminism as a sensibility instead of a fixed set of theories, we can use it to explore the ways that women are constructed and construct themselves in particular ways *and* make sense of those constructions. Gill (2007) points to several "relatively stable features" that shape postfeminist discourses. She lists them as "femininity is a bodily property; the shift from objectification to subjectification; the emphasis on self-surveillance, monitoring, and discipline; a focus upon individualism, choice, and empowerment; the dominance of the makeover paradigm; a resurgence in ideas of natural sexual difference; a marked sexualization of culture, and an emphasis upon consumerism and the commodification of difference (p. 149). These common themes can help us analyze women's lives and the representations of them that circulate in popular media. Popular media plays a highly significant role in shaping women's conceptions of what is possible, and thus it is important to study as a sort of pulse-point for dominant attitudes and beliefs (and possible attitudes and beliefs, along with preferred attitudes and beliefs). In the next section, I draw on salient elements of Gill's (2007) definition of postfemininist sensibilities to show the importance of studying cultural texts like *Fifty Shades of Grey* (2011) through a postfeminist lens.

FEMININITY AS BODILY PROPERTY/INDIVIDUALISM, CHOICE AND EMPOWERMENT

In the postfemininist sensibility of "Femininity as Bodily Property," women's femininity is perceived as a choice that is freely made as well as a burden that needs to be controlled in order to fit within proscribed definitions. Gill (2007) argues that femininity is supposedly women's property and source of power (p. 149).

In this framework, women own their bodies and make their choices on a free-will basis, but these "free-will" choices are uncannily similar to the dominant norm of what a sexy female body is represented as. "Femininity as Bodily Property" dovetails nicely with the sensibility of "Individualism, Choice, and Empowerment" because the choices women make are seen as their source of empowerment. Daily choices are viewed by many young women as a form political action (Budgeon, 2001; Mann, 1994; Showden, 2009), while some more traditional feminists critique that view as being based in a neoliberal philosophy that problematically leads women away from collective action and toward a focus on consumer choices rather than political action.

In *Fifty Shades of Grey* (2011), Anastasia's relationship to her body reflects these tensions/contradictions. At some points, she insists that her body is her own to make decisions about; yet at other times, it seems that Christian owns and controls her body. The Contract that Christian gives her, which Anastasia never formally signs but nonetheless allows to shape her behavior, lays out the parameters of the Dominant/Submissive relationship that Christian demands, including what and when to eat, how to groom herself, what to wear, how and when to look at Christian, and when and how often to exercise. For instance, it states "the Submissive will keep herself clean and shaved and/or waxed at all times. The Submissive will visit a beauty salon of the Dominant's choosing at times to be decided by the Dominant and undergo whatever treatments the Dominant sees fit" (James, 2011, p. 106). In part, these rules work to discipline an unruly self into a submissive, compliant body/self. But since the Contract insists that both parties consent to the premises, it suggests that Anastasia is freely choosing the objectification through her adherence to the rules, if not her "official" signature. As Gill (2007) argues "in this modernized neoliberal version of femininity, it is absolutely imperative that one's sexual and dating practices be presented as freely chosen" (p. 154), even if these practices give women a false sense of empowerment – as can be seen in Anastasia's resistance to signing the Contract and her occasional rebellion against it.

For the most part, Anastasia abides by the rules. Christian's Contract and his revisions, then, define what a "sexy body" is and shapes Anastasia's own view as well. She makes herself over into that image. At one point when Anastasia is going on a date with Christian, Kate says "We need to make sure you're simply irresistible for this evening" (James, 2011, p. 85) to which Anastasia's subconscious responds "*Oh no*. this sounds like it will be time consuming, humiliating, and painful" (James, 2011, p. 85). The end result of this makeover is described a complete shaved and groomed body that fits with Christian's expectations listed in the Contract. Even though grooming in the way that the Contract, Christian, and society expect her to goes against her grain, Anastasia still falls in line with it, in order to gain the empowerment that is supposed to accompany it. At another point, Anastasia "chooses" to groom herself in a similar manner, putting on make-up even though it "intimidates" her (James, 2011, p. 213). This particular incident shows that Anastasia has internalized the standards because she makes the choices and performs the actions without Kate's urging or help. When Kate sees her wearing make-up, a clingy dress and stiletto heels, she tells Ana that "you scrub up well" and that "you'll have him eating out of your hand" (James, 2011, p. 214). At times, Anastasia is presented as an uninformed, easily molded mind who, while she rebels, ultimately adheres to dominant cultural definitions of what is sexy because she does not have her own concepts of/surety about herself that are strong enough to counter these. In fact, her definitions of self easily fall in alignment with Christian's, and the fact that she pleases him becomes her singular source of power. Whether this perception of power gives her agency or not is left open for interpretation, but the incidents show that Anastasia is trying to find her way in a complicated terrain.

The critics are divided on their interpretations of Anastasia's behaviors in this regard. Ramsland (2012) argues that "Ana is at the center of a narcissistic fantasy that she controls" (p. 219), "getting to feel powerful by bringing a wealthy, creative, and controlling man to his knees" (p. 220). Throughout the book, she is shown to use her femininity (usually presented as a childish or naive girlishness) to change him from the Dark Knight/"fifty shades of fucked up" (James, 2011, p. 269) to a man who complies more easily to heterosexual norms – or "hearts and flowers" as Christian continually refers to them. For example, Anastasia uses her girlishness to control Christian when she puts her hair up in pigtails to protect herself "from Blackbeard" (James, 2011, p. 126). At another point, she uses an assault of kisses to prevent him from beating her (James, 2011, pp. 348–349). So, even though she disciplines herself into a femininity that is traditional and defined externally through Christian's Contract and societal norms, she uses that femininity to work to change Christian into what she wants him to be, which is, in the book, presented as a form of empowerment.

What an analysis of *Fifty Shades of Grey* highlights, then, is that there is not a simplistic definition of women's empowerment and not a singular route to agency for women. When the neo-liberal individual is relied upon, the complexities of identity production is oversimplified, but postfeminist sensibilities of "Femininity as Bodily Property" and "Individualism, Choice, and Empowerment" can help us understand the multiple and sometimes competing discourses about women's "agentic sexuality" (Harris, 2010, p. 123).

SELF-SURVEILLANCE AND DISCIPLINE

Closely linked to "Femininity as Bodily Property" and "Individualism, Choice, and Empowerment" is the postfeminist sensibility of "Self-Surveillance and Discipline." In our current cultural moment, women are asked to constantly discipline themselves so that their choices align with cultural regulations imposed upon them, even as this self-surveillance is supposed to be seen as a freely chosen, personal choice. Women are required to internalize external belief systems. Gill (2007) argues that while self-surveillance has always existed, the current moment is distinctive becaquse of the "increased self-surveillance" that has been extended to "entirely new spheres of life and intimate conduct," including one's interior life (p. 155).

The dialogue between Anastasia's subconscious and inner goddess is evidence of her interior life and the struggle to regulate and transform herself through self-surveillance and discipline. The intensity and ubiquity of the two voices highlight the increased impact of the internalized self-surveillance to which Gill (2007) points. Christian uses technology and his wealth to watch Anastasia and to make her fall into compliance with his wishes, but his surveillance can only go so far; she must internalize his desire for her to act, think, and even feel in certain ways in order for these elements to truly become a central part of her identity. This is where her subconscious and her inner goddess come into play. As Fire (2012) writes, "inside of Ana is the 'subconscious,' who glares at her over her wing-shaped spectacles' judging herself harshly and critically and her 'inner goddess,' who wants to embrace life, dive into new experiences, and find where her passion and pleasure lies (p. 130). Her subconscious is a judgmental voice that represents more traditional values. Putting Anastasia down and trying to force her to control herself and her wayward behavior, her subconscious is presented as a disempowering voice. On the other hand, her inner goddess is the completely adventurous sexpot who can be found stamping her foot impatiently when Anastasia is not making choices that fulfill her inner sexual desires. The inner goddess represents Anastasia's confidence, emphasizing free-will choice and the potential empowerment that is supposed to come with it.

At one point in the novel, Christian presents Anastasia with two choices that echo not only her two inner voices, but the two ends of the continuum of roles women are given in our culture. When asked why he gave her a copy of *Tess of the d'Urbervilles*, Christian answers "It seemed appropriate. I could hold you to some impossibly high ideal like Angel Clare or debase you completely like Alec d'Urberville'" (James, 2011, p. 95), to which Anastasia answers "'If there are only two choices, I'll take the debasement.' I whisper, gazing at him. My subconscious is staring at me in awe" (James, 2011, p. 95). Even though Sands (2012) argues that the inner goddess is the angel and the subconscious is the devil (p. 70), both are parts of societally acceptable femininity, thus the two voices highlight the struggles that women go through in every day life to abide by old expectations of the "good" girl and yet also live up to current male expectations to be "up for it" at all times – the latter image also being conceived of as the source of new feminine power. Both of these parts are required in the contemporary feminine identity in order to fulfill the dominant expectations of femininity in the culture, but women must continually use self-surveillance and discipline to find and maintain a balance between the two. Women must be sexy but not too sexy, in control of their bodies yet out of control enough in order to do things that men want them to, and innocent enough to not be slutty. They must be hyper-vigilant about being desirous but not being too desirous. It is clear, as Gill (2007) points out, self-surveillance and discipline now relate to many areas of intimate and public life for women.

Critics are once again conflicted in their interpretations of Anastasia's behaviors in *Fifty Shades of Grey* (2011). Levkoff (2012) praises the book for its embracing of women's sexuality, which has not always been accepted in culture:

Our fantasy lives, our personal lives, the things innately ours, have become pathologized, politicized, and publicly demonized. Our culture can't handle women who own (and embrace) their sexuality. It hasn't been too kind to women who want sex (or merely want to talk about it). We have a word for them: 'sluts'. (Levkoff, 2012, p. 360)

Anastasia's subconscious buys into this cultural view of women who want sex, calling herself a "'ho'" while her inner goddess acknowledges her sexual desire for Christian (James, 2011, p. 145). Countering such judgments, though, Levkoff (2012) argues that our inner goddesses are crucial because "we need to remember that we are more than just someone's spouse or mother. We have names; we are sex goddesses. We are definitely not sluts" (Levkoff, 2012, p. 362). She argues, therefore, that Anastasia's inner goddess – and the conversations that *Fifty Shades of Grey* (2011) has inspired amongst women readers – are empowering because it reminds women of the importance of their sexual natures and their own identities outside of their relationships to others, suggesting that they "own" their sexuality outside of the power relationships that sex occurs within. Further, Frampton (2012) asks "who wouldn't be better with a little more inner goddess waving pom-poms in her brain?" (p. 277). Self-surveillance, then, becomes for Levkoff (2012) and Frampton (2012) not a disempowering practice but one that ensures women are meeting their own sexual needs – as Anastasia's inner goddess advocates.

Others, however, suggest that the "up for it" sexuality that is inherent in work like *Fifty Shades of Grey* (2011) gives only an illusion of control. Harris (2010) argues that "contemporary up for it" female sexuality subjectivities" may seem to empower but actually require women to internalize "regimes of disciplinary power" through embracing notions of neoliberal individualism that imply choice but do so within limited narratives of what is possible (p. 116). In other words, it may seem as if women are choosing their own sexual freedom, but they are actually making their lives knowable through dominant narratives that limit their choices (Harris, 2010, p. 116). Thus, as Gill (2007) emphasizes, they are disciplining their selves through constant surveillance to make sure they align themselves with cultural norms about femininity, but simultaneously perceive it as free-will choice. These conflicting interpretations highlight the paradoxes that women now face in the current cultural moment, paradoxes that must be brought to light and questioned if women are to find agency for themselves in the milieu in which they find themselves.

SEXUALIZATION OF CULTURE

One final postfeminist sensibility that is important to highlight is the "Sexualization of Culture." *Fifty Shades of Grey* (2011) represents porn culture made popular. No longer are books with significant BDSM elements relegated to seedy, wrong-side-of-town kinds of stores. Instead, women are reading the book in checkout lines at the grocery store and are openly talking about sexual issues that were once considered non-mainstream and even deviant (Day, 2012, p. 29). The book represents an opening of the discourse about sex in our culture, but critics have multiple interpretations of the effect of this. As Hutcherson (2012) argues that *Fifty Shades of Grey* "has single-handedly given millions of women permission to explore erotica, get in touch with their inner sexpot, and try new ways to heat up the bedroom with their partners" (p. 109). Some argue that the representation of BDSM in the book is empowering, with BDSM being presented as a way "to play with both gender and power in creative, intelligent ways" (Bussel, 2012, p. 147). Midori (2012) likewise argues that "the book has brought the notion of sex toys, whips, bondage, and erotic roleplay into mainstream" (p. 138) which is a good thing, according to her, because it helps to improve people's sex lives (p. 140). BDSM has now become more mainstream, allowing people more freedom and choices without feeling shame. In fact, Graham (2012) argues that the book is so popular because "it encourages freedom of expression" (p. 135).

Yet, there are problems with the way the sexuality is represented in the book. Although seeing benefits in the book, Hutcherson (2012) also points out limits, suggesting that it is problematic to present that women should be able to have orgasms at the command of their partners. She further argues that the representation of BDSM in the book is problematic likewise because it is tied to Christian's controlling nature. BDSM is not necessarily centered on the kind of uber-control, stalking, abusive behavior that Christian displays. Hutcherson (2012) points out that "Anastasia allows Christian to abuse her emotionally and physically. She does not give consent to the spankings she receives, so this is not BDSM play, but abuse. She allows herself to be treated poorly by this man simply because she doesn't want to lose him. What a poor message to send to young female readers" (p. 112). Armintrout (2012) argues that one of the most worrying messages of the book is that "being completely dominated and controlled by a man is a natural part of a mature relationship" (p. 86). Armintrout (2012) contends that if a friend or sister of ours was dating someone like Christian, we might not be so quick to think he was the perfect man; instead, we might feel compelled to call the police and report his behavior (p. 89). She asks, when considering the full range of Christian's behaviors, "do you pick up the vibrator and fantasize about him, or do you pick up the phone and call the police?" (p. 89).

As Sanzo (2012) asks, "Right now millions of housewives are questioning their own reactions (irrational or otherwise) to Christian Grey. *Why do we love this guy so much?*" (p. 62). When female readers and critics alike try to answer this question and determine why *Fifty Shades of Grey* (2011) is so attractive to female readers, many of them arrive at a similar reasoning: Christian Grey is a modernized, sexualized version of the Bryonic hero. His is a hypersexualized version of Mr. Rochester in *Jane Eyre*, Rhett Butler in *Gone with the Wind*, Mr. Darcy *in Pride and Prejudice,* and Heathcliff in *Wuthering Heights* (Sanzo 2012). So, these critics are arguing that the sexualization of culture that is represented in romance novels is nothing new in the porn erotica that is now so popular, even though what is discussed/ presented has been upped a notch. The "extraordinary proliferation of discourses about sex and sexuality across all media forms" (Gill, 2007, p. 163), then, is a sign that previous trend are both continuing and advancing as what is being discussed is expanding in an increasingly sexualized culture. While this might empower women through offering them more choices, it may also cause them to be more objectified. It is important, thus, to study the ways these paradoxes work in women's daily lives.

CONCLUSION

So what can we learn from using Gill's (2007) postfeminist sensibilities – and their relationship to neoliberalism – to study *Fifty Shades of Grey* (2011)? Postfeminism highlights for us the complexity of the current cultural moment for women. It's important to consider the multiplicity of options/discourses that are both feminist and anti-feminist (Gill, 2007). Instead of seeing women who "engage in the sexualization of culture as either cultural dupes (as a form of false consciousness) or agentic sexuality" (Harris, 2010, p. 116), we need to "engage with the complex and contradictory nature of discourses around contemporary active female sexuality" (Harris, 2010, p. 116). What this quote highlights is that we need to avoid simplistic interpretations of women's choices and the impact of those choices. Any given choice may have multiple consequences, including both empowerment and disempowerment. And depending on the context, a choice that can be empowering in one context can be disempowering in another. So, postfeminist sensibilities in and of themselves are not either good nor bad; instead, they index the complexities that women face as they navigate the current terrain. When neoliberalism is added to/intersects with postfeminism, though, the choices are more limited by an overemphasize on free-will over the limitations that cultural constructs place on choices.

Fifty Shades of Grey (2011) illustrates that there are multiple versions of "agentic femininity," as Harris (2010) puts it: "In noting the multiple forms of sexually agentic femininity we recognize that cultural discourses are not monolithic and uniform. They are instead composed of varying discourses. These discourses shift in meaning, produce multiple readings and are intertextual in their relationships with other discourses and in the production of new ones" (Harris, 2010, p. 123). The conflict that Anastasia feels about the relationship and the critics' multiple interpretations of the book and its impact on women in our culture illustrate that there are indeed multiple discourses about sexual agency in circulation currently. Using Gill's (2007) postfeminist sensibilities as an analytic perspective (p. 148) helps us understand those competing and multiple discourses as they operate in one text that has had a large cultural impact.

DISCUSSION QUESTIONS

1. Consider how fan-fiction can be a form of empowerment for women. Why is this an outlet women enjoy?
2. What are other novels or characters from novels which take on a postfeminist agenda? How do you know this?
3. How can postfeminism be exemplified in other forms of pop culture such as movies, music etc?

REFERENCES

Armintrout, J. (2012). Every breath you take. In L. Perkins (Ed.), *Fifty writers on fifty shades of grey* (pp. 81–90). Dallas, TX: BenBella Books.

Brooks, A. (1997) *Postfeminisms: Feminism, cultural theory and cultural forms.* London: Routledge.

Budgeon, S. (2001). Emergent feminist identities. *European Journal of Women's Studies, 8*(1), 7 28.

Burkett, M., & Hamilton, K. (2012). Postfeminist sexual agency: Young women's negotiations of sexual consent. *Sexualities, 15*(7), 815–833.

Bussel, R. K. (2012). Kink and condescension: Fifty shades of BDSM backlash. In L. Perkins (Ed.), *Fifty writers on fifty shades of grey* (pp. 145–151). Dallas, TX: BenBella Books.

Christian, M. (2012). The game changer. In L. Perkins (Ed.), *Fifty writers on fifty shades of grey* (pp. 17–26). Dallas, TX: BenBella Books.

Day, S. (2012). The brown paper bag. In L. Perkins (Ed.), *Fifty writers on fifty shades of grey* (pp. 27–30). Dallas, TX: BenBella Books.

Evans, A., Riley, S., & Shankar, A. (2010). Technologies of sexiness: Theorizing women's engagement in the sexualization of culture. *Feminism and Psychology, 20*(1), 114–131.

Felthouse, L. (2012). Label, schmabels, I'll take the publicity! In L. Perkins (Ed.), *Fifty writers on fifty shades of grey* (pp. 31–35). Dallas, TX: BenBella Books.

Fire, S. (2012). Sexual empowerment at the water cooler. In L. Perkins (Ed.), *Fifty writers on fifty shades of grey* (pp. 127–131). Dallas, TX: BenBella Books.

Frampton, M. (2012). My inner goddess. In L. Perkins (Ed.), *Fifty writers on fifty shades of grey* (pp. 273–278). Dallas, TX: BenBella Books.

Gill, R. (2007). Postfeminist media culture: Elements of a sensibility. *European Journal of Cultural Studies, 10*(2), 147–166.

Graham, H. (2012). Fifty shades of women. In L. Perkins (Ed.), *Fifty writers on fifty shades of grey* (pp. 133–136). Dallas, TX: BenBella Books.

Gresh, L. (2012). The McDonald's of lust. In L. Perkins (Ed.), *Fifty writers on fifty shades of grey* (pp. 115–119). Dallas, TX: BenBella Books.

Gwynne, J. (2011). "Baby, I'm not quite finished yet": Postfeminism and the negotiation of sexual boundaries in the contemporary erotic memoir. *Journal of Gender Studies, 20*(4), 371–381.

Harris, A. (2010). Mind the gap: Attitudes and emergent feminist politics since the third-wave. *Australian Feminist Studies, 25*(66), 475–484.

Harrison, K., & Holm, L. (2013). Exploring grey zones and blind spots in the binaries and boundaries of E.L. James' fifty shades Trilogy. *Feminist Media Studies, 13*(3), 558–562.

Hutcherson, H. (2012). Fifty ways of looking at sex in fifty shades. In L. Perkins (Ed.), *Fifty writers on fifty shades of grey* (pp. 109–113). Dallas, TX: BenBella Books.

James, E. L. (2011). *Fifty shades of grey*. New York, NY: Vintage Books.

Levkoff, L. (2012). The professional poster child. In L. Perkins (Ed.), *Fifty writers on fifty shades of grey* (pp. 357–362). Dallas, TX: BenBella Books.

Love, S. (2012). Whose shades of grey? In L. Perkins (Ed.), *Fifty writers on fifty shades of grey* (pp. 221–226). Dallas, TX: BenBella Books.

Mann, P. (1994). *MicroPolitics: Agency in a postfeminist era*. Minneapolis, MI: University of Minnesota Press.

Martin, A. (2013). Fifty shades of sex shop: Sexual fantasy for sale. *Sexualities, 16*(8), 980–984.

McRobbie, A. (2004). Postfeminism and popular culture. *Feminist Media Studies, 4*(3), 255–264.

Midori. (2012). Fifty shades of snark. In L. Perkins (Ed.), *Fifty writers on fifty shades of grey* (pp. 137–141). Dallas, TX: BenBella Books.

Perkins, L. (2012). Introduction: Fifty ways to look at fifty shades. In L. Perkins (Ed.), *Fifty writers on fifty shades of grey* (pp. 1–4). Dallas, TX: BenBella Books.

Ramsland, K. (2012). Being stretched: The risks and riches of a "Limit-Experience." In L. Perkins (Ed.), *Fifty writers on fifty shades of grey* (pp. 213–220). Dallas, TX: BenBella Books.

Rose, M. J. (2012). Between the covers. In L. Perkins (Ed.), *Fifty writers on fifty shades of grey* (pp. 7–11). Dallas, TX: BenBella Books.

Sanzo, J. (2012). The byronic hero archetype and Christian Grey: Why America's favorite sadist is nothing new. In L. Perkins (Ed.), *Fifty writers on fifty shades of grey* (pp. 57–66). Dallas, TX: BenBella Books.

Satyal, R. (2012). Crass is in session. In L. Perkins (Ed.), *Fifty writers on fifty shades of grey* (pp. 121–125). Dallas, TX: BenBella Books.

Showden, C. (2009). What's political about the new feminisms? *Frontiers, 30*(2), 166–198.

Tsaros, A. (2013). Consensual non-consent: Comparing E.L. James' fifty shades of grey and Pauline Reage's story of O. *Sexualities, 16*(8), 864–879.

Wright, S. (2012). Fifty shades of sexual freedom. In L. Perkins (Ed.), *Fifty writers on fifty shades of grey* (pp. 237–241). Dallas, TX: BenBella Books.

JENN BRANDT AND SAM KIZER

9. FROM STREET TO TWEET

Popular Culture and Feminist Activism

The 2017 Women's March (also known as the Women's March on Washington), which took place worldwide on January 17, 2017, was the largest single-day protest in U.S. history. The 2017 march, along with its subsequent marches and other social protests such as the #MeToo Movement, have thrust feminism and activism into an international spotlight. As a *movement* for social, political, and economic gender equity and justice, feminism is inherently activist in nature. Although activism has become more mainstream in recent years, for many, the word "activist" conjures up many of the same stereotypes associated with "feminist": shrill, radical, and outside the bounds of what is acceptable. Whether marching with picket signs, chained to buildings, or hugging trees, the *idea* of the activist (and feminist) put forth by popular culture is often one of extremes. Even more favorable representations are often seen as the brunt of the joke, overeager, or with their judgment clouded by their earnestness. In reality, however, most people have had some experience with activism, whether it be signing a petition, taking a stand on an issue, or even simply calling someone out on a racist or sexist joke. This chapter will explore the "everyday activism" of feminism, focusing specifically on digital feminisms, social media, and the role of the Internet in contemporary feminist thought.

THE "FIRST WAVE" AND ORIGINS OF FEMINIST ACTIVISM

Feminism's history of social justice and activism originated with the "woman's rights" movement (which is ofter referred to as the first wave of feminism) and its connection to the Abolitionist Movement. Early U.S. feminists, such as Elizabeth Cady Stanton, Susan B. Anthony, Lucretia Mott, and Sojourner Truth, were concerned about social inequalities, the dynamics of race and gender, and the legal status of women under the law. Alongside the fight to end slavery was a desire to improve women's social status, particularly in relation to contract rights associated with marriage

© KONINKLIJKE BRILL NV, LEIDEN, 2019 | DOI:10.1163/9789004414259_009

and property laws. A defining moment of this movement was the Seneca Falls Convention of 1848, which resulted in, among other things, Stanton's "Declaration of Sentiments and Resolutions." Using the form of the "Declaration of Independence" as its basis, the "Declaration of Sentiments and Resolutions" demands that women have "all the rights and privileges which belong to them as citizens" of the United States. In closing, Stanton acknowledges the challenge ahead, writing,

> In entering upon the great work before us, we anticipate no small amount of misconception, misrepresentation, and ridicule; but we shall use every instrumentality within our power to effect our object. We shall employ agents, circulate tracts, petition the State and national Legislatures, and endeavor to enlist the pulpit and the press in our behalf. We hope this Convention will be followed by a series of Conventions, embracing every part of the country. (1997, pp. 80–81)

Stanton's "Declaration of Sentiments" not only articulates the goals and aims of the women's rights movement, but also laid the groundwork for the inclusion of activism in the very foundation of feminist theory. The efforts of these early activists would eventually result in the Nineteenth Amendment to the U.S. Constitution, which granted women the right to vote in 1920.

"CONCIOUSNESS-RAISING" AND ACTIVISM IN THE SECOND WAVE OF FEMINISM

Many of the popular representations and misconceptions we have today of activism and feminism come from what is considered the start of the second wave in the U.S. in the 1960s. Under the banner of "the personal is political," second wave feminist groups like New York Radical Women and Redstockings organized "consciousness-raising groups" to mobilize women in an active critique and response to existing power structures and institutions. These informal groups gave rise to the organized protests, marches, and sit-ins that became visible markers of the "women's liberation" era of the 1960s and 1970s. During this time there was a deep divide in the feminist movement, between those who would come to be known as "liberal feminists" (affiliated with groups such as the National Organization of Women (NOW) and the National Women's Political Caucus (NWPC), and their more "radical" sisters. Whereas liberal feminists aimed to seek reform within existing power structures – fighting anti-discrimination laws, lobbying to get more women into elected positions – radical feminists felt the best plan of action was not to bring forth change from *within* the system, but to take down the system itself. While the word "radical" would come to be associated with fringe and/or extreme viewpoints, the women originally identified with the word's etymological origin "root," with an emphasis on grass-roots activism and getting at the "root" of the problem. At its core, grass-roots activism is local in nature, with individuals and communities banding together to work toward a common goal.

A key component of second wave feminism was the use of consciousness-raising (CR) as a platform for activism. The goal of consciousness-raising was to use women's lived experiences as the foundation for radical thinking and radical action. As "an ongoing and continuing source of theory and ideas for action," Kathie Sarachild (1973) argued consciousness-raising was "both a method for arriving at the truth and a means for action and organizing. It was a means for the organizers themselves to make an analysis of the situation, and also a means to be used by the people they were organizing and who were in turn organizing more people" (pp. 148–149). An understanding of the origin of consciousness-raising is important, as it speaks to both the strength and weakness of second wave feminist activism.

Part of what made consciousness-raising so "radical," Sarachild argued, was not only its emphasis on women's lived experiences, but that it did not depend upon immediate results. Thinking and action, Sarachild stressed, should not be limited to "that which we can do immediately. Action must be taken, but often it must be planned – and delayed" (p. 150). While stressing forethought is certainly prudent, the lack of immediate action coupled with the spread of consciousness-raising into "women's groups," meant that much of the political aims and content began to disappear as time went on. The more "mainstream" consciousness-raising became, group organizing took a back seat to individual therapy. Although this shift may seem subtle, the implications were much greater; as "women's liberation" become "personal freedom," the locus of change became less about radical, political action and more about individual change and choice.

"BECOMING THE THIRD WAVE"

A brief history of second wave feminism and consciousness-raising is necessary, as it is a useful lens through which to view contemporary feminist activism and its relationship to social media and the Internet. In both instances, the two rely on a model of collective rhetoric, where, "the collaborative interaction of many voices creates new meanings for individuals' experiences"

(Dubriwny, 2005, p. 398) and, in turn, gives those "individual experiences new meanings by moving them into the realm of social reality" (p. 401). With each, there is an emphasis on individual experience translating into larger, more collective action. This understanding of a need for action was a large factor in the impetus and articulation of a "third wave" of feminism. In her landmark article "Becoming the Third Wave" (1991), Rebecca Walker writes, "I connect with my own feelings of powerlessness. I realize that I must undergo a transformation if I am truly committed to women's empowerment. My anger and awareness must translate into tangible action" (p. 87). She goes on to say that we must, "understand power structures with the intention of challenging them" and turn "outrage into political power" (p. 87). With this call to action, Walker ends her piece declaring a new wave of feminism – the third wave.

In its early years, third wave feminism's emphasis on personal empowerment was distorted through the 1990's popular culture of "girl power," which resulted in the media's emphasis on "personal choice," as opposed to political change. In many ways this emphasis on "girl power" – defined by 1990's popular culture most notably through the British pop group the Spice Girls – was in response to the Riot Grrrl movement that emerged in the Pacific Northwest in the early 1990s. Growing out of the punk movement and music scene, Riot Grrrl was in many ways a descendent of the consciousness-raising and radical feminism of the second wave. The culture was one of creativity and DIY – with music, zines, and a style that focused on women's empowerment, rebelling against negative stereotypes of women and femininity, calling out sexism, and speaking out about sexual assault.

Along with Walker's piece and the Riot Grrrl movement, Jennifer Baumgardner and Amy Richards' *Manifesta: young women, feminism, and the future* (2000) and *Grassroots: A Field Guide For Feminist Activism* (2005) came to define the third wave of feminism and to articulate its continued emphasis on activism. As Baumgardner and Richards explain, "A regular women becomes an activist when she rights some glaring human mistake, or recognizes a positive model of equality and takes the opportunity to build on it" (p. 282). They go on to add, though, that undirected action alone is not enough to lead to tangible outcomes or success, rather, "clear intention, a realistic plan, and an identifiable constituency distinguish political activism from random acts" (p. 295). Their activist outline for intention, planning, and community is important, and has particular relevancy to contemporary feminist activism and its relationship to social media and the Internet.

DIGITAL FEMINISMS

The commercial growth and popularity of the Internet occurred simultaneously with the development of the third wave. While the initial goal of tech-savvy feminists was to get more women on the web, more recently the focus has been on the connectivity and potential for intersections of women, feminism, and the Internet. When Marianne Schnall registered the domain name "Feminist.com" in 1994, only 15% of Internet users were women. As an online site for feminist resources, connectivity, and information, both the site and the Internet introduced feminist resources to individuals who were not intentionally searching for "feminism" or "activism." Users got "the chance to grasp their connection to feminism without first having to confront and overcome their biases against it," contends Amy Richards, who authored the site's original "Ask Amy" column. "The process itself demystifies feminism" (p. 521). Perhaps even more importantly, though, the "Internet makes it easy to become informed, active, *heard*, to feel part of the political process rather than passive victims of it" (Richards, 2003, p. 521). Reflecting specifically on the activist potential of the Internet, researcher Laura Illia (2003) argues that, "Cyberactivism grows around issues selected through the interconnection of many kinds of players: traditional pressure groups that go online, spontaneous aggregation, and individuals" (p. 327). This mixture of participants reflects Richards's assertion that the Internet has the potential to bring people to feminism and activism without their initial intention toward these directions. The interconnectedness of these groups creates what Illia refers to as an "immediate and spontaneous network of relationships" that operates on local, national, and global levels (p. 326). This allows participants to shift back and forth between online and offline activism across geographic lines in real time.

As a result, "cyberfeminism" has emerged to refer to online and digital activities that explicitly support issues of gender awareness and/or an active engagement with feminist politics. As Jessie Daniels (2009) notes, however, "Cyberfeminism is neither a single theory nor a feminist movement with a clearly articulated political agenda. Rather, 'cyberfeminism' refers to a range of theories, debates, and practices about the relationship between gender and digital culture" (p. 102). Just as it would be irresponsible to think of terms such as "woman," "man," or "gender" as monolithic categories, it is important to note that it is negligent to think of cyberfeminism as a uniform movement. Hence the standard acceptance of the term "cyberfeminisms," or more recently, digital feminisms. This is particularly true when one considers the vastly different ways in which individuals are using digital media, social networking, and the Internet for both personal and political ends. When looking at the trajectory of feminism, we can see the ways in which the Internet has transformed consciousness-raising and other forms of activism.

The greater exposure of women's issues and feminist concerns via the Internet and digital media has resulted in an increased argument for a fourth wave of feminism. For example, Kira Cochrane (2013), author of the book *All the Rebel Women: The rise of the fourth wave of feminism*, situates and defines the fourth wave through online activism. She writes:

> This movement follows the first-wave campaign for votes for women, which reached its height 100 years ago, the second wave women's liberation movement that blazed through the 1970s and 80s, and the third wave declared by Rebecca Walker, Alice Walker's daughter, and others, in the early 1990s. That shift from second to third wave took many important forms, but often felt broadly generational, with women defining their work as distinct from their mothers'. What's happening now feels like something new again. It's defined by technology: tools that are allowing women to build a strong, popular, reactive movement online.

Although Cochrane articulates a fourth wave defined by technology, many feminists reject the wave metaphor entirely, finding it outdated; essentialist; and/or too heavily tied to white, academic notions of feminism. Instead, they embrace digital feminisms as a more inclusive term to discuss the intersections of contemporary feminism and digital media. While online spaces continue to serve as a means to bring exposure to feminist concerns and coordinate activism, digital feminism also stresses an increased visibility for marginalized communities, while bringing greater exposure to these issues to individuals who occupy more privileged spaces.

Therefore, through social media, activism has become more accessible than ever before, as the Internet has created a space for social justice to permeate popular culture. As a tool for activism, the Internet not only brings feminist concerns to the public's attention, but also encourages and supports mediated discourse regarding issues exploring the intersections of gender, race, class, and sexuality. What follows is a discussion of two of the most popular platforms of social media – Facebook and Twitter – and a demonstration of how the Internet has made feminist activism a part of popular culture and people's everyday lives.

DIGITAL FEMINISMS AND FACEBOOK

Founded in 2004, Facebook's current mission is to "share and make the world more open and connected" giving people an opportunity to "express what matters to them" (2014). Indeed, with more than one billion active users, this mission is certainly being realized in a social media giant that far surpasses its humble beginnings at Harvard University. While the site originally functioned as a "Hot or Not" dating and ratings site for Harvard students, it quickly expanded its form and function as it spread to other colleges, universities, and individuals with a student email address, before eventually being available to anyone over the age of thirteen. Mark Zuckerberg's Facebook has completely permeated popular culture; people have the ability to communicate in ways never dreamed of just a decade ago. Today individuals, businesses, celebrities, politicians, organizations, and just about anything or anyone you can think of has a Facebook page, creating an intermingling of personal experiences and professional interests that is all but inescapable.

When considering the potential for feminist activism with respect to social media, it is important to remember that, "any piece of technology reflects implicit assumptions of the people/business that designed it, along with the explicit design/ commercial goals of the product" (Harquail, 2010). Facebook, in particular, reflects this caution. From criticisms that its algorithms filter which posts and news its users see, to the Cambridge Analytica scandal that brought light to ways in which users' private information and data is being sold, to "fake news" and reports of Russia using Facebook to interfere with the 2016 elections, Facebook has come under increased scrutiny from users and the government alike. That being said, despite its initial intentions and current corporate status, Facebook has also developed in ways that allows users to organize around a cause, raise awareness, and voice political concerns. Stand-alone pages such as "Pop Culture Feminism" use Facebook as a vehicle to create conversations about media representations of gender, whereas other groups use Facebook in tandem with additional online platforms and to supplement face-to-face interaction. Organizations such as the Rape, Abuse, & Incest National Network (RAINN), the Gay and Lesbian Alliance Against Defamation (GLAAD), the National Organization of Women (NOW) all have active Facebook pages with lively forums and infographics that users can share on their own pages. The "sharing" connects individuals and organizations that might not otherwise come into contact, spreading both the organizations' reach and the potential for activism.

145

In 2018, Facebook launched a Breaking News interface on its platform, allowing users to quickly access news about events around the world in real time. Video content, from both anchor desks and reporters on the ground; comments; and viewer interaction became seamlessly integrated with mobile technology and could be updated rapidly. Individual users and organizations alike can now share breaking news stories to their pages which creates multiple channels for community engagement, a key tenet of feminist activism. Perhaps most important is that the breaking news feature covers everything from local to international stories, thus making clear that critical global events are not confined to the United States. A major downside to this platform, though, is that the news organizations themselves get to determine what is and is not "breaking" news; in other words, what is deemed important and worthy of immediate attention is decided by media producers who might not have the interests of the larger population in mind. Feminist news organizations such as Bitch Media and Women's Media Center are usually quick to highlight this discrepancy and expand upon the breaking news stories Facebook covers, offering a launching point for individuals and activist groups to engage with the content. Breaking News has greatly enhanced both the breadth and depth of knowledge surrounding current events while simultaneously opening up new, interconnected avenues for feminists to engage in conversations about how to best approach these happenings.

One of the earliest tests of Facebook Breaking News' effectiveness and of its potential for feminist activism occurred shortly after its launch. Hurricane Florence made landfall on September 14, 2018, causing statewide flooding in North Carolina (at least two dozen flooding records were broken) and widespread destruction of property and infrastructure. The storm stalled over the area for a week, augmenting the already incredible impacts. It was the aftermath, though, that truly showcased the storm's power: due to standing floodwater, mosquitos the size of half-dollar coins swarmed cities, agricultural and sewage waste infiltrated the drinking water supply, and tens of thousands of residents were left without housing (Beitsch, 2018; Golgowski, 2018). Facebook Breaking News not only made the sharing of information and aid easily accessible, but also opened an effective avenue for feminists to organize around social issues the hurricane brought to light, particularly the intersections of racism and environment. Activists took to Facebook to point out how many impacted communities were rural farming towns with predominantly poor Black and Latinx populations. Furthermore, these towns are disproportionately impacted by environmental deregulation, often being "dumping grounds" for agricultural and industrial waste that are not permitted in the wealthy white cities (Richardson, 2018). U.S. Immigration and Customs Enforcement targeted these regions after the storm, specifically attempting to harass and arrest Latinx people without work visas who were seeking shelter (Richardson, 2018).

The geographic terrain that Florence impacted is also a deeply political one, with the lives and livelihoods of poor people of color caught in the crosshairs of state policy and global climate change, and the conversations surrounding these politics on Facebook led to the creation of the A Just Florence Recovery coalition. The coalition is a network of hundreds of advocacy and activist groups in North Carolina who collaborate to provide aid, foster community building, and offer access to hurricane relief resources. Since September 2018, they have hosted news conferences and summits where storm survivors can meet with organization leadership and state legislators, and even established a volunteer network to help displaced families find shelter, food, and transportation. Facebook remains a primary platform through which the coalition's many groups can network, broadcast their meetings, and reach people in need of their resources. All of these direct, tangible responses to disaster developed out of engaging with Facebook Breaking News stories about the hurricane, highlighting that airing frustration and fear online can indeed translate into material action on the ground.

Ignoring the ethical implications of Facebook itself (if you post it, they own it) and disregarding Mark Zuckerberg's and the site's characterizations in *The Social Network*, it is no question that Facebook has changed the way mediated communication occurs, and feminist consciousness-raising is responding accordingly, although not without lingering pitfalls. As has been observed, "Many technologies can be co-opted so that they facilitate unintended purposes. Truly revolutionary technology has social justice and liberation built in" (Harquail, 2010). Still, the ease of accessing and posting information on Facebook makes it an obvious choice for feminist-oriented users to raise the consciousness of others; no part of popular culture goes undiscussed, and in turn, Facebook users are actually engaging in a large-scale cultural critique in hopes of achieving greater social justice.

DIGITAL FEMINISMS AND TWITTER

Twitter founder Jack Dorsey's first tweet was sent out in 2006, but it was not until the 2007 South by Southwest Interactive festival that Twitter established itself as one of the most innovative social media platforms. Prior to this point, Twitter went largely unnoticed, as its few users at the time did not realize its potential on mobile networks; at the festival, however, the creators demonstrated those capacities and Twitter's popularity and usage exploded. The ability to "live tweet" events, in particular, proved particularly noteworthy, and attendees at the festival were able to immediately post content for all other users to see. Through this, festivalgoers could organize meetups and engage in dialogue with other folk and event organizers; this was even further enhanced when hashtags were introduced later that year, making it even easier for users to track Twitter activity during an event, or related to a specific cause or popular culture topic. This innovation laid the groundwork for immediate, rapid-response communication, which proved incredibly beneficial to organizing collective action.

Twitter was in 2007, and still is now, the premier mainstream microblogging service through which users can post snippets of information and rapidly share it with their network of followers. Content spreads rapidly, and with 78% of users actively tweeting from their mobile devices, much of the information is posted long before other mediums, even Facebook, get ahold of it. With such technology, feminists have realized Twitter's potential as a consciousness-raising agent, especially in the sense that popular culture and feminist activism can be merged instantly at ones fingertips. The 2012 controversy between Susan G. Komen for the Cure (formerly known as The Susan G. Komen Breast Cancer Foundation) and Planned Parenthood is a clear case of this, where the speed of Twitter was instrumental in garnering feminist support, funding, and change.

In a heated election year where women's health and reproductive freedoms seemed to be at the front of battle lines, Komen drew attention on January 31, 2012 when it announced that it would no longer be granting money to help fund cancer screening services at Planned Parenthood. Karen Handel, a Republican who was appointed Komen's senior vice president for public policy in April 2011, made it no secret that she is against many of the policies and services of Planned Parenthood, and the announcement of such a dramatic cut in funding had many people quickly arguing that Handel – and Komen – were putting politics before the welfare of women's health. While Komen's move may not have been all that surprising, what no one expected was the way that Planned Parenthood – through social media – would fight back. Almost immediately, angry responses from individuals began popping up on Twitter, Facebook, and Tumblr, decrying Komen's decision. Planned Parenthood quickly joined in with its own official responses, as well as posting links to the media's coverage of the story, re-Tweeting pro-@PPact Tweets, all the while reminding individuals how they, too, could help support Planned Parenthood.

When all was said and done, Planned Parenthood received over $400,000 in just 24 hours, as well as a $250,000 pledge from Michael Bloomberg. As donations to Planned Parenthood continued to pour in, and amidst continued public pressure, Komen announced on February 3 that it "will continue to fund existing grants, including those of Planned Parenthood, and preserve their eligibility to apply for future grants." On February 7, as a result of the controversy, Handel resigned from Komen. Discussing the matter in an interview with *The Daily Beast* on February 10 Handel conceded, "Komen doesn't have the strength [of Planned Parenthood] in the area of social media."

Clearly, by Handel's own admission, it can be seen that the Internet and social media have the potential to coordinate and facilitate quick and decisive action. This type of impact is similar to the consciousness-raising of the second wave. Both relied on individual experiences and collective rhetoric not only to bring national awareness to feminist issues, but also with the intention of bring about measurable change. In this more recent case, many of the pro-@PPact Tweets detailed personal testimonials associated with Planned Parenthood, with supporters using their own experiences to influence others.

In addition to being a platform for fundraising, Twitter has also proven to be a leader in creating and sustaining national conversations on a number of social issues. Responding to the acquittal of George Zimmerman in the murder of Trayvon Martin, #BlackLivesMatter was founded by three radical Black women activists: Alicia Garza, Patrissa Cullors, and Opal Tometi Sparking national discourse surrounding how law enforcement agencies disproportionately target, arrest, and kill Black people in the United States with no regard for due process, the Black Lives Matter network pays special attention to the ways in which anti-racist movements may still exclude vulnerable Black populations, especially Black trans women. Thus, #BlackLivesMatter is often deployed to highlight intersectional concerns facing these communities (Black Lives Matter, 2019). Systemic racism is nothing new and is deeply interwoven into the history, culture, and legal infrastructure of the U.S., and #BlackLivesMatter utilized Twitter to bring these issues to the forefront of popular culture and organize action on the ground in response.

Since 2013, #BlackLivesMatter has grown steadily, with its founders hosting forums on Twitter and in communities throughout the country discussing how state-sanctioned violence impacts Black lives. It was the 2014 murder of Mike Brown in Ferguson, MO, however, that propelled the movement into the mainstream. Immediately after Ferguson police officer Darren Wilson fatally shot Brown, #BlackLivesMatter issued an urgent call on Twitter asking for as many of its members as possible to converge in the area. Garza, Cullors, and Tometi engaged Twitter not only as a rallying cry, but also as an organizational tool: each organizational chapter was given a role in the action, a plan for how to get to Ferguson and back, and resources for what to do in their own communities after leaving Missouri. More than 600 activists participated. Twitter effectively functioned as the networking tool for this "Black Life Matters Ride" while simultaneously ensuring that #BlackLivesMatter gained national and international traction. Perhaps most importantly, the activism in Ferguson served as a catalyst for social change that is still being engaged to this day (Black Lives Matter, 2019). Several states have since passed legislation to hold law enforcement more accountable for their actions and Black Lives Matter has more than 40 chapters worldwide (Luibrand, 2015). #BlackLivesMatter continues to use Twitter to recruit new Black leaders and activists, push anti-racist public policy, and honor all Black lives in the United States and beyond.

Perhaps the most visible sign of digital feminist activism in recent years has been #MeToo, more formally known as the "Me Too Movement." Founded in 2006 by activist Tarana Burke, Burke began using the phrase "Me Too" on the social network site MySpace to bring awareness to the prevalence of sexual assault, particularly in low-income and African American communities. Burke's goal was to highlight how commonplace these crimes are, while also helping to create a sense of community and support for survivors. As a survivor herself, Burke's activism is centered on being an advocate for not only herself, but also for others who may not be ready or comfortable sharing their stories publicly, but may be empowered through the stories and empathy of others. On October 15, 2016, actress Alyssa Milano, responding to the allegations of sexual harassment and assault by Hollywood film producer Harvey Weinstein, urged her Twitter followers, "If you've been sexually harassed or assaulted write 'me too' as a reply to this tweet." By noon the next day, Twitter had confirmed to CNN that the #MeToo hashtag had been tweeted more than a half million times. The flood of "#MeToo"s on social media in the days and weeks that followed – from both celebrities and average citizens – highlighted both the extent to which sexual harassment and assault are commonplace in our society, as well as the potential for platforms like Twitter to spark global conversations (as evidenced by the fact that the hashtag has been translated into over 80 languages) and action.

Milano's celebrity status, as well as the retweet and #MeToo responses of a number of other Hollywood stars, certainly helped bring attention to this issue. Milano, though, would go on to acknowledge Burke as the original founder of the movement, and the women would work together to make sure that the movement behind #MeToo was more than just a hashtag. In the months that would follow, Burke spoke nationally at the Women's March and on a number of media outlets, and given her background in activism and survivor support, has been able to use #MeToo to develop an activist movement that, while rooted in the digital, carries into physical spaces. Currently the Me Too Movement website (https://metoomvmt.org) serves as a resource for survivors and advocates, providing an online space for activism, but also a guide for community-based action adaptable for different communities.

CONCLUSION

The above cases are examples of successful online campaigns that complement the more commonplace 'grassroots' activism that occurs daily. It should be noted, though, that on an individual level, the influence and reach of social media is unclear. Despite an increase in availability, roughly a third of adults in the U.S. do not have broadband Internet access in their home, with "racial minorities, older adults, rural residents, and those with lower levels of education and income" less likely to have Internet service at home (Pew Research Center). With this in mind, for proponents of the fourth wave and digital feminisms to focus exclusively on the Internet as a means for understanding the movement is exclusionary, repeats essentialist tenets of the second wave, and ignores deeper systems of privilege.

There is also the concern that the public nature of social and digital media makes feminists and activists vulnerable in the 21st century in ways they were not in the past. In addition to the broad misogyny that exists in online spaces through tweets, memes, and social media posts, there are also more targeted attacks on feminists and activists, including threats; hacking of social media accounts, which may or may not lead to false impersonations; doxing, the practice of making personal information public; and public shaming. Not to mention the misogyny and violence associated with online subcultures such as the "manosphere" and Incel groups, which work to actively undermine and harm women, the LGBTQIA+ community, feminists, and social justice activists.

While the success of the examples discussed in this chapter should not be undermined, it is important to remember that, as with the consciousness-raising movement of the second wave, "Thousands, perhaps hundreds of thousands, of women in the United States have participated in consciousness raising, without becoming revolutionaries or even movement activists" (Rosenthal, 1984, p. 323). The same can be said of those who "Like" things on Facebook or the somewhat passive nature of "hashtag activism" on Twitter. That is not to say that using Facebook, Twitter, or other forms of social media to raise awareness for feminist concerns is a bad thing. Indeed, in this day and age, it is essential. But, similar to the ways in which consciousness-raising lost its political bite as it devolved into a space for airing of personal grievances without any goal or purpose in sight, the Internet can serve as a space for a similar lack of direction.

It would be a mistake to take Facebook and Twitter – commercial sites that attract specific types of users – as representative of an entire movement. Further, unlike the original intention of consciousness-raising groups to provide a space for analysis, the pace of Internet culture tends to focus on sound bytes, as opposed to depth of thoughts and/or prolonged analysis. Or, as Meghan Murphy, founder of the award-winning feminist blog *Feminist Current*, notes, "Twitter is not for nuance or humanity. It is for sharp words, glib remarks, and inspirational quotables – feminist greeting card style."

The goal, then, is to integrate and build upon these communities, while being mindful of their limitations. Using the Internet to mobilize action and raise awareness is necessary and good, but there has to be a deeper meaning, direction, and force behind such movements if the fourth wave and digital feminisms are going to make any sort of lasting or permanent change. Consciousness-raising on social media provides a vast and rapidly expanding foundation on which feminists and feminisms can thrive, and thus these movements have been provided a multifaceted mediated space in which to further their causes and permeate popular culture. Indeed, Facebook, Twitter, and scores of other social networks work individually and collectively to raise consciousness and advocate for social justice and radical inclusion, and the largely approachable discourses on these platforms yields increased visibility of these ideals. On the Internet, users need not be academic thought leaders or highly referenced feminist figures to engage in feminist activism; rather, by virtue of expression feminist ideals online, they become a part of a larger discourse, a digital collective, that seamlessly merges feminisms and social media to engage, critique, challenge, and change popular culture.

DISCUSSION QUESTIONS

1. One major criticism of digital feminism is that it hinges purely on rhetoric and does not actually advance social change, especially at the grassroots

level. Yet, we know that digital feminisms are becoming essential for feminist movements to sustain themselves. How can/should we bridge this gap? What current online grassroots movements effectively demonstrate a correlation between digital feminism and lasting social change?

2. Some digital feminist activists, in particular radical feminists on Tumblr, have been labeled "Social Justice Warriors" (SJWs) and are often scrutinized by mainstream feminist movements and popular culture. Perform an Internet search for 'social justice warriors.' What are your findings? Are negative perceptions of this group grounded? How can relationships between SJWs and digital feminism at-large be improved?

3. Recent digital feminist activity has garnered national and international attention. Search for news stories and articles on #YesAllWomen, #WhyIStayed, #MeToo, and #BlackLivesMatter. How were these movements portrayed in media? How did they respond to these representations? What can current and future digital feminisms do to combat such intensive criticism?

4. In conjunction with Question 3, opponents of digital feminisms can easily 'hijack' hashtags to fit their own agenda. This was most readily seen in late 2014 when anti-feminist movements converted #BlackLivesMatter to #AllLivesMatter. What are the problems of this and how can we respond to them? What can be done when digital feminisms are derailed like this?

5. Across all social media, hate speech is seemingly inescapable wherever digital feminism is present. Do you ever respond to discriminatory or hateful comments online? If so, how do you approach other Internet users who aren't aligned with feminist ideology? What are other ways you can engage in feminist activism and discussions online?

REFERENCES

Baumgardner, J., & Richards, A. (2000). *Manifesta: young women, feminism, and the future.* New York, NY: Farrar, Straus, and Giroux.

Beitsch, R. (2018). Few wells are tested for contamination after massive flooding from Hurricanes Florence and Michael. *The Huffington Post.* Retrieved from https://www.huffingtonpost.com/entry/hurricane-wells-contamination_ us_5c13c2ffe4b0cce3ea29d165

Black Lives Matter. (2019). *Herstory.* Retrieved from https://blacklivesmatter.com/about/ herstory/

Cochrane, K. (2013, December 10). The fourth wave of feminism: Meet the rebel women. *The Guardian.* Retrieved from http://www.theguardian.com/world/2013/dec/10/fourth-wave-feminism-rebel-women

Daniels, J. (2009). Rethinking cyberfeminism(s): Race, gender, and embodiment. *WSQ: Women's Studies Quarterly, 37*(1–2), 101–124.

Dubriwny, T. N. (2005). Consciousness-raising as collective rhetoric: The articulation of experience in the redstockings' abortion speak-out of 1969. *Quarterly Journal of Speech, 91*(4), 395–422.

Facebook. (2014). *Mission*. Retrieved from http://www.facebook.com/facebook/info

Golgowski, N. (2018). North Carolina has a massive mosquito problem after Hurricane Florence. *The Huffington Post*. Retrieved from https://www.huffingtonpost.com/entry/north-carolina-mosquito-problem_us_5bb10a32e4b0343b3dc1352e

Hanna, K. (2003). Gex X survior: From Riot Grrrl rock star to feminist artist. In R. Morgan (Ed.), *Sisterhood is forever: The women's anthology for a new millennium*. New York, NY: Washington Square Press.

Harquail, C. V. (2010, September 30). Facebook for women vs. Facebook designed by feminists: Different vs. revolutionary. *Authentic Organizations: Aligning Identity, Action, and Purpose*. Retrieved from http://authenticorganizations.com/harquail/2010/09/30/if-women-had-designed-facebook/#sthash. UBQruCQb.dpbs

Illia, L. (2003). Passage to cyberactivism: How dynamics of activism change. *Journal of Public Affairs, 3*(4), 326–337.

Just Florence Recovery. (2018). *About*. Retrieved from: https://justflorencerecovery.org/about/#

Luibrand, S. (2015, August 7). How a death in Ferguson sparked a movement in America. *CBS News*. Retrieved from: https://www.cbsnews.com/news/how-the-black-lives-matter-movement-changed-america-one-year-later/

Murphy, M. (2013, December 18). The trouble with Twitter feminism. *Feminist Current*. Retrieved from http://feministcurrent.com/8403/the-trouble-with-twitter-feminism/

Pesta, A. (2012, February 10). Komen official Karen Handel calls planned parenthood a 'gigantic bully.' *The Daily Beast*. Retrieved from http://www.thedailybeast.com/articles/2012/02/10/komen-exec-karen-handel-calls-planned-parenthood-a-gigantic-bully.html

Pew Research Center. (2018). *Internet/Broadband fact sheet*. Retrieved from http://www.pewinternet.org/fact-sheet/internet-broadband/

Richards, A., & Schnall, M. (2003). Cyberfeminism: Networking the net. In R. Morgan, (Ed.), *Sisterhood is forever: The women's anthology for a new millennium*. New York, NY: Washington Square Press.

Richardson, Z. (2018). Black activists demand justice in aftermath of Hurricane Florence. *Workers World Party*. Retrieved from https://www.workers.org/2018/10/10/black-activists-demand-justice-in-aftermath-of-hurricane-florence/

Rosenthal, N. B. (1984). Consciousness raising: From revolution to re-evaluation. *Psychology of Women Quarterly, 8*(4), 309–326.

Sarachild, K. (1973). Conciousness-raising: A radical weapon. In A. Koedt, E. Levine, & A. Rapone (Eds.), *Radical feminism*. New York, NY: Quadrangle Books.

Shapeero, T., (Director) & Hong, G. (Writer). *NBC*.

Stanton, E. C. (1997). Declaration of sentiments and resolutions. In S. E. Cady, A. D. Gordon, & S. B. Anthony (Eds.), *The selected papers of Elizabeth Cady Stanton and Susan B. Anthony* (Vol. 1). New Brunswick, NJ: Rutgers University Press.

Third Wave Foundation. (2014). *History*. Retrieved from http://www.thirdwavefoundation.org/about-us/history/

Walker, R. (1992). Becoming the Third wave. *Ms Spring*, 86–87.

ADDITIONAL READING

Anderson, K. J. (2014). *Modern misogyny: Anti-feminism in a post-feminist era*. London: Oxford University Press.

Banet-Weiser, S. (2015). Confidence you can carry!: Girls in crisis and the market for girl empowerment organizations. *Continuum: Journal of Media and Cultural Studies, 29*(2), 1–12.

Baumgardner, J., & Richards, A. (2000). *Manifesta: Young women, feminism and the future*. New York, NY: Farrar, Straus and Giroux.

Berger, M. (Ed.). (2006). *We don't need another wave: Dispatches from the next generation of feminists*. New York, NY: Seal Press.

Bly, L., & Wooten, K. (2012). *Make your own history documenting feminist and queer activism in the 21st century*. Los Angeles, CA: Litwin Books.

Boylorn, R. M. (2008). As seen on TV: An autoethnographic reflection on race and reality television. *Critical Studies in Media Communication, 25*(4), 413–433.

Bromley, V. (2012). *Feminisms matters: Debates, theories, activism*. Toronto, ON: University of Toronto Press.

Brown, J. A. (2013). Panthers and vixens: Black superheroines, sexuality, and stereotypes in contemporary comic books. In S. C. Howard & R. L. Jackson (Eds.), *Black comics: Politics of race and representation* (pp. 133–150). New York, NY: Bloomsbury Academic.

Butler, J. (1990). *Gender trouble: Feminism and the subversion of identity*. New York, NY: Routledge.

Butler, J. (1993). Critically queer. *GLQ: A Journal of Lesbian & Gay Studies, 1*, 17–32

Butler, J. (2013). For White girls only? Postfeminism and the politics of inclusion. *Feminist Formations, 25*(1), 35–38.

Carlton, D. (1994). *Looking for little Egypt*. Bloomington, IN: IDD Books.

Carruthers, C. (2018). *Unapologetic: A Black, queer, and feminist mandate for radical movements*. Boston, MA: Beacon Press.

Chouliaraki, L. (2013). *The ironic spectator: Solidarity in the age of post-humanitarianism*. Cambridge: Polity Press.

Cobbett, M. (2014). Beyond 'victims' and 'heroines': Constructing 'girlhood' in international development. *Progress in Development Studies, 14*(4), 309–320.

Coleman, R. R. M. (2011). "ROLL UP YOUR SLEEVES!": Black women, black feminism in feminist media studies. *Feminist Media Studies, 11*(1), 35–41.

Collins, P. H. (2009). *Black feminist thought: Knowledge, consciousness, and the politics of empowerment* (3rd ed.). New York, NY: Routledge.

Collins, P. H. (2013). *On intellectual activism*. Philadelphia, PA: Temple Press.

Crozier-De Rosa, S., & Mackie, V. (2019). *Remembering women's activism*. New York, NY: Routeledge.

Dale, C., & Overell, R. (2018). *Orienting feminism: Media, activism and cultural representation*. Cham, Switzerland: Palgrave Macmillan.

Dáil, P., & Wells, B. (2018). *We rise to resist: Voices from a new era in women's political action*. Jefferson, NC: McFarland & Company, Inc.

Desai, K. (2016). Teaching the third world girl: Girl rising as a precarious curriculum of empathy. *Curriculum Inquiry, 46*(3), 248–264.

Dicker, R., & Piepmeier, A. (Eds.). (2003). *Catching a wave: Reclaiming feminism for the 21st century*. Boston, MA: Northeastern University Press.

Dines, G., & Humez. J. M. (Eds.). (2014). *Gender, race, and class in media: A critical reader* (4th ed.).Los Angeles, CA: Sage Publications.

Douglas, S. (2010). *Enlightened sexism: The seductive message that feminism's work is done*. New York, NY: Times Books.

Eric-Udorie, J. (2018). *Can we all be feminists?: New writing from Brit Bennett, Nicole Dennis-Benn, and 15 others on intersectionality, identity, and the way forward for feminism*. New York, NY: Penguin Random House.

Ferrera, A. (2018). *American like me*. New York, NY: Simon and Schuster.

Finley, L. L., & Stringer, E. R. (2010). *Beyond burning bras: feminist activism for everyone*. Santa Barbara, CA: Praeger.

Foucault, M. (1975). *Discipline and punish: The birth of the prison*. New York, NY: Vintage.

Gardiner, J. K. (Ed.). (2002). *Masculinity studies & feminist theory: New directions*. New York, NY: Columbia University Press.

Gay, R. (2014). *Bad feminist*. New York, NY: Harper.

Gillis, S., Gillian, H., & Munford, R. (Eds.). (2004). *Third wave feminism: A critical exploration*. New York, NY: Palgrave.

Griffin, R. A. (2014). Black women and gender violence in for colored girls: Black feminist reflections on the power and politics of representation. In J. S. C. Bell & R. L. Jackson (Eds.), *Interpreting Tyler Perry: Perspectives on race, class, gender, and sexuality* (pp. 169–186). New York, NY: Routledge.

Harding, S. (2004). *The feminist standpoint theory reader: Intellectual and political controversies*. New York, NY: Routledge.

Hawkesworth, M. (2018). *Globalization and feminist activism* (2nd ed.). Lanham, MD: Rowman & Littlefield.

Hernandez, D., & Reman, B. (2002). *Colonize this! Young women of color and today's feminism*. New York, NY: Seal Press.

Hesford, W. (2014). Facing Malala, facing ourselves. *JAC: A Journal of Rhetoric, Culture, and Politics, 33*(3–4), 407–423.

hooks, b. (1981). *Ain't I a Woman: Black women and feminism*. Boston, MA: South End Press.

hooks, b. (2002). *Feminism is for everybody: Passionate politics*. London: Pluto Press.

Kearney, M. C. (Ed.). (2011). *The gender and media reader*. New York, NY: Routledge.

Khoja-Moolji, S. (2018). *Forging the ideal educated girl: The production of desirable subjects in Muslim South Asia*. Oakland, CA: University of California Press.

Kimmel, M. (1987). *Changing men: New directions in research on men and masculinity*. Newbury Park, CA: Sage Publications.

Kimmel, M., & Messner, M. (1989). *Men's lives*. New York, NY: Macmillan Publishing.

Koffman, O., & Gill, R. (2013). 'The revolution will be led by a 12-year-old-girl': Girl power and global biopolitics. *Feminist Review, 105*, 83–102.

Lepore, J. (2015). *The secret history of Wonder Woman*. New York, NY: Vintage Books.

Martin, C. E., & Sullivan, J. C. (2010). *Click: When we knew we were feminists*. New York, NY: Seal.

McAllister, M. P., Sewell, E. H., & Gordon, I. (2001). *Introducing comics and ideology*. New York, NY: Peter Lang.

McCammon, H., & Banaszak, L. (2018). *100 years of the Nineteenth Amendment: An appraisal of women's political activism*. New York, NY: Oxford University Press.

McRobbie, A. (2008). *The aftermath of feminism: Gender, culture, and social change.* Thousand Oaks, CA: Sage Publications.

Moeller, K. (2018). *The gender effect: Capitalism, feminism, and the corporate politics of development.* Oakland, CA: University of California Press.

Moeller, K. (2019, January 4). The Ghost Statistic that Haunts Women's Empowerment. *The New Yorker.* Retrieved from https://www.newyorker.com/science/elements/the-ghost-statistic-that-haunts-womens-empowerment

Moynagh, M., & Forestell, N. (Eds.). (2012). *Documenting first wave feminisms: Volume 1: Transnational collaborations and crosscurrents (Studies in gender and history).* Toronto, ON: University of Toronto Press.

Mulvey, L. (2009). *Visual and other pleasures* (2nd ed.). New York, NY: Palgrave Macmillan. Senkovich, N.

Muscio, I. (1998). *Cunt: A declaration of independence.* Seattle, WA: Seal Press.

Nicholson, L. (Ed.). (1997). *The second wave: A reader in feminist theory.* New York, NY: Routledge.

Shriver, M., Morgan, O., & Skelton, K. (Eds.). (2014). *The Shriver report: A woman's nation pushes back from the brink.* New York, NY: Palgrave Macmillan.

Perry, I. (2003). Who(se) am I?: The identity and image of women in Hip Hop. In G. Dines & J. Humez (Eds.), *Gender, race, and class in media: A critical reader* (pp. 136–148). Thousand Oaks, CA: Sage Publications.

Rebollo-Gil, G., & Moras, A. (2012). Black women and Black men in hip hop music: Misogyny, violence and the negotiation of (white-owned) space. *Journal of Popular Culture, 45*(1), 118–132.

Rich, A. (1980). Compulsory heterosexuality and lesbian existence. *Signs, 5*(4), 631–660.

Rose, T. (2008). *The Hip Hop wars: what we talk about when we talk about Hip Hop-and why it matters.* New York, NY: Basic Civitas Books.

Saini, A. (2009) Annals of the black superheroine. *Bitch: Feminist Response to Popular Culture, 45,* 35–41.

Sheridan-Rabideau, M. P. (2008). *Girls, feminism, and grassroots literacies activism in the GirlZone.* Albany, NY: State University of New York Press.

Smith-Prei, C., & Stehle, M. (2016). *Awkward politics: Technologies of popfeminist activism.* Montreal, Canada: McGill-Queen's University Press.

Steinem, G. (2014). Our revolution has just begun. *Ms. Magazine,* 27–31.

Switzer, H. (2018). *When the light is fire: Maasai schoolgirls in Contemporary Kenya.* Champaign, IL: University of Illinois Press.

Switzer, H., Bent, E., & Endsley, C. (2016). Precarious politics and girl effects: Exploring the limits of the girl gone global. *Feminist Formations, 28*(1), 33–59.

Trier-Bieniek, A. (2013). *Sing us a song, piano woman: Female fans and the music of Tori Amos.* Lanham, MD: Scarecrow Press.

Van Nieuwkerk, K. (1995). *"A trade like any other": Female singers and dancers in Egypt.* Austin, TX: University of Texas Press.

Vickery, J., & Everbach, T. (2018). *Mediating misogyny: Gender, technology, and harassment.* Cham, Switzerland: Palgrave Macmillan.

West, C., & Zimmerman, D. (1987). Doing gender. *Gender, 1,* 125–151.

West, L. (2016). *Shrill: Notes from a loud woman.* New York, NY: Hachette Books.

Westmarland, L. (2001). *Gender and policing: Sex, power, and police culture.* Portland, OR: Willan Publishing.

Wiegman, R. (2002). Unmaking: Men and masculinity in feminist theory. In J. K. Gardiner (Ed.), *Masculinity studies & feminist theory: New directions* (pp. 31–59). New York, NY: Columbia University Press.

Weiner, S., & Jacobs, E. (2017). *Why I march: Images from the Women's March around the world*. New York, NY: Abrams Image.

NOTES ON CONTRIBUTORS

EDITOR

Adrienne Trier-Bieniek, Ph.D., is the author and editor of several books focused on gender and culture including *The Politics of Gender* (Brill, 2018), *The Beyoncé Effect* (McFarland Press, 2016), *Feminist Theory and Pop Culture* (Sense Publishers, 2015), and *Gender and Pop Culture: A Text-Reader* (Sense Publishers, 2014). She is the author of *Sing Us a Song, Piano Woman: Female Fans and the Music of Tori Amos* (Scarecrow, 2013). In addition to numerous book chapters and journal publications, Adrienne has written for the news website *Huff Post*. She has been interviewed by NBC News, NPR, Reuters, USA Today, The Tampa Bay Times, and the Orlando Sentinel on topics such as violence against women, gender and music, health, and popular culture. She can be reached at www.adriennetrier-bieniek.com.

AUTHORS

Emily Bent, Ph.D., is an Assistant Professor in Women's Studies and Gender Studies at Pace University. Her research examines the intersections of girlhood, human rights, and activist politics, and has been published in *Girlhood Studies, Feminist Formations, Global Studies of Childhood*, and *Sociological Studies of Children and Youth*. Her forthcoming article in *Signs: Journal of Women in Culture and Society* explores how Emma González contributes to the project of public feminism. Her current book project, *Feminist Girls: The New Politics of Age and Gender at the United Nations*, chronicles girl-activist practices in the girls' rights movement over the decade.

Patricia R. Boyd, Ph.D., is an Assistant Professor at Arizona State University. She first read *Fifty Shades of Grey* one weekend when she was stuck at home with a cold and her husband brought them home to distract her. Her current research interests revolve around three key themes: feminist and post-feminist theories/practices, pedagogical theories, and new media engagements. She is currently working on a book entitled *Celebrity Endorser Identities: Changing Practices in the Current Cultural Moment* (Mellen Press, forthcoming) addressing the ways that celebrities' identities are impacted by the products they endorse. A sampling of her work includes

"Transformative Capacities within Webs of Power: Women's Discussion of Books and Identity Online" which was featured in *Jellic*, and "'The 21st Century Way to Meet and Socialize': Discursive Constructions of Black Heterosexual Male Identities in Online Personal Ads."

Jenn Brandt, Ph.D., is an Associate Professor of Women's Studies at California State University, Dominguez Hills. Brandt's work focuses on gender and cultural studies in literature, popular film, and television. She is the co-author of *An Introduction to Popular Culture in the US: People, Politics, and Power.*

Carrie L. Buist, Ph.D., is an Assistant Professor of Criminal Justice at Grand Valley State University. Her current research interests include queer criminology, pop culture, prisons, gender, and feminism. She has published articles in *Culture, Health, and Sexuality*, *Crime and Justice*, *Critical Criminology*, and is the co-author of the award winning book, *Queer Criminology*.

Nicole B. Cox, Ph.D., is an Associate Professor in the Communication Arts Department at Valdosta State University, where she teaches media studies courses. Her research explores depictions of gender, identity, and culture. Her most recent project focuses on representations of masculinity in southern culture; she currently is examining the use of item songs in Bollywood cinema and the NFL's "NO MORE" campaign. She has previously written on *The Real Housewives, Sons of Anarchy, Orange Is the New Black*, and *Slumdog Millionaire.*

Lauren J. DeCarvalho, Ph.D. is an Assistant Professor in the Department of Media, Film & Journalism Studies at the University of Denver, where she teaches film and media studies. Her research explores depictions of intersectional identities and her most recent project focuses on narratives of incarcerated women, both onscreen and off. Currently, she is examining *Wentworth*, but she has written previously on *Girls, Enlightened, Veep, Sons of Anarchy*, and *Orange Is the New Black.*

Rachel Alicia Griffin, Ph.D., is an Associate Professor of Race and Communication at the University of Utah. As a critical/cultural scholar who has earned several honors, her research interests span Black feminist thought, critical race theory, sexual violence, and the social institutions of sport, media, education, and the U.S. presidency. Dr. Griffin has published in journals including *Women's Studies in Communication*, *Critical Studies in Media Communication*, the *International Journal of Qualitative Studies in Education*, and *The Howard Journal of Communications*. She is also the co-editor of *Adventures in Shondaland: Identity Politics and the Power of Representation* (Rutgers University Press, 2018). Her pending research project is a co-authored monograph titled *Marginalization and the Modern Presidency: Presidential Communication, Identity Politics, and the Battle for 'Real' America*. She has delivered well over 100 anti-sexual violence and Inclusive Excellence presentations on campuses and at conferences nationally and internationally.

April Kalogeropoulos Householder, Ph.D., is the Director of Undergraduate Research and Prestigious Scholarships and is an adjunct faculty member at the University of Maryland, Baltimore County. She is the author of several articles on intersectional feminism and popular culture, and co-author of the book *Feminist Perspectives on Orange is the New Black*, with Adrienne Trier-Bieniek. Her research and teaching focuses on feminist/queer film and media, pop culture, and the modern Greek diaspora.

Sam Kizer, M.A., is a doctoral student in the Department of Gender Studies at Indiana University Bloomington. His research primarily interrogates how autism is socially constructed through mass media, education, and disability rights discourses. Currently, he is examining how autistic people understand and perform sexual desire. His work has appeared in the *Canadian Journal of Disability Studies* and he has presented nationally at the Popular Culture Association/American Culture Association's national conference and the National Women's Studies Association annual conference.

Angela M. Moe, Ph.D., did her doctoral work in Justice Studies from Arizona State University in 2001 and is currently a Professor of Sociology at Western Michigan University where she also holds an advisory affiliation with the Department of Gender and Women's Studies. Initially trained as a criminologist focusing on intimate partner victimization, her more recent interdisciplinary, and largely ethnographic, work has traversed an array of subject matter related to women, health and the body. She has published over two dozen articles in sociology, criminology, social work and humanities based outlets and is a steadfast proponent of prevention and awareness related to family victimization within her community.

Jean-Anne Sutherland, Ph.D., is an Associate Professor of Sociology at the University of North Carolina Wilmington. Her research spans two areas; the sociology of mothering and, sociology through film. She has published work on mothering, guilt and shame in *Sociology Compass*, *The Encyclopedia of Motherhood*, and in *Mama Ph.D.: Women Write about Motherhood and Academic Life*. She is co-editor (with Kathryn Feltey, University of Akron) of *Cinematic Sociology: Social Life in Film*, a sociology text that uses film as a lens to explore core sociological concepts and the ways in which social life is represented in film.

Tia C. M. Tyree, Ph.D., is a Professor at Howard University within the Department of Strategic, Legal and Management Communications. Her research interests include African American and female representations in mass media, hip hop, rap, reality television, film and social media. She has published chapters in multiple books and several key journals, including *Women and Language*, *Journal of Black Studies*, *Howard Journal of Communications*, *International Journal of Emergency Management* and *Journalism: Theory, Practice & Criticism*. She is also co-editor of *Social Media: Pedagogy and Practice*; *Social Media: Culture and Identity* as well as *HBCU Experience – The Book*.

Melvin L. Williams, Ph.D., is an Assistant Professor of Communication Studies at Pace University, where he teaches undergraduate courses in critical media studies, popular culture, and race and ethnicity in the media. As a communication scholar and celebrated culturist, he examines the intersections of race, gender, and sexuality in popular culture, specifically, how minority communities use its mediums to address disparaging media representations. Dr. Williams has published research in several books and journals, including *Feminist Theory and Pop Culture*, *Race, Gender, and Class: The Journal*, *Spectrum: A Journal on Black Men*, *The Journal of Hip-Hop Studies*, and most recently, *The Journal of Sports Media*.

Printed in the United States
By Bookmasters